Advancement in Library and Information Science

Advancement in Library and Information Science

Editor

Vaishali Khaparde
Head and Associate Professor
Dept of Library and information Science
Dr Babasaheb Ambedkar Marathwada University
Aurangabad 431004
Maharashtra, INDIA

Ess Ess Publications
New Delhi

Advancement in Library and Information Science

ISBN: 978-81-7000-660-2

Rs.1075/-

First Published 2012

Published by:
Ess Ess Publications
4831/24, Ansari Road,
Darya Ganj,
New Delhi-110 002.
INDIA
Phones: 23260807, 41563444
Fax: 41563334
E-mail: info@essessreference.com
www.essessreference.com

Cover Design by *Patch Creative Unit*

Printed and bound in India at Salasar Imaging Systems.

CONTENTS

Dr. S. P. SATARKAR
M.Sc., M.Lib.Sc., Ph.D.
University Librarian
SWAMI RAMANAND TEERTH
MARATHWADA UNIVERSITY,
'Dnyanteerth', Gautaminagar,
Vishnupuri, **NANDED** - 431 606.

Foreword

25.11.2011

It was a matter of great pleasure for me to go through the papers included in the book "Advancements in Library and Information Science." The papers highlight the changing scenario of library and information science precisely.

The subject Library and Information Science has a peculiarity to incorporate useful innovations from different subjects. It has incorporated concepts from Economics, Management Science, Computer Science, Communication Technology and so on. This was done for providing better and efficient services to its users. It is accepted fact that, the subjects which refine its contents survive and become popular. People from library and information science have always kept this principle in their minds. I feel that, present book is one of the attempt in this direction.

The book is having 24 articles. These articles are written by the professionals in library and information science, not only from India, but also from abroad. The authors from outside India, include professionals from Sri Lanka, Kenya and Swaziland. This has increased the utility of the document at international scenario. This is essential considering the present era of globalization.

The book highlights the nascent concepts like Web 2.0, Total quality Management and its application in libraries, Digital libraries, Open repositories, RFID technology used in libraries, Information literacy, Social networking etc. All these areas are recent one and hence the book will be useful to grasp these ideas by the professionals. The practicing librarians can implement these techniques to strengthen the library services.

Another feature of this book is inclusion of few articles of case studies. Case studies share experience of one professional with others. This is proved as best way of efficient communication. These case studies have increased the utility of the document.

I am sure that, the book will be of immense use to the professionals in Library and Information Science.

Dr.S.P.Satarkar
UniversityLibrarian and Head,Library and Information Science,
Swami Ramanand Teerth Marathwada University,
NANDED (Maharashtra) 431606

Fax & Phone : (02462) 229560 • Resi : (02462) 241446 • Email :suresh_satarkar@reddiff.com
Phone EPABX : (02462) 229242, 229243 Ext. 135 • Mobile : 94228 72646

PREFACE

Library and Information Science is an interdisciplinary field that applies the practices, perspectives and tools of management, information technology, education, and other areas to libraries the collection, organization, preservation, and dissemination of information resources and the political economy of information.

The impact of information technology is now being visible among the people who are using computers in library for advancement and up-gradation of traditional knowledge resource. It has become a necessity in present day context. The growing demands from the users have created new tools and techniques, which would definitely create a history in the documentation processes in the future digital libraries. The networking in the library is now emerging at a great extent. Use of computer, internet and electronic mail systems are making people closer to each other.

The book 'Advancement in Library and Information Science' presents an excellent collection of (24) articles on various facets of Library and Information Studies. The articles highlight advancement in Library and Information field with up-to-date data and subject coverage. The contributors are eminent library and information science professionals, from different parts of India and out of India. The articles included in this volume maintain a high academic standard.

The book commences with a foreword by Prof. Satarkar S.P. Librarian of SRTM University, Nanded. He is very eminent personality in LIS profession. We express our humble thanks and gratitude of Prof. Satarkar S. P. for writing the foreword to this volume in the midst of his busy schedule of programme.

The (24) articles presented in this volume are grouped under 7 thematic categories. They are: Library Automation, Information Communication Technology, Intellectual Property Right, Library and Information Management, Library and Information Science Education and Library and Library Profession, Statistical Research Methods in Library and Information Science, Information Literacy.

Under the first category Library Automation, there are four articles, which focuses on digital libraries and library automation. The second category. In ICT there are three articles they focus on the web2.0. The next category is IPR and it includes only one article. Library and Information Management include six articles, which are related to preservation and conservation, various types of libraries management. The next category is Library and Information Science Education and LIS Profession which consist three articles. The sixth category is Statistical Research Methods in Library and Information Science it includes two articles. The last category is Information Literacy that includes three articles.

For this endeavour, we have contacted eminent library professionals from all the parts of the country and abroad.

We also express our indebtedness to Ess Ess Publication, New Delhi for their willingness to execute this work and publish it in a meticulous manner.

No doubt, this book will be an asset to Library and Information education and research at different levels. It is hoped that the Library and Information professionals would accept this valuable publication whole heartedly.

Dr. (Mrs.) Khaparde Vaishali Sovind

LIST OF CONTRIBUTORS

Adhe G. D.
Associate Professor & Head
Dr. Babasaheb Ambedkar, College Of Arts & Commerce,
Nagsenvana Aurangabad.
adhegovind65@gmail.com.

Anita Jain
Chief Librarian
Jaipur Engineering College And Research Centre Sitapura,
Tonk Road, Jaipur (Rajasthan) INDIA.
anitajain.lib@gmail.com.

Bharat Kumar
Assistant Librarian,
Management Development Institute,
Gurgaon – 122007, India
bharat.kumar@hotmail.com,
bharatkumar@gmail.com.

Prof. (Dr.) R.D. Biradar
Director, School of Commerce and
Management Science

Chopkar H.D.
Librarian,
Podar International School, Aurangabad.

Dr. Dharamraj K. Veer
In-Charge University Librarian,
Dr. Babasaheb Ambedkar Marathwada University,
Aurangabad, (MS), India

Fayaz Ahmad Loan
Documentation Officer,
Centre Of Central Asian Studies,
University Of Kashmir, Srinagar (J&K), India.
fayazlib@yahoo.co.in.

Golwal Madansing D.
Librarian,
Nya.Tatyasaheb Athalye Arts,
Yed.S.R.Sapre Commerce & Vid.D.Pitre Science College
Deorukh - 415804 Ratnagiri. *Mgolwal4@Gmail.Com.*

Gul Sumeer
Assistant Professor,
Department of Library and Information Science,
University of Kashmir, India.

Henry D S Kinya
Librarian,
Africa Nazarene University Nairobi –Kenya
hhkinya5@gmail.com.

Jadhav Vandana S.
Assit. Professor,
Vidyadhan Mahavidyalay CIDCO Aurangabad.
vandisjadhav@gmail.com.

Ad. Kalbande S.S.
Assistant Professor,
Mastyodary Law College, Jalna, (MS), India

Khandare Rahul B.
Librarian,
Sardar Vallabhabhai Patel Arts & Science College Ainpur,
Tal. Raver, Dist. Jalgaon (Maharashtra)
rahulkhandare39@yahoo.in.

Khaparde Vaishali S.
Associate Professor & Head,
Dept. Of Dept.Of Lib & I Sc,
Dr. Babasaheb Ambedkar Marathwada University,
Aurangabad (MS), India.
vaishali_khaparde@rediffmail.com.

Kulkarni J.
Assit. Librarian
SRTM University,
Nanded.

Md. Nurul Islam
Librarian,
DNC College, Murshidabad,
West Bengal
islam.mdnurul430@gmail.com.

Mohamed Majeed Mashroofa
Senior Assistant Librarian,
South Eastern University of Srilanka,
Srilanka

Mukhyadal B. G.
Lecturer (Cont.)
Dr. Babasaheb Ambedkar,
College of Arts & Commerce Nagsenvana,
Aurangabad.
bgmukhyadal@gmail.com.

Nabi Hasan
Deputy Librarian,
Indian Institute of Technology Delhi,
New Delhi-16
hasan@library.iitd.ac.in.

Sagare Ganesh D.
Librarian
R.C. Patel Institute of Technology Shirpur,
Dhule, Maharashtra, India.
sat123_pad123@yahoo.co.in.

Satish L. Padme
Assistant Librarian,
Dr. Babasaheb Ambedkar Marathwada University,
Aurangabad, Maharashtra, India

Shafi Muzamil
Professional Assistant,
College of Teacher Education (Cet),
Maulana Azad National Urdu University (Manuu)
Srinagar.
muzamil_shafi@rediffmail.com.

Shahista P.
Assit. Librarian,
Dr. Babasaheb Ambedkar Marathwada University,
Aurangabad (MS) India.

Shelke Santosh M.
Librarian,
Shri Bhagawan Homoeopathic Medical College,
N-6, CIDCO, Aurangabad.
sms8220@gmail.com.

Shyam M. Sarsare
Project Fellow, Swami Ramanand Teerth Marathwada University,
Nanded, (MS), India

Sonwane S. S.
Assistant Professor
Dept. of LIS Dr. Babasaheb Ambedkar,
Marathwada University Aurangabad.
Shashank65@Yahoomail.Com.

Tariq Ahmad Shah
Research Scholar,
Department of Library And Information Science,
University of Kashmir, India.
Tariqahmadshah@Gmail.Com.

Thiyam Satyabati Devi
Assistant Librarian,
Cataloguing Head I /C University Of Swaziland,
Swaziland.
sdthiyam@uniswa.sz, satya115@rediffmail.com.

Vaishnav A. A.
Prof & Head (Retd.)
Dept. of LIS Dr. Babasaheb Ambedkar,
Marathwada University Aurangabad.
ashwinivaishnav15@gmail.com.

Waghmare Sanjay S.
Assit. Prof.
Dagdojirao Deshmukh Arts, Commerce & Science College,
Waluj, Aurangabad.

UNIT 1

LIBRARY AUTOMATION

1

Concept of Digital Library: A Comprehensive Study

Anita Jain
Chief Librarian
Jaipur Engineering College and Research Centre Sitapura,
Tonk Road, Jaipur (Rajasthan) INDIA
E-mail: anitajain.lib@gmail.com

ABSTRACT

Fast development in information technology and communication played a vital role in globalization. Library functions and management is also effected by this revolutionary changes and emerged it as "Digital Library". Its main object is to fulfill the demand of library users with relevant updated and accurate information at economic cost and at universal norms. The history of civilization is the history of all improved means of communication through library function from print paper to its digital form the paperless electronic viewed. Its management is specific & coordinated through specialist. The process of digitization basically involves converting a physical object in to electronic viewed through its main tools MARC, Internet resources & searching, a collection of net work and searching information through search engine. . This trend started in advanced countries about five decades ago and two decades ago in India.

Key words: Globalization, Electronic Devices, Transforming, Transforming information, LAN & WAN, CD-ROM, WINISIS, GENESIS WEB, APACHEWEB SERVER, MARC.

1. INTRODUCTION

Through the fast development in the field of Information Technology & means of communication the countries of global world are coming nearer to nearer now a days. That time has gone when it was told that how one can reach or approach to the distant part of the country and world. Now with in no time one can easily approach to any where in the world. This could only be possible due to the revolutionary changes in the means of communication through IT. As each & every field of the life is effected by this revolutionary development then how the services of library can be aloof & untouched from this change. In fact application of IT can eassily be seen in the field of library, the treasures of knowledge, resultant that library services have become more efficient and effective as well.

The emerging trends in digital technologies and their applicability to information handling activities added new challenges to knowledge professionals for providing qualitative success to its users. [(1)](DESIDOC Vol. 29, No.2(2009)-RS R Varalakskhmi). It has brought a revolutionary changes in the field of modern library functions. [(2)] Due to this application the concept of digital library are coming up and Digital libraries are being set & maintained by using the of Internet services and by developing library software.

2. WHAT IS DIGITAL LIBRARY

Due to the development in the field of electronic science and technology, the library functions & system have all together changed and have been transformed in digital library. Not only this but this emerging trend is trying to develop the uniform system of entire library functions and activities all around the glob. Though it is very difficult due to the different languages even then efforts are being done and are in progress.

In this way digital library is said to be a collection controlled and access of informations through the electronic device, system and format by adopting universal patterns and modes Clifford lynch, a well known expert on Internet and web technologies has defined the digital library "The digital library not just one entity,but multiple sources seemlessly integrated". [3] (Lynch Clifford and Hector Garcia – Molimma. IITA Digital Library Workshop Reston, VA, MAY – 18-19,1995)

In this way the digital library offer a platform where in methodologies of information development and database management can be maintained. It has reduced the growing costs of cataloging , preserving and making accessible of read ables. The vast collections of readable materials are stored and preserved for the very longest period through this digital form and device with paperless system based on computer network technology and communication facilities. It can be termed as supplementary facility to traditional library for better retrieval and faster communication. One can easily, directly & transparently access the library facilities without the specific knowledge of librarian ship. In the broader sense it can be defined as paperless library totally based on electronic computer technology, in which all library functions and activities can be activated without the help & specific knowledge of librarian ship. Its goal is to be a universal access. As & when it will be possible then it will be called as global universal digital library. Although digital libraries have a long way to go before they reach their full potential, there has been significant development in the past decade.

3. OBJECT OF DIGITAL LIBRARY

It has vital objects due to its electronic computerised working and resources. Digital information objects may be in a variely of formets such as electronic journals, web pages, refrence materials, images, audio-video readables etc. Its main object is to fulfill the demand of library users by providing relevant, comprehensive upto-date and accurate information at an economic cost at the right time. Digital objects are equivalent conceptually to the items that may be found amongest library holdings. Its main object is to set & run the library management at universal norms, principles & practice. To fulfill this object efforts have been made by library congress washington D.C. In 1966, there after U.K. France, Germany, Canada & Australia have come forward. Now there are 60 countries in the world have taken effective steps to-wards formation of bibliographic formets. Now efforts are being made to reconcile the different formets.

4. HISTORY OF DIGITAL INFORMATION RESONANCE

Communication is a regular & unending process. From the birth to death not only man but even all living being use to communicate their feelings & thoughts at each & every moments of life. Without communication no one can live for a moment. From the symbolic wall drawing and painting age to the age of alphabetical age of language expresses through speech and printing technology the process of communication had passed through drastic changes due to the development of science of technology. It is all due to the developed human mind's creation. The storage or so called collections of exchangeable valuable feelings & thoughts emerged the concept of library, which has now turned up in digital form of collection to use for making this communication process continue to generation to generation. In this way the history of library starts from the emergence of human life & shall continue till its existence in the universe. Its patterns & form of shape remained in variably changed according the means & sources of the collected readable materials. It is all due to the technological development, so occurred due to the inventions and creations time to time. In this way it is a long way to move from ancient past to the unpredictable future. Since 1940s several thinkers have forecast the replacement of print on paper by the electronic media. Their dreams and forecast turned in reality inform of digital library. Nanotechnology may convert it in Neno library or pocket library, laptop library is available due to its digitalization. The history of civilisation in the history of all improved means of communication through stored & preserved documents, which are only available in libraries. The developments of libraries from print-paper based to digital form seems an illustration of man's never ending desire to improve means of communication.

5. CHARACTERISTICS OF DIGITAL LIBRARIES

A Digital libraries are electronic viewed of the conventional archival. By converting all library functions and activities in to electronic version with the greater sense of exchange, communication and value added professionals elevations. It is a paperless library in which information and reading material is stored in digital form. The user can directly obtain the material by accessing library functions without the help of any librarian. The user can also copy the required readable from master version by using electronic system and technology. The transformational effects of digital technology can easily be seen in-

(a) Collection of document, which make it permanent and quick handling and accessible as well.

(b) Individual working without any specific knowledge of librarian ship.

(c) Transforming and transporting of information with in and outside the country. This is an important characteristics of digital library which helps in seeking the required information's to use.

The telecommunication is facilitating the use of electronic methods. The mechanism of publishing and printing of readable from the master version made the library function very easy & fast. It is only due to the Internet facility available with in libraries & with its user.

6. MANAGEMENT OF DIGITAL LIBRARY

While adopting digitization techniques in libraries some important factors are earnestly needed in managing the whole process of electronic device and techniques. Not only to storage and distribution of data i.e. documents in digital form but it is essential to preserve them for a long term in such a way that the scanned image of documents will be remain visible for a long time to come. Apart from this standardization for wholesale conversion of documents in digital format is imperative. To fulfill the objective, motive & institutive aim behind digital library it requires a specific management in which specialist in IT, Electronics, internet administrators and librarians are employed. The cordial and expertise efforts of all these experts will make this mission successfully achieved and fulfilled. The managers of digitization jobs have to keep in mind these aspects and their point of view must be global & universal. It is a very careful issue for the success of digitization process. For efficient management it is essential to have high speed local server with fast connectivity to internet, full text search engines with efficient indexing facilities, web server and FTP servers and electronic document management facility. The relational databases also needed to support a variety of digital formats. Management of digitized documents for preservation is an important issue in relevance of technical obsolescence. The preservation of the storage medium of data should be in such a way that may be helpful in transferring from one storage medium to another storage medium and which can easily be accessed to context i.e. easy to translate data from one format to another during such migration there should not be any loss of documentary information. As it is very difficult and not possible at present to have a common standards libraries need to make CD ROM and optical disk back-ups. Management of digital libraries would include all kinds of documents i.e. published unique printed documents, which should be selected by the committee of experts for scanning without violating copyright regulations. In this regard it is important that it should have the means of revenue generation for the maintenance of digital library. Each institution has to keep in mind that any sensitive documents that create controversy and affect a sanctity and gravity of any group, society and country, should not be scanned for its wider use. The selection committee should undertake a final quality check iterance of the authenticity and accuracy of information. In this way the management should be objective, selective and remunerative as well for digital library.

7. PROCESS OF DIGITAL LIBRARY

The process basically involves converting a physical object i.e. printed text, manuscript , image or sound & film and video recording., image or electronic photograph by using scanner or digital camera and safely store them in CD's or drivers i.e. pen drives etc. This whole process is called digitization or digitalization. To facilitate and to complete the whole process of creating digital information resources i.e. digitalization it is basically required that all the library functions must be computerized with scanners, CD writer and internet connection. Networking facilities like LAN & WAN must also be available in library. CD-ROM and multimedia stations should be installed. These requirements will reduce expenditure in converting text to digital form. To make the best use of this process a separate web page may be created for library highlighting its services and collections on internet. It will increase the use of its resources. Though there are problems to be faced like compliance with standards of widely distributed linkages and value added services are interposed at many implementation stages even then this process will definitely increase the capacity and capability of library for providing responsive and high quality on line services. CD-ROM (Compact Disc Read One Memory) technology had made this process more easy, vital & fast. It has attracted the publishers, the libraries and the user with its unique features of large storage capacity and its interactive search facility. Hussain K.H. Rahnam Nair R and Raveendran AK have assessed its impective importance for digital library. In their published paper "CD-ROM full text publishing" mentioned "By the mid 80s, CD-ROMs made profound impact on libraries...affecting library services and operations in academic libraries" Beheshti J, large A and Moukdad H have called it as a "transient technology" Now it has invariably considered as a valuable and important storage device. In the recent past the role of this technology has become more prominent and vital, with spread of DVDs, in content to digital library It came to be known as a dv-stressing collections device to meet out the automation requirements of the libraries and information processing centers will done version of CDS-ISIS is widely used. This database creation software is known as "WINISIS" and can easily accessible on web through "GENISIS WEB". This software is widely used and developed by UNESCO since 1995. The present "WINISIS version, 1.5 build 3" has been introduced in 2003. The most important feature of this software is capability to handle an unlimited number of databases and users are free to design according to their requirements. Many libraries, Museums in the world are using this software now a days through "*Apoche Ineb Server*". Few databased sodeveloped by Mishra Kumar & Tripathi Libraries P.K. Kelkar Library IIT Kanpur by using ININSIS/ GENISIS software, can be seen in following figures.

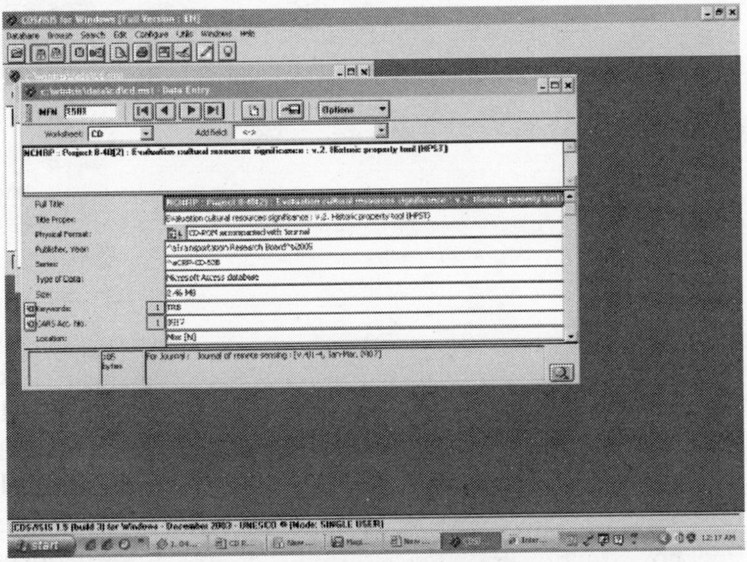

Fig. 1. Data Entry Worksheet

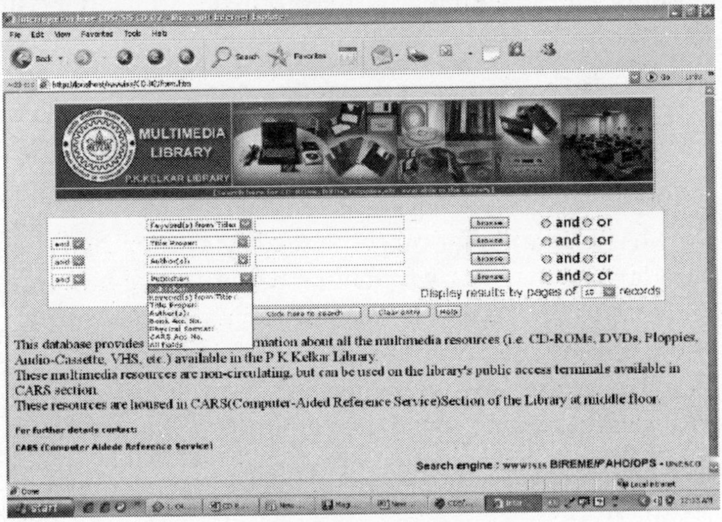

Fig. 2. Query Form

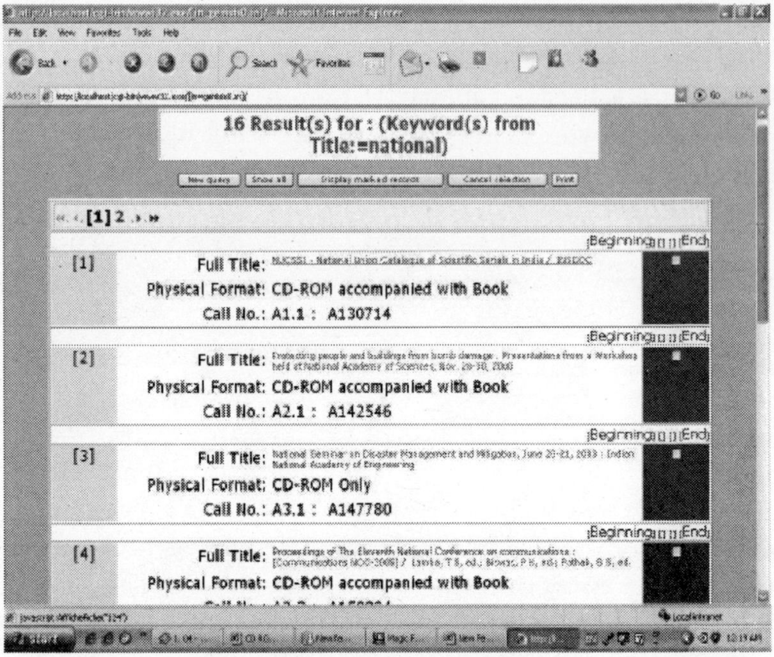

Fig. 3. Detail display of search result

For effective and meaningful process of digitalization, the following tools play important role

A. MARC

B. Internet resources and searching

C. Developing Digital Library

A. MARC

MARC Stands for machine readily cataloging it helps to standardize the library functions at one common & agreed standard to the used by all libraries by exchanging bibliographies information among computerized library systems. It can be saw well interpreted cataloging record of data contains a guide to tell the computer what type of data fallow" BY the help of this all type of library application programs can be applied to the library data basic.

Averred of marc records are developed by library congress, which now called USMARC. The standing of marks is more then 35 years. Library congress in satiation de was the first to produce MARC records in October 1966 there after U.K. France Germany, Canada and Australia have devised separate MARC formats.

In this way thee were 60 countries in the world using bibliographies formats based on MARC.

Later on it was felt necessary to create one MARC format to facilitate the bibliography exchange of records because every country has developed their own MARC format & country then from one to another was the big problem, ten MARC –21 come in as a harmonized CANMARC and USMARC. The national Library of Canada and library congress worked to gather and record all the format differences the familiar terms of marc are: Fields (ii) Sub fields (iii) Indicators (iv) content Designators

The bibliographic data of catalogued item has been deiced in logically into fields and subdued into sub field each type of data with in the field is called sub fields that is predated by a code for batter identification. The indicators are the two speeches, which is a number from 0 to 9. There are only two indicators in field. A contact designators is a collection terms used refer to the tags, sub field codes and indicators.

In the way MARC has its vital important is providing a standard format for the global exchange of bibliographic information available in machine readable format in the library world ride.

B. Internet Resources and Searching

The internet is a collection of net work i.e. compilation of national, regional and foreign net works are commuted through "gateways". It is based on server models which stored and provide the information required by the clients.

It is a fantastic tool for closely associated was used the world wide wave for transmitting a wide verity of information it is based on web technology and dependency of internet increasing day by day as provide batter security and hire bandwidth at a lower price due to its technological advancement as we inter the twenty first century the internet will have to offer faster access and become more powerful useful reliable and less congested .

It is necessary to have search engine for searching information on internet. The search use software program search for robots, spiders or crawlers. Since there is a large number of useful information available in the library and its is improves to physically examine all the books million of pages and billions of words or the wave and its difficult to search all those wave pages without the help of search engine /direction which is common by called "subject catalogue" the wave directories are organize according to the main topics and sub topic e.g. Arts, science health, business act. Wave search engine is like on index of a book from which one can local individual appearances of search words and document also over the wave through search techniques.

Concept of cataloging of resources available in the library physically is also now possible for cataloging the internet resources. The need was felt in order to create bibliographic resources of the resources available on internet and to make it available through on line catalogues. Through computer, internet recount, modem and simple communication software one can reach to library resources on internet. The utility of internet resources can be assessed in proper and effective routine functioning of library by locating the subject wise directories.

C. Developing Digital Libraries

A digital library resources is on assemblage of digital computing , storage, and communication machinery to gather with the software needed to reproduce emulate and extend the resources provided by conditional library. The concept of a digital library is not merely equivalent to a digitized collection with information management tools. Association of research libraries has identify the fine elements of digital libraries

(i) The digital library is not a single entry
(ii) It requires technology to oink the resources of a many.
(iii) Its linkages are transparent to the end users.
(iv) Universal access to digital libraries is a goal.
(v) Digital library collections are not limited to document surrogates.

The digital libraries will provide more enterable access, anywhere, any time. It will be cheaper there frient libraries. There is a great need for adopting various standards and best practices to build interoperable digital libraries. Digital information needs to be achieved and preserved for future use. It is a digital publishing tools connected from one digital format to another to suite the requirements of a particular digital library.

This process is called as digitization or digitalization. The first step is computing paper documents in to a digital library collection is to obtain images of all pages of all publications in digital format by scamming then through scammer, a digital image of each paper is reamed and transformed into image. The main tool of such electronic system of recording, storing transmission and communication of information records computer, keyboard, web search engine or web directory and the internet system through which one can get authentic and well evaluated information due to this system library function become more effective, efficient and standardized on the basis of national and international norms, formats and marks. It is a boon for the library system, services and management.

8. ADVANTAGES OF DIGITAL LIBRARIES

The development of digital libraries seems an illustration of man's never ending desire to improve his means of communication. The digital library is an advanced information highway in this regards which easily provide quick, accurate and updated authenticate information as and when and where in the world at minimal cost required by users by using searching and browsing mechanisms. Its CD ROM technology is a permanent optical - based storage device through which documents can stored and preserved for a very long time and can randomly access at a very low cost. It is a reliable medium requires less shelf space. It is economical and practically viable now a day. Due to its easy transportation, it becomes attractive in days - to competitive world. Its sources not get exhausted with unlimited use. Presentation of information can do with in a reasonable time with its easy, effective and speedily multiple accesses. One can easily download the required information due to its networking capability.

Due to its multiple use it is advantageously useful in providing education, training and career planning etc; as large volumes of data and information's can easily be stored and transferred. In this way it develops a distributed learning environment for the benefit to its users. Above all, the quality of information service can be improved and maintained through the digital resources. Advocates of digital libraries use to say that digital library contribute in many ways such as its resources can assist in the process of knowledge creation.

Though there are many problems and challenges to be faced in this process of transmission of data information's from its collection centre to its users, such as compliance with standards of widely distributed linkages and value - added services are interposed at many stages, even then the multimedia capability of digital is clearly a distinct advantage for recording, storing and preserving information's in a wide verily of formats. Here it is worth while to mention that difference of opinion regarding its value and utility may exists but every body like to adopt and adept new technologies hence it is not an end in it self. The digital resources need to be organized into a digital library and the principle of resource selection; collections and organization for access and retrieval applicable to other resources as well. The real benefits to technology, especially for libraries, will be in improving resources and services. Now there can be no dispute about the importance of digitization and digital resources despite of this facts that in completion of this process of digitalization there are many challenges and practical problems may come and arise to face. In facing and over coming over the difficulties new technology will definitely be helpful and will certainly brought huge improvement in providing physical accesses to published information resources especially on the web.

9. DEVELOPMENT OF DIGITAL LIBRARIES IN INDIA

The modern libraries not only contain books and periodicals but also contain a large verify of non book items in the form of digital resources, which can be classified in two segments - visual and audio. The visual can further be seen in still photographs and moving film elips & strips

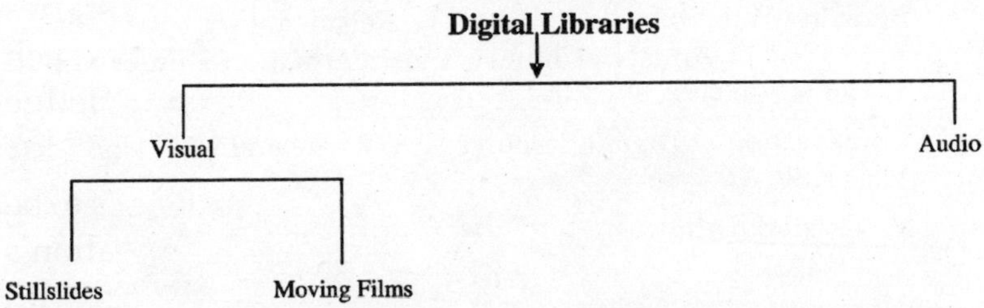

This trend started in U.S.A. U.K. And other advanced countries about fine decade ago. The pace of growth of

scientific information had also become faster.

In India this transformation of library started two decades ago. In early 1990 Indian Institute of Technology Kanpur library known as P.K. Kelkar library had transformed in to digital library by using Winisis and Genisis web software. A well planned and systematic efforts had been made in this regard. Likewisw central Drug Research Institute Library (CDRI Library) Lucknow, and College of Engineering Panchvati Nasik (Maharashtra) invited such an efforts during the year 2000 through different modules of LIBSYS. There after this wave spread over in the country with its faster speed now at last 800 libraries in the countries have been changed into digital libraries.

10. REFERENCES

- DESIDOC Vol. 29, No. 2 (RSR Varalaksksmi).
- Digital library and information developments, Kusum Verma, Delhi, Vista International Pub. House 2008.
- Lynch Clifford and Hactor Garcia - Molimma IITA Digital Library Work Shop Reston, VA, May - 18/19-1995
- Hussain K.H. Raman Nair R and Raveendran A.K. CD-Rom full text publishing - information studies, 8 (3)(2002)Paper on line accessed at eprints, relis.org/archive/0006219/01/IS2002 pdf.
- Beheshti J, Large A and moukdad H, designing and developing multimedia CD-ROMs: lesson from the online information review, 25(4)(2001)229-240.
- CD ROM collection management and development of web interface by using WINISIS/GENISIS at P.K. Kelkar library , IIT kanpur, published in Annals of library and information studies vol 55 December 2008PP265-274.
- Conservation of Digital Resources P.S. Bodke and KN Nandurkar Page No. 170
- WWW.ukoin.ac.uk

2

Digital Library Use: A Case Study of R. C. Patel Institute of Technology

Satish L. Padme
Assistant Librarian, Dr. Babasaheb Ambedkar Marathwada University Library, Aurangabad, Maharashtra.
Sagare Ganesh D.
Librarian, R. C. Patel Institute of Technology Shirpur, Dhule, Maharashtra, India.

ABSTRACT

Libraries are established in order to meet multifarious needs for information of the society, hence they play a vital role in the societal development by providing proper and useful information to the people contained in the books and in other types of reading sources.

The rapid growth and uses of information communication technologies has changed the library scenario in their source and services .The IT revolution has changed the traditional library in to computerized library, then automated library ,electronic library and most recently in to a Digital Library. Digital library directly offered directly access to the content of a wide variety of intellectual works. Including text, audio, video and, data. ; and may offer a variety of services supporting search, access and collaboration .in last decade the genesis and development of digital libraries have rapidly increase because they offer convenience, expanded access, and search capabilities not present by traditional libraries .

Present paper systematically analyses the definition of Digital library, concept of Digital library& digital library services, importance of digital library, about R. C. Patel college Digital library, Infrastructure of digital library in a R. C. Patel college of engineering, digital library Sources. Year wise use of Digital library by UG and PG student and Faculty, Average use of digital library per day, per month, purpose of using digital library services. In Present study survey method was adopted by the author.

Keywords: Library, IT, Electronic library, Digital library, R. C. Patel college of Engineering.

1. INTRODUCTION

Now we are living in 21st century and this age is called as information age which is based on the IT revolution has changed the traditional library into computerized library and computerized library into electronic library, then it change in to Digital library. Digital library is an organized collection of digitized material including text, images, video and audio, along with methods for access and retrieval and for selection, creation, organization, and maintenance of the collection. Aims of DL are improved access, Preservation, Application environment in any kind of institutional library. DL provide and infrastructure for publishing and managing content so it is discovered easily and effectively.

Present study focuses on the use of Digital library by the Engineering college student of R. C. Patel institute of Engineering. In which attempts have been made to know the digital library Sources. Yearwise use of Digital library by UG and PG student and Faculty, Average use of digital library per day, per month, purpose of using digital library services.

2. DIGITAL LIBRARY: DEFINITION

Digital library could be referred to as computerized network system where all the information is stored in electronic format, which can be accessed and transmitted through networks enabling retrieval of desired information by a large number of users."

3. IMPORTANCE OF DIGITAL LIBRARY

In this modern complex and corporate world everyone need quality information within the shortest time. it is not possible to the traditional libraries to satisfy the need of user. Digital library provides almost all information required by the user. Digital libraries with various technologies namely audio, video, computer, Internet, multimedia, satellites, TV cable, interactive video, telephone line etc. greatly support the higher education

4. ABOUT RC PATEL INSTITUTE OF TECHNOLOGY

The library is automated with SLIM software and will be connected to the main server to the hostel via WiMax network so that students can access OPAC (Online Public Access Catalog) through the hostel terminals. Reprographic facility is also made available to the students and faculty members. Library digitized. The library remains open for the entire duration of the college timings and provision is also made for 24 hrs access during University Examinations. The Library is self-sufficient with all the academic requirements and has a sound collection of National/ International Journals, Books, Educational CDs and CBTs.

5. OBJECTIVES OF THE STUDY

- To assess the contemporary use of electronic information resources by the faculty member

- To study the use of web services in RCPIT digital library by the faculty members
- To know the time spent for resources searching by the faculty member of RCPIT
- To examine the types of approaches databases and search techniques used by the faculty members
- To know the satisfaction of faculty members
- To highlight the problem in searching of e-resources

6. METHODOLOGY

Survey method has been adopted to study the various aspects. A structured questionnaire was design to collect the data from the faculty member of R .C. Patel institute of technology from all branches of Engineering. keeping in mind basic objectives of study.

7. ANALYSIS OF DATA

Out of 80 teaching faculty members includes Assistant professor, Associate professors, and professors from different faculties of engineering only 64 (80%) responded with the filled in questionnaire .data collected through questionnaire was scrutinized, classified, and tabulated for better understanding.

7.1. Computer Knowledge of Faculty Members

The present study attempted to ascertain the knowledge of computers of faculty member. These studies show that all the respondents were computer literate, which is a healthy sign for any organization. In addition, the study attempted to know about the extent of computer knowledge of faculty members.

Table 1. Extent of Computer Knowledge

Extent	*No. of respondents*	*Percentage*
Excellent	30	47%
Good	22	34%
Fair	10	16%
Satisfactory	2	03%
Total	**64**	**100%**

The analysis of Table 1 shows that as high as 30 respondents, representing 47% of total respondents had excellent computer knowledge. Further the computer knowledge of 22 respondents 34% was good followed by 10 respondents 16% with fair computer knowledge, and 2 respondents 03% with satisfactory computer knowledge. The results show an encouraging picture of faculty member of RCPIT on extent of computer knowledge.

7.2. Frequency of Using the Digital Library

DL& their sources has become an important tool for teaching and research. Literature on all the field of knowledge is available on internet, which is very useful for faculty members to enrich their knowledge. The present study attempts to find information on the use of DL, frequency, purpose. Table 2 clearly reveals that most of the faculty members. i.e. 47 out of 80 (73%) were using it on daily basis. Further 16% respondents were using it on weekly basis 6% were using it on monthly basis, and 5 % use it when they require it.

Table 2. Use of D.L & Facilities

Frequency	*No. of respondents*	*Percentage*
Daily	47	73%
Weekly	10	16%
Monthly	04	06%
As when required	03	05%
Total	64	100%

7.3. Purpose of Use Digital Library facilities

Regarding the purpose of DL Facilities ex. Internet and other services use the analysis of table 3 shows that as high as 61 respondents out of 64 (95%) opined that they use services for study and research .it is followed by 03 responses 05% for email, and general information.

Table 3. Purpose of Use Digital Library facilities

Purpose	*No. of responses*	*Percentage*
Study and research	61	95%
General information,	03	05%
Total	64	100%

7.4. Use of e-resources

E-resources along with print resources have become an integral part of a library collection. In addition, a remarkable shift of choice from print resources to e-resources have taken place by users for information accordingly, a large number of e-resources are being acquired by libraries but it is a fact that use of e-resources is not satisfactory in most of the libraries, the main reason is the lack of awareness among the users. The present study attempt to highlight on this matter in the table no.4.

Table 4. Use of e-resources

Response	*No. of Responses*	*Percentage*
Yes	62	97%
No	02	02%
Total	**64**	**100%**

Table no. 4 clearly indicate that out of 64 respondent 62(97%) were aware of e-resources and only 2% respondents not aware about e-resources the result implies towards a positive sign regarding use of e-resources by the faculty members of RCPIT, Shirpur.

7.5. Type of e-resources frequently used

The analysis of data in Table no. shows that e-journals and e-databases were the most use e-resources by the respondents as seen their responses which are 19(30%) and 20(31%) respectively. it is followed by use of e-articles(14%) ,e-books (11%) ,e-thesis-dissertation,(8%),e-newspapers, magazines(2%) ,and further 5% responses indicates the use of all mentioned e-resources by the Teaching faculty member of RCPIT

Table 5. Type of E-resources Frequently Used

E-resources	*No. of Responses*	*Percentage*
E-databases	19	30%
E-journals	20	31%
E-articles	9	14%
E-books	7	11%
E-news Papers/magazines	1	02%
E-thesis	5	08%
All	3	05%
Total	64	100%

7.6. Purpose of Using E-resources

The main purpose of using e-resources by the faculty members of RCPIT is to all purposes .it shows that as high as 58 responses, out of 64 representing91% followed by (3%) study, teaching and research work,(3%) for writing paper (3%) for presentation in seminar/ conferences / workshop.

Table 6. Purpose of Using E-resources

Purpose	*No. of Responses*	*Percentage*
Study and teaching Research work	2	03%
Paper writing for publication	2	03%
Seminar ,workshop presentation	2	03%
All	58	91%
Total	**64**	**100%**

7.7. Knowledge of Copyright

Copyright and intellectual property right is two core legal issues related to any arbitrary and indiscriminate use of any documents. Faculty members should have the knowledge of these while using the e-resources .realizing its importance, the present study collected data on these. Analysis of table no.7 reveals that a majority of 55 respondents (86%) have knowledge regarding the copyright and IPR issues whereas 09 respondents (14%) did not have any knowledge regarding the copyright and IPR issues, which quite surprising.

Table 7. Knowledge of Copyright

Knowledge on copyright/IPR	*No. of Respondents*	*Percentage*
Yes	55	86%
No	09	14%
Total	**64**	**100%**

7.8. Problem in E-resources Searching

The distribution of faculty members according to their problems in resources searching is shown in following table no.9.

Table 8. Problem in E-resources Searching

Problem in e-resources searching	*No. of Respondents*	*Percentage*
Lack of terminology	10	15.8%
Lack of technical experience	19	29.6%
Lack of command	30	46.8%
Problems not create	05	07.8%
Total	**64**	**100%**

It is evident from table no.8 that the problems faced by the faculty members in e-resources searching are lack of command (46.8%), lack of technical experience (29.6%), and lack of terminology (15.8%), and (7.8%) faculty members did not have any problems in e-resources searching .Hence it can be concluded that most of the faculty members are facing the problems of lack of command.

7.9. Satisfaction of faculty members

The distribution of faculty members according to their satisfaction of DL services of RCPIT is shown in Table no.9.

Table 9. Satisfaction of Faculty Members

Opinion of Faculty	*No. of Respondents*	*Percentage*
Satisfied	35	54.7%
Almost satisfied	26	40.6%
Dissatisfied	03	4.7%
Total	**64**	**100%**

It is evident from table no. - that (54.7%) of the faculty members are satisfied with regards to RCPIT Digital library services , (40.6%)of the faculty members are Almost satisfied about services and (4.7%) of the faculty members are not satisfied about DL services. Hence it can be concluded that most of the faculty members (95.3%) are satisfied or almost satisfied about DL services of RCPIT.

8. CONCLUSION AND SUGGESTIONS

The library environment has currently undergone drastic change in terms of Digital library their collection and services .the proliferation of Digital library has had a significant impact on the way the academic community uses, stores, and preserves information. Faculty member attitude seem to be a very positive towards Digital libraries get way to provide assistance in accessing e- resources.

In today's Information age faculty members and students are heavily dependent on Digital libraries and their e-resources for satisfaction of their information need within time and to keep themselves up-to-date in their subject area.

The study reveals that the faculty members of RCPIT, Shirpur, are using the Digital library and their e-resources satisfactorily .at the same time the Digital library of RCPIT is playing an important role into provide the quality library services and in promotion, assistance, and guidance in accessing the e-resources. Still there is enough scope for central library to develop its infrastructural facilities for accessing e-resources, procurement of more e-resources as per requirement, motivating user for accessing open source e-resources.

9. REFERENCES

- Doraswamy M. Web search pattern in digital libraries by faculty members of engineering colleges: A Survey. Indian journal of library and information science, 2009, 3(2), 103-107.
- http://www.rcpit.ac.in/main.asp?mpage=library.htm
- Satpathy, S. & Rout, B. Use of E-Resources by the faculty members with special reference to CVRCE, Bhubaneswar. DESIDOC journal of Library and Information Technology, 2010, 30(4), 11-16.
- Swain, D. K. & Panda, K. C. Use of e-services by faculty members of business schools in state of India: A study. Collection Building, 2009, 28(3), 108-16.http://www.emeraldinsight.com accessed on 10 July 2011.
- T. Ashok Babu, T... Etal. vision of future library and information *systems,* Chennai: viva Books private Ltd. 2000.

3

RFID (Radio Frequency Identification) in Libraries

Chopkar H. D.
Librarian, Podar International School, Aurangabad, (MS), India
Dr. (Mrs.) Khaparde V. S.
Associate Professor & Head, Dept.of Lib & I Sc. Dr. Babasaheb Ambedkar Marathwada University, Aurangabad (MS) India

ABSTRACT

Radio Frequency Identification (RFID) is a new generation Identification and Data collection technology that helps to automate business processes and allows identification of large number of objects like books, using radio waves. RFID is used in libraries primarily to automate the book handling process including checkout, inventory maintenance and check in when combined with automatic or computer assisted sorting equipment, RFID facilitates and speeds up book sorting. Automating this process allows librarians to spend more time with customers increasing customer satisfaction. This paper discovers the technology, Components of RFID System, advantages and disadvantages of RFID in library.

Keywords: Library Automation, Radio Frequency Identification (RFID), Library Security, Library collections;

1. INTRODUCTION

Radio Frequency Identification (RFID) is a generic term is used to describe a system that transmits the identity (in the form of a unique serial number) of an object or person wirelessly, using radio waves. It's grouped under the broad category of automatic identification technologies. Radio frequency identification combines radio frequency and micro-chip technologies to create a smart system that can be used to identify secure and inventory items. RFID invented in 1969, patented in 1973, first used in harsh industrial environment in 1980s', and standards presented in 2001, is the latest addition of technology to be used in the libraries for a combination of automation and security activities in the well maintenance of documents either inside the library or goes out-of library. RFID uses wireless radio communication to uniquely identify objects or people, and is one of the fastest growing automatic data collection (ADC) technologies , which is comprising one or more reader/ interrogators and RF transponders in which data transfer is achieved by means of suitably modulated inductive or radiating electro-magnetic carriers. In addition it can be used as a data carrier, with information being written and updated to the tag on the fly. RFID systems carry data in suitable transponders, generally known as tags, and retrieve data, by machine-readable means, at a suitable time and place to satisfy particular application needs.

RFID is a combination of radio frequency and microchip. RFI chips are of particular interest, because they have become smaller and smarter to the point where they can be added every kind of document and can be read and updated from a distance.

2. DEFINITION

Radio Frequency Identification uses a semi conductor (microchip) in a tag or label to transmit stored data when the tag or label is exposed to radio waves of the correct frequency.

3. COMPONENTS OF RFID SYSTEM

A comprehensive RFID system has components

3.1. Tag

The heart of the system is the RFID tag, which can be fixed inside a books back cover or directory to CDs and videos. This tag is equipped with a programmable chip and an engraved antenna and microchip with a capacity of at least 64 bits.

There are three types of tags

1) Read only
2) WORM
3) Read/Write

Tags are read only, if the identification is encoded at the time of manufacture and not rewritable. WORM (write-once-read-many) tags are programmed by using organization, but without the ability to rewrite them later. Read/write tags, which are chosen by most libraries, can have information changed or added. In libraries that use RFID, it is common to have part of the read/write tag secured against rewriting.

3.2. Readers

It consists of one RF module (providing the signal process of transmitting or receiving) one control module and one coupling element through an input/output interface, to connect with applications; another very important feature is the power supply. Passive tags do not contain power and all the power for the process must converted from radio waves that are the provided by the reader. Active tags contain a battery. Compared with passive tags, active tags provide more distance for induction, but life still depends on batteries.

The properties of radio waves are frequency dependent. They depend on the frequency of the electromagnetic spectrum. Just as the structure of memory cards or smart cards depend on the mode of memory and structure.

Readers in RFID in library are used in the following ways.

I. **Conversion Station :** where library data is written to the tag.

II. **Staff workstation to circulation :** used to charge and discharge library materials.

III. **Self check-out station:** used to check out library materials without staff assistance.

IV. **Self check-in station :** used to check in library materials without staff assistance.

V. **Exit sensors :** to verify that all materials living the library has been checked out.

VI. **Book-drop reader :** used to automatically discharge library materials and reactivate security.

VII. **Sorter and conveyor :** automated system for returning materials to proper area of library.

VIII. **Hand-held reader :** used for inventorying and verifying materials is shelved correctly.

3.3. Antenna

The antennas produces radio signals to activate the tag and read write data to it. Antennas are the channels between the tag and the reader, which controls the system's data acquisitions and communication. The electromagnetic field produced by an antenna can be constantly present when multiple tags are expected continually. Antennas can be built into a doorframe of receive tag data from person's thing passing through the door.

3.4. Server

The server is the heart of some comprehensive RFID systems. It is the communications gateway among the various components. It receives the exchanges information with the circulation database. Its software includes the SIP/SIP2 (session initiation protocol) APIs (Application Programming Interface) NCIP (National Circulation Interchange Protocol) or SLNP necessary to interface it with the integrated library software but no library vendor has yet fully implemented NCIP APPROVED BY NISO. The server typically includes a transaction database, so that reports can be produced.

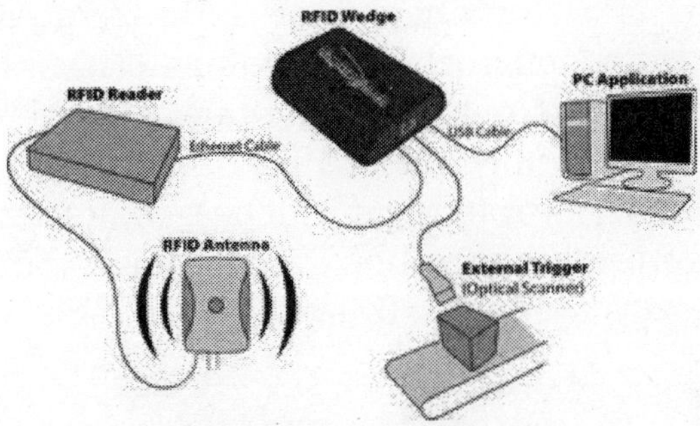

Fig. 1. Components of RFID System

4. RFID USE IN LIBRARY

RFID technology is primarily intended to reveal a current change in the library user service from the semi-automated to the fully-automated mode. It is a fast growing technology used in libraries for enhanced circulation capabilities, better inventory control, reliability, minimizing theft of document and provides batch access and storage of mass data. It facilitates better programming possibilities than barcode readers and also promotes operational efficiency and precision. RFID technology has further advantages over barcode readers such as faster circulation transaction and perfect tracking. This technology has the benefit of a simplified self-charging/discharging, highly reliable, high-speed inventorying and automated identification of materials. It enhances the rate of utilization of journals and book sorting. It also affords a faster inventory check, a better user information and web interface ,and book dropping and sorting, weeding the collection, shelf reading, collection development, location missing items and cleaning up of the collection, videos and CDs. It gives real time visibility for library inventory and reduces valuable staff time spent scanning barcodes for charging and discharging items without affecting the essence of the library service. RFID is the latest technology to be used in library theft detection systems.

RFID is a combination of radio frequency-based technology and microchip technology. The information contained on microchips in the tags affixed to library materials is read using radio frequency technology. A reader (sensor scanner or interrogator) looks for antennas on the tags and retrieves information from the microchips through them. The tags used in RFID systems can replace both EM

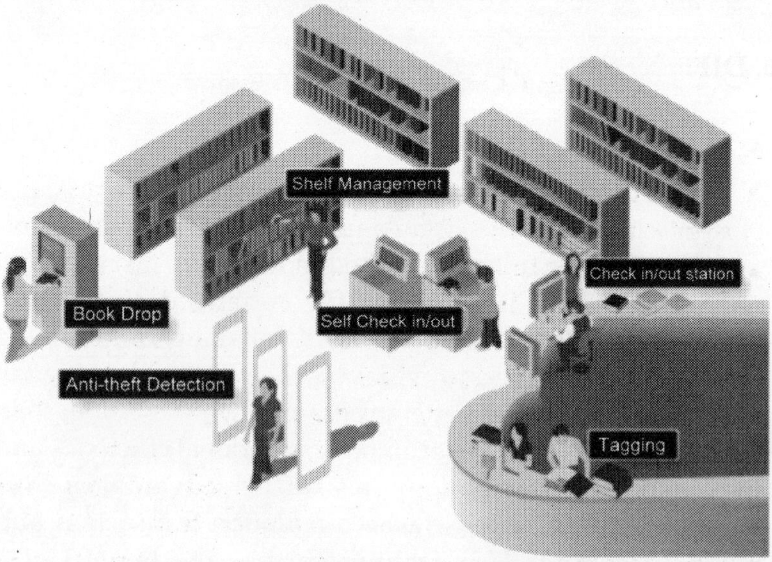

Fig. 2. RFID in Library Management

(Electro-Mechanical) or RF (Radio Frequency) theft detection barcodes and targets although the hybrid system that 3M introduced in 2000 replaced only barcodes and retained the EM strips in the belief that EM is superior to RFID for security.

5. SIX SENTENCE ABOUT RFID FOR LIBRARY

1. RFID tags replace both the EM security strips and barcode.
2. Radio frequency anti-theft detection is innovative and safe.
3. Simplify patron self check-out / check-in.
4. High-speed inventory and identify items which are out of proper order.
5. Long-term development guarantee when using open standard.
6. Ability to handle material without exception for video and audio tapes.

6. DIFFERENCE BETWEEN BARCODE AND RFID

- Information can be read from RFID tag much faster than from barcodes
- Several items in a stack/counter can be read at the same time using RFID.
- Items do not have to be handled one-by-one nor removed from the shelves.
- Inventory-taking is no longer a tedious operation
- RFID can stand more than 10,000 read/write
- RFID can have theft bit which can be done in two stages "ON/OFF".
- Shelf verification/rectification can be done on daily basis.
- Need not open/remove books to capture information

- Items are identified on upper and lower shelves more comfortably.

7. BASIC TECHNOLOGY COMPARISON BARCODES VERSUS RFID

RFID	*BARCODE*
• Can be read and write	• Read only
• No line of sight required	• Needs direct visible contact to reader
• Multiple items can be read simultaneously (anti-collision)	• Single items scan
• Items attendant data (mobile data-carrier)	• Database look-up is always necessary
• Guaranteed data retention of at least 10 years	• Limited lifetime due to printing
• Stock verification made easier as No need of taking the books out from shelf. We can read multiple books from the shelf at a time.	• Stock Verification takes time because of the fact that each book has to take out from shelf and then scanned with the scanner.

8. ADVANTAGES

8.1. Rapid Check-out/Check in

The use RFID reduces the amount of time required to perform circulation operations. The most significant time savings are attributable to the facts that information can be read from RFID tags much faster than barcodes and that several items in a stack can be read at the same time, while initially unreliable, the anti-collision algorithm that allows an entire stack to be check out or check-in. The other time savings realized by circulation staff are modest unless the RFID tags replace both the EM security strips or RF tags of older theft detection systems and the barcodes of the library management system.

8.2. High-speed Inventorying

Unique advantage of RFID systems is their ability to scan books on the shelves without tipping them out or removing them. A hand-held inventory reader can be moved rapidly across a shelf of books to read all of the unique identification information. Using wireless technology, it is possible not only to update the inventory, but also to identify items which are out of proper order

8.3. High reliability

The readers are highly reliable. Some RFID systems have an interface between the exit sensors and the circulation system to identify the items moving out of the library. Were a patron to run out of the library and not be intercepted, the library would at least know what had been stolen. If the patron card also has an RFID tag, the library will also be able to determine who removed the items without properly charging them. This is done by designating a bit as the "theft" bit and turning it off at time of charge and on at time of discharge.

8.4. Simplified Patron Self-charging/Discharging

For patrons using self-charging, there is a marked improvement because they do not have to carefully place materials within a designated template and they can charge several items at the same time. Patron self-discharging shifts that work from staff to patrons. Staff is relieved further when readers are installed in bookdrops

8.5. Automated Materials Handling

RFID technology is automated materials handling. This includes conveyor and sorting systems that can move library materials and sort them by category into separate bins or onto separate carts. This significantly reduces the amount of staff time required to ready materials for reshelving. Given the high cost of the equipment, this application has not been widely used.

8.6. Fast Track Circulation Operation

The use of RFID reduces the amount of time required to perform circulation operations. The most significant time savings are attributable to the facts that information can be read from RFID tags much faster than from barcodes

8.7. Tag life

RFID tags last longer than barcodes because nothing comes into contact with them. Most RFID vendors claim a minimum of 100,000 transactions before a tag may need to be replaced

9. DISADVANTAGES

9.1. High cost

The major disadvantage of RFID technology is its cost

9.2. Removal of exposed tags

The RFID Tags can not be concealed in either spine or gutter of the books and are exposed for removal. If a library wishes, it can insert the RFID tags in the spines of all except thin books; however, not all RFID tags are flexible enough

9.3. Accessibility to Compromise

It is possible to compromise an RFID system by wrapping the protected materials in two or three layers of ordinary household foil to block the radio signal. It is also possible to compromise an RFID system by placing two items against one another so that one tag overlays another. That may cancel out the signals. This requires knowledge of the technology and careful alignment.

9.4. Exit Gate Sensor Problems (Reader)

While the short-range readers used for circulation

charge and discharge and inventorying appear to read the tags 100 percent of the time, the performance of the exit gate sensors is more problematic. They always don't read tag at up to twice the distance of the other readers. There is no library that has done a before and after inventory to determine the loss rate when RFID is used for security.

9.5. User privacy concerns

Privacy concerns associated with item-level tagging is another significant barrier to library use of RFID tags. The problems with today's library RFID system is that the tags contain static information that can be relatively easily read by unauthorized tag readers. This allows for privacy issues described as tracking and hotlisting.

9.6. Lack of standard

The tags used by library RFID vendors are not compatible even when they conform to the same standards because the current standard only seek electronic compatibility between tags and readers.

10. BEST PRACTICES FOR LIBRARIES

As libraries are implementing RFID systems, it is important to develop best practices guidelines to utilize the technology in best way and to keep the privacy concern away.

1) The library should be open about its use of RFID technology including providing publicly available documents stating the rational for using RFID, objectives of its use and associated policies and procedure and who to contact with question.
2) Signs should be pasted at all facilities using RFID. The signs should inform the public that RFID technology is in use, the type of usage and a statement of protection of privacy and how this technology differs from other information collection methods.

3) Only authorized personnel should have access to the RFID system
4) No personal information should be stored on the RFID tag.
5) All RFID readers in the library should be clearly marked.
6) Information describing the tagged item should be encrypted on the tag even if the data is limited to a serial number.
7) All communication between tag and reader should be encrypted via a unique encryption key.

11. CONCLUSIONS

Libraries have become a driving force in the development of RFID for the mass market. This technology was first used in other sectors, such as logistics, airline luggage automation and parcel distribution. The leading role for libraries is understandable, since libraries share their knowledge in the development of these systems. Also the benefits have been greatest in the library community. It is important to know that the software is far more refined today. Developments in RFID technology continue to yield larger memory capacities, wider reading ranges, and faster processing. The interest in RFID as a solution to optimize further the automation and tracking of documents are gathering momentum at an increasing pace, with more libraries joining the trails. RFID is increasing in popularity among libraries, as the early adopters of this technology have shown that, it makes good economic sense, both for large and small libraries.

12. REFERENCES

- Boss R.W (2003) RFID Technology for libraries. *Library technology report, 39(6),6-58.*

- Coyle, M (2005) Management of RFID in libraries. *Journal of academic librarianship*, 31(5), 486-509.
- Hussain, A (2007) RFID in libraries. *IASLIC Bulletin*, 52(1), 49-59
- Molnar, D; Wagner D.A (2004) Privacy and security in library RFID: issues, practices and architectures. Retrieved from *www.cs.berkeley.edu_dmolnar/library*.
- Narayanan, A; Sing S and Somasekharan, M (2005) Implementing RFID in library: methodologies, advantages and disadvantages.
- Singh, J; Brar, N and Fong, C (2006) The state of RFID applications in libraries. *Information Technology and Libraries*, 25(1), 24-32.
- Syed Md.Shahid (2005) Use of RFID Technology in libraries: a new approach to circulation, tracking, inventorying and security of library materials. *Library philosophy and practices*, 8(1).
- Ward, Matt (2006) RFID: Frequency, standards, adoption and innovation. *JISC Technology and Standards Watch* 16-17.
- Yu, S.C.and Shin, H. (2007) RFID implementation and benefits in libraries. The Electronic Library, 25(1), 54-64.
- *www.rfid-library.com/en/default_e.html.*

4

Digital Library Sources and Services in Information Age

Rahul B. Khandare

Librarian, Sardar Vallabhabhai Patel Arts and Science College Ainpur, Tal. Raver, Dist. Jalgaon (Maharashtra)

ABSTRACT

Digital libraries provide instant access to digitized information by utilizing the avenues of information technology. Unlike printed books, digital libraries are multimedia and data retrievable can be brought under net-surfing in the sea of information and are aided by hypermedia and hypertext programmes and experimental expert systems. Doorways to libraries are becoming gateways to the world as digital content, through new and constantly changing technology, becomes available. The term digital library is now widely accepted to mean the use of digital technology in the provision of library services and operations, which include acquisition, organization, storage conservation and dissemination of Information to users.

KEYWORDS: digital library, hardware, software's, greenstone, fedora.

1. INTRODUCTION

The advent of information technology has paved the way for digital libraries. There are a number of terms used by authors to represent the concept of digital library as polyglot.library, electronic library desktop library, online library, library without walls, virtual library etc. of these, digital library is the commonly used terminology by majority of authors. Digital libraries are heterogeneous in nature. These include work related to information and how to digitize, store, find, link, visualize, use, publish, manage and share information. Digital libraries provide instant access to digitized information by utilizing the avenues of information technology. Unlike printed books, digital libraries are multimedia and data retrievable can be brought under net-surfing in the sea of information and are aided by hypermedia and hypertext programmes and experimental expert systems.

2. DEFIFNITIONS OF DIGITAL LIBRARIES

Digital library may be defined as; According to Larson; "Digital libraries as not single, stand able and repositories, of digital data. Instead, they are a heterogeneous collection of network-based repositories using a variety of protocols for user's interaction, data encoding and transmission."

According to Griffin; "An organized collection of multimedia data with information management methods they represent the data as useful information and knowledge to people in a variety and organizational contexts".

3. NEED OF DIGITAL LIBRARIES

There are numbers of reasons of building up digital libraries, such as information explosion, dwindling budgets of the library, space problem, high information demand, available technologies, etc. as we know, today despite of having well-stocked libraries and well equipped resource centers, users demand for information is never met. Digital library can provide programmatic solutions to the problems faced by traditional libraries in managing their print-based collection like shrinking budget, time barrier and so on.

The world wide web and other web based technologies, use friendly interfaces, advances in online storage technologies etc. have worked as a catalyst in accelerating the pace of digitization and the some features for need of digital libraries that why digital libraries needed.

4. CHARACTERISTICS OF DIGITAL LIBRARIES

The different features of digital library may be defined as follows;

Collections : Digital library contain fixed, permanent documents, because of these, current libraries will not only have more dynamic collections, but also digital environment will made enable of quick handling and or ephemeral information.

Work : Digital library worked by individual alone.

Transforming of information : Breaking the physical boundaries of data transfer within and outside the countries. It is viewed that the support for communication and collaboration is as important as information seeking activities community or set or communities.

Digital resources of information : The digital resources can be online and off line, such as internet, e-journals, e-books, LAN-WAN, CD-ROMs, audio visual aids.

- Translation of a document may express essentially the same information, e.g. versions of classic literature in different languages.
- Each stored item is valuable, often with part of its residual assigned by its authors' assignees.
- Users are usually elsewhere than the information they

want, and often wish to correlate things from several sources.

- Item are put into libraries because, while each is thought valuable for futures references, the specific individuals who will read it and times when this will occur are not known.

5. ADVANTAGES OF DIGITAL LIBRARIES

No physical boundary : The user of a digital library need not to go to the library physically; people from all over the world can gain access to the same information, as long as an Internet connection is available.

Round the clock availability a major advantage of digital libraries is that people can gain access 24/7 to the information.

Multiple accesses : The same resources can be used simultaneously by a number of institutions and patrons. This may not be the case for copyrighted material: a library may have a license for "lending out" only one copy at a time; this is achieved with a system of *digital rights management* where a resource can become inaccessible after expiration of the lending period or after the lender chooses to make it inaccessible (equivalent to returning the resource).

Information retrieval : The user is able to use any search term (word, phrase, title, name, and subject) to search the entire collection. Digital libraries can provide very user-friendly interfaces, giving clickable access to its resources.

Preservation and conservation : Digitization is not a long-term preservation solution for physical collections, but does succeed in providing access copies for materials that would otherwise fall to degradation from repeated use. Digitized collections and born-digital objects pose many preservation and conservation concerns that analog materials do not. Please see the following "Problems" section of this page for examples.

Space : Whereas traditional libraries are limited by storage space, digital libraries have the potential to store much more information; simply because digital information requires very little physical space to contain them and media storage technologies are more affordable than ever before.

Added value : Certain characteristics of objects, primarily the quality of images, may be improved. Digitization can enhance legibility and remove visible flaws such as stains and discoloration.

Easily accessible.

6. DISADVANTAGES OF DIGITAL LIBRARIES

Copy right : Digitization violates the copy right law as the thought content of one author can be freely transfer by other without his acknowledgement so one difficulty to overcome for digital libraries is the way to distribute information. How does a digital library distribute information at will while protecting the copyright of the author?

Initial cost is high : The infrastructure cost of digital library i.e. the cost of hardware software leasing communication circuit is generally very high.

Efficiency : With the much larger volume of digital information finding the right material for a specific task becomes increasingly difficult.

Environments : Digital libraries cannot reproduce the environment of a traditional library many people also find reading printed material to be easier than reading material on a computer screen.

Preservation : Due to technology developments a digital library can rapidly become out of date and its data may become inaccessible.

- Libraries are vary of the new technology
- The first and important problem is of IPRs where the

library authorities have to discuss with publishers and authors on their aspect to evolve some mechanisms.

- Lack of expert to handle and operate the latest technology.
- Technological changes are also coming very fast in which everyone is expected to be shortcoming for implementing various programmes. So it is not feasible to change all the resources in to digital forms by the common libraries.

7. INFRASTRUCTURE PROPOSED FOR DIGITALIZATION PROCESS

On the basis of existing digital library initiatives, the following infrastructure proposed;

1. Hardware
   - High end servers-2
   - CD/DVD servers-1
   - CD/DVD writer-1
   - Client/server
2. Compatible operation system
3. Software
   - DIENST (*http://www.cs.cornell.edu/edlrg/diensstoverview.htm*)
   - EPRINTS (*http://software.eprints.org/download.php*)
   - GREENSTONE (*http://www.greenstone.org/english/home.html*)
   - ROADS (*http://roads.lut.ac.uk*)
   - SITESEARCH (*http://www.sitesearch.oclc.org*)
4. Scanners
   - A3 size-1
   - A4 size-1
   - Digital camera-1

5. Outsourcing of digital resources
6. Fiber optic connectivity
7. Manpower
8. Training staff and users

8. RESOURCES OF DIGITAL LIBRARY

- High speed internet connectivity
- Library should create the bibliographic database of print and non-print materials and such database to be made available via LAN and WAN
- Subscription E-journals
- Acquisition of need based digital resources in the form of CD-ROM, optical disk and multimedia version;
- Subscription E-Books
- Electronic text and journals
- E-mail and bulletin board
- Facility to access commercial databases via online in the related areas; and
- Internet –web

9. SERVICES OF MODERN DIGITAL LIBRARY

A modern digital library provides the following services to its users regardless of their geographical location;

- Book circulation
- Inter library loans
- Photography of documents
- On-line/off line reservation
- User membership, user's queries
- Reference support for subject searches
- A advanced librarian
- User education and training programmes

- Current awareness services
- Assistance in using computer facilities
- Access to library catalogues, databases, internet
- Publisher awareness service
- List of new publication received
- Electronic reference desk
- Assistance with bibliographic packages
- Flexible methods of submitting requests, e.g. via telephone, facsimile, e-mail, www, post.
- Electronic delivery to requesters workstation, where possible.

10. COLLECTION OF DIGITAL LIBRARY

- Metadata describing the data and having facility to provide links to other related databases;
- Open communication protocols for information retrievals
- Information access tools like; browsers, display and search engines;
- Electronic publishing tools
- Data compression
- Digital storage devices
- Scanning and conversion technology
- Multimedia for integration technologies
- Privacy and security
- Inter operability over the libraries
- Advanced information retrieval tools like indexing routing and filtering of information and
- Intellectual property rights.

11. EXAMPLES OF DIGITAL LIBRARIES

There are some examples of digital libraries has given below;

- American Memory from the Library of Congress; *http://lcweb2.loc.gov/ammem/ammemhome.html*
- University of California at Berkeley; *http://elib.cs.berkeley.edu/*
- Internet Public Library ; *http://www.ipl.org*
- New York Public Library; *http://digital.nypl.org/*
- LDL @ DRTC, Bangalore; *https://drtc.isibang.ac.in*

12. DIGITAL LIBRARY SOFTWARES

Some commonly used open source digital library software's are –

- Green Stone Digital Library Software
- E-prints
- D space
- Ganesha Digital library
- Keystone digital library suite
- Fedora
- Post Nuke
- Refbase
- Word Press
- Drupal & Bricks

12.1. Greenstone Digital Library Software

Green Stone is a suite of software for building and distributing digital library collections. It runs on all versions of windows, UNIX, MACOS-Y and apache. The greenstone digital library system has two separate interactive interfaces-

I. The reader's interface – who can be accessed by end users and operators within a web server.

II. The librarian interface - which is a Java based Graphical user interface (GUI) which makes material gathering, adding metadata, designing the searching and browsing facilities that collection will offer the users and build and serve the collection easier.

12.2. Eprints

EPRINTS is an open source of software package for building open access repositories. It is primarily used for institutional repositories and scientific journals. It can successfully run under Linux and Mac OSX. EPrints is developed at the School of Electronics and Computer Science, University of Southampton, UK.

The key features are:

- It is open-source software distributed under GPL licensing.
- It has multilingual support and one available on Linux platform
- It requires MySQL and Perl.
- It supports OAI-PMH protocol therefore good for creating distributed repositories.
- Metadata is stored in DBMS and on request displayed in XML format.
- One digital object can have more than one file.
- Authentic users can be created with rested responsibility.
- Work-flow can be established and online editors can edit the metadata.
- Online submission is supported in other words it supports self-archiving.
- The repository displays the recent additions.
- The software supports simple search by name of author, title and so on.

- Advanced search supports uncontrolled key word search and full text search.
- Collection can be created of preprints, post-prints, audio-visual streams and so on.

12.3. DSPACE

DSPACE– is a digital repository system that captures, stores, indexes, preserves and redistributes an organization's search data. The DSPACE OSS makes submission easy and supports the long term preservation of the digital material stored in its repository. It accepts all form of digital materials including text such as article, reprints, technical reports, working papers, conference papers, e-thesis, database, images, audio files, video files, learning objects and reformatted digital library collections. It runs on UNIX or LINUX operating system. It is used by many institutions, libraries archives, cultural heritage institution, government agencies and corporations. DSpace developed jointly by MIT Libraries and Hewlett-Packard Labs. The key features are:

- It is open source software distributed under GPL.
- It has very good multilingual support and it is platform independent.
- The software is written in JAVA and the system runs on Tomcat JSP server (an open source web server for Java Server Pages)
- A DSpace repository can be divided into communities. Communities can have several collections and can have sub collections. Collection contains items.
- Community, collection, and item have persistent identifiers called handles.
- Items can be described according to Dublin Core elements. Metadata can be modified even after submission.
- Batch ingestion (batch upload) of the items is possible.

- Batch export is also possible in the METS format but this is yet to be evolving fully.
- DSpace provides authorization. Each user of DSpace should have authorization he/she wishes to upload a document.
- DSpace requires mail server for posting automatically generated mails regarding activities to authorized persons.
- Workflow can be defined within the DSpace and persons can be authorized to submit, edit and view.
- Searching is done in DSpace according to metadata submitted but it also supports full-text search.

12.4. Ganesha Digital Library OSS

Ganesha Digital Library OSS enables institutions and users to share their knowledge as well as simultaneously access and utilize knowledge. It supports fast information searching.

12.5. Keystone Digital Library Suite

Keystone Digital Library Suite - is a family of open source digital content management, portal management and information discovery software packaged together to provide libraries, museums and archives with state of the digital library services. It supports the Firebox, Internet Explorer, Mozilla, Netscape, opera and safari web browser for accessing its functionality.

12.6. Fedora OSS

Fedora OSS runs on Linux, windows and Tonot 2.4. It supports word PDF, HTML and GIF file format. Fedora is a general-purpose digital repository system developed by Cornell University Information Science and the University of Virginia Library.

Key features are:

- Fedora is an open source web services based framework for managing and delivering digital content.
- It provides different views for the same document. For example, different level of resolution and size of the same image can be viewed.
- Fedora can be used as a component in the creation of applications such as institutional repositories and course management systems.
- Fedora is written in Java and runs as a web application in Tomcat.
- The storage layer uses a RDBMS (MySQL) and file system.
- Fedora supports FOXML (XML format specific to Fedora) and METS extension as object ingest and export formats.
- It supports batch ingest and batch export.
- User authentication is restricted to Administrator and Anonymous users.

12.7. Postnuke

Postnuke is software that creates an impressive, dynamic website and provides the web master with a site that can be administered with a minimal amount of HTML knowledge through a web browser. Installing modules, blocks and themes can increase Postnuke's functionality. For e.g. we can add a forum, a gallery and contact form. We can also change entire site look by changing themes. All this is possible with just a few clicks in the administrative panels.

12.8 Ref Base

Ref base is web based institutional repository and reference management software which is often used for self archiving.

12.9. Word Press

Word Press is a state-of-the-art semantic personal publishing platform with a focus on aesthetics web standards, and usability. It has been designed for blogging, but it is flexible enough to create all kinds of websites. It is written in PHP- a web programming language that mixes with HTML to produce dynamic web pages, and it has a host of template functions and plug-in that makes it easy to customize.

12.10. Drupal

Drupal is a free software package that allows an individual or a community of users to easily publish, manage and organize a wide variety of content on a website.

The built-in functionally combined with dozens of freely available add-on modules, will enable features such as: Content Management System. Blogs, collaborative authoring environment, forums, peer-to- peer networking, Newsletters, podcasting, picture galleries etc.

12.11. A Brick (Building Resources For Integrated Cultural Knowledge Services)

A brick (Building resources for integrated Cultural Knowledge Services) is an OSS framework for the management of distributed digital assets.

The OSS is an effective system in the hands of intelligent librarians to satisfy their users to a great extent.

13. CONCLUSION

Digital Collection of information with multimedia features, offer faster and easy access to large number of users. With the advent of information society, libraries being the part of society are gradually bringing in the speculated changes in their structure, function and services. The traditional libraries are shifting towards Automation,

Automated ones towards electronic, electronic ones moving to digitize their collection and ultimately a virtual library is the end mark of the process. The objective is - Speedy access of information instead of information storage. Access to maximum information instead of building large collection. A shift from mere storage house to electronic access points.

REFERENCES

- Dalve, Daya B. and Vaishnav A.A. (2010). New dimensions in library management proceeding of national seminar.
- Devarajan G. (1999). *Information technology in libraries.* New Delhi: Ess Ess publications.
- Singh, M.P. (2004). *Use of Information technology in library and information science.* Delhi: Abhijit publications.
- Singh, Sonal (2010). *Digital library collection and resources.* Lectured delivered in 10 th refresher course in LIS organized by ASC, Dr. B.A.M.U. Aurangabad.
- Tripathi, Aditya (2009). *Digital library collection and resources.* Lectured delivered in 9 th refresher course in LIS organized by ASC, Dr. B.A.M.U. Aurangabad.
- Verma, Naresh Chandara. (2007). Digital library information resources and services in modern era. *Journal of library and IT*. Vol. 3.
- *www.wikipedia.org(accessed* on 2/9/2011)

5

Net Generation: What The Academic Librarians Need to Know to Educate Them

Mohamed Majeed Mashroofa
Senior Assistant Librarian,
South Eastern University of Sri Lanka

ABSTRACT

This study describes various characteristics of Net Generation, their requirements, learning styles and information skills. This paper takes the form of a literature review and commentary on Net Generation and how the academic Librarians should prepare to educate them. The purpose of this study is to understand the Net generation and to explore their requirements in order to upgrade teaching pedagogies and library services. This article reviews selected literature on Net Generation and identified the paths and ways how to approach the Net generation for effective teaching and learning. It concludes that this generation students possess certain key traits that influence their learning styles. Accordingly teaching techniques and information sources and services should be polished and upgraded. It recommends that when the students enter into the university academics should analyze their ICT skills, Information behavior and the expectation towards library and learning perspectives in order to develop the existing services and to improve the teaching paradigms.

KEYWORDS: Net Generation, academic Librarians, library services, information sources, ICT skills.

1. INTRODUCTION

Net Generation or millennial particularly those aged 18-22 who make our undergraduate population today are characterized as technologically savvy and wanting results instantly and easily. Traditional teaching methods and library services may be ineffective on this generation. It is pivotal role of educationists to identify the requirements of students in order to adjust and develop the faculties or universities. Information and Communication Technology (ICT) rapidly develops day by day. The present day students widely access to digital media and the internet; they learn, work, think and create differently than the previous generations. Glass(2007) in Shaw, S.(2008) says that people who grow up in different time periods have very different sets of beliefs, values attitudes and expectations which in turn impact their behavior generally and in the workplace. Many parents complain that trying to get the children to study without radio, television and internet is rarely successful. Educating the Net generation is a privilege and a challenge.

The internet has led to the kind of global village of information and communication. Many researches in USA and other western countries have proven that the present day students are technologically savvy and they widely use instant messaging, blogs, wikis, computer games and social networks or sites. It is the pivotal role of educationists of our country to identify how the students conceptualize and use these new tools. With this knowledge university can create contexts for technology use that enhance learning, improve students' services and enrich students' social lives.

Net Generations are born around the time when PC was introduced. Generation Y is the term used for most recent demographic group. Net Generation is alternatively called as Millennial whose birth years fall between 1982 and 2000. People who born during the period was also called as the "Dot-Coms" the "Echo boomers", the "i Generation", Generation D" (D-Digital) and the " Nexters". Many pieces of research have been carried out in Western countries to identify the characteristics of this generation in many aspects such as behavior, social, cultural, learning and teaching.

2. CLASSIFICATION OF GENERATIONS

Oblinger and Oblinger (2005) has classified various generations as follows.

Matures : People who born in 1900-1946 are described as "Greatest Generation" They have the attributes of command and control as well as self-sacrifice. They respect for authority, prefer family and community involvement. They dislike technology.

Baby Boomers : People who born in 1946-1964 are described as" Me Generation". They are characterized as optimistic and workaholic. They like to have responsibility and they are work ethic. They have the attitude "can-do". They dislike laziness.

Generation X : People who born in 1965-1982 are described as "Latchkey Generation". They are independent and skeptical. They like freedom and capable of multitasking. They balance the work and life. They dislike red tape and Hype.

Net Generation : People who born in 1982-1991 and they are described as "Millennial". They are characterized as hopeful and determined. They like public activism and latest technology. They are very close with their parents. They dislike anything slow and negativity.

Post-Millenials : People who born in 1995-present.

Many other scholars such as Howe and Strauss(2000), Lancaster and Stillman (2002), Martin and Tulgan (2002), Tapscott (1998) and Zemke et al.(2000) have classified generations differently.

According to Howe and Strauss (2000), Millennial generations are the people born in 1982-2000.

3. CHARACTERISTICS OF NET GENERATION

Oblinger and Oblinger (2005) has described the characteristics of Net generation as follows.

They are digitally literate : Able to use intuitively a variety of IT devices and navigate the internet. They are comfortable using technology without an instruction manual.

They are more visually literate : Able to express themselves using images. They can weave together images, text and sound. Their ability to move between the real and virtual is instantaneous, expanding their literacy beyond text. Because of the availability of visual media, their text literacy may be less well developed than previous cohorts. They refuse to read large amount of text.

They are capable for multitasking : They can be online while simultaneously watching T.V., talking on the phone or listening to the radio. That means they are capable of using many Medias simultaneously.

Connected : They feel the world has been a connected place. Net genres are always connected.

Immediate : They are very fast. They expect immediate response. They can move one activity to another quickly sometimes performing simultaneously. They value speed than accuracy.

Experimental : Net Genres prefer to learn by doing rather by being told. They learn well through discovery. Their exploratory style enables them to better retain information and use it in creative and meaningful ways.

Social : Prolific communicators and have more social interaction. They always teaming up in internet games, posting web diaries through blogging, forwarding jokes and e-mails. Face book has made their circle of friends even larger.

Teams : They prefer to learn in teams. Peer-to-peer approach is common.

Structure : They are very achievement oriented. They work towards the goal. They want parameters, rules, priorities and procedures to achieve the goal. Their preference is for structure rather than ambiguity.

Engagement and experience

Visual and kinostic

Many of these characteristics are most commonly observed with the students even if they are coming from developed countries or developing countries. Location is not a matter. Every where technology is rapidly developing.

Savage T. (2003) in Oblinger and Oblinger (2005) has described that for the Net Gen, the internet is like oxygen: they can't imagine being able to live without it.

4. TECHNOLOGY AND LEARNING

Net Genres learn differently from their predecessors. They are bored in the traditional classroom. Because, they're grown up in digital environment. They are capable of using multiple media simultaneously. For example, accessing websites, listening to music, ,text messaging and working with face book at a same time is possible to them. In addition they are multi resources; a variety of digital and print resources are used by them. But mainly they rely on media rich resources.

Further they have different characteristics and habits of learning. They are independence and autonomy in their learning styles. They prefer reading lecture notes online and view interactive media such as power point presentation and digital images. In addition they like to work in groups / team work. They need for instant gratification and short attention span. Also they emphasize learning by doing through technology.

Now technology is developing such a rate traditional ways of teaching and learning are not supporting teachers and students to the fullest capacity. To give a new dimension of teaching and learning IT can be used effectively. Faculties must understand the Net Genres/ their learning styles and their expectation towards the teachers and faculty. Net Genres are distinctly different in their characteristics and learning expectations. Their lives immersed in multitasking in technology rich cultures and they are assumed to be active

Digital Native Learners	*Digital Immigrant Teachers*
Prefer receiving information quickly from multiple multimedia sources	Prefer slow and controlled release of information from limited sources
Prefer parallel processing and multitasking	Prefer singular processing and single or limited tasking
Prefer processing pictures, sounds and video before text	Prefer to provide text before pictures, sounds and video
Prefer random access to hyperlinked multimedia information.	Prefer to provide information linearly, logically and sequentially.
Prefer to interact / network simultaneously with many others	Prefer students to work independently rather than network and interact.
Prefer to learn "just in time"	Prefer to teach "just in case" (it is on the exam)
Prefer instant gratification and instant rewards	Prefer deferred gratification and deferred rewards
Prefer learning that is relevant, instantly useful and fun	Prefer to teach to the curriculum guide and standardized tests

experiential learners. They learn by doing. They prefer 'hands-on" and not linear in fashion. Trial and error is the metaphor they use for learning like in computer games.

They value action and use a take-action approach. They expect information and ideas to be shared openly and freely and created in multimodel ways. (Doren,R. and Asselin, M.(2010).

Millenials have unique characteristics towards learning. Therefore, traditional classroom teaching is no longer effective with these students. Jukes and Dosaj (2003) in Clarke, T. and Clarke E.(2009) has differentiated how digital students learn and how non digital teachers teach. Non digital teachers are known as digital immigrants.

It is obviously true that there is a gap in between the preferences of digital natives and the way of teaching of digital immigrant teachers. Therefore, digital immigrant teachers should adjust and sail the boat as per the preferences of digital native learners'. Majority of faculty members and academic librarians are digital immigrants. They have to find ways to integrate electronic teaching (and learning) into our established rhythms, strategies and purposes. It will not replace older forms of learning or teaching rather enhances the effectiveness of the existing system.

5. LEARNING PEDAGOGY

Net Generation have some more characteristics with new technologies. They are fascination with new technology, need for group activity, emphasize on extracurricular activities. (Howe and Strauss (2000).

The traditional teaching paradigm the teacher is a master and commander delivers lectures by chalk and talk or power point slides. This method emphasizes acquisition of facts, memorization, repetition and recall. This is mainly text based and focused on logical sequence of knowledge. This is believed as "one-size fit-all". Brown (2005) in

Skiba,D.J.&Barton A.J.(2006) says the "Net generation requires a learner centered model of education with a shift from traditional teaching paradigm to a constructivist learning paradigm". Engaging students in construction of knowledge is widely accepted and adopted in all over the world through helping students to gain knowledge. The key idea of constructivism is students should generate their knowledge through experience based activities, rather than being taught by teachers. Faculties have to consider the following aspects in educating these students.

1. Their Digital Literacy
2. Experiential and Engaging
3. Interactivity and Collaboration
4. Immediacy, connectivity and Communication

6. INSTRUCTIONAL TECHNOLOGY

Using technology for instruction is differing from one another. Faculties neither insist a lecturer to adopt a specific technology nor denying the use of technology if he / she wish to apply. But totally it depends on the person who handles it. How students can be motivated by using technology?

- Connect the learner with social context
- Relate the curricula to their experiences, cultures and goals,

Generally faculties develop and implement most of the content and teaching practices. Hence there is a gap between learning and what the faculties know and do. This gap impacts

- the development of materials for interactive technology,
- what faculty incorporate into their teaching and
- the design of the curriculum.

It is necessary to approach the development of

infrastructure technologies and programming with the same rigor, discipline and habits of inquiry that the faculty bring to their own research agendas.

We should not prepare a student only to pursue a career in his/ her field but also foster the desired qualities of a liberally educated person regardless of discipline. We must prepare our students for lives of creativity, citizenship and social responsibility as well as success in a workplace through increasingly shaped by science and technology. A graduate should be informed, open minded and empathetic in nature.

7. ROLE OF ACADEMIC LIBRARIES

In addition to the above mentioned technological shift from teaching to digital natives, academic libraries should change the collection development strategies, too. Especially they should move to electronic resources from traditional print resources. Mode of services have to be redesigned according to the changing demands of the millenials. There should be a move to electronic databases, e-books, virtual research environments as well as digitized versions of traditional and rare resources. Apart from this academic librarians should teach information literacy to create critical thinkers. Especially they have to consider on how to use different types of information sources, how to build and plan effective search strategies, how to manage information, how to evaluate and use information for their learning and research purposes. To achieve the expected outcomes librarians have to apply technology in teaching and consider the learning styles of the present day students as described above such as constructivism, trial and error, hands on practice, gaming , interactivity, collaboration and communication..

8. RECOMMENDATION

We are living in highly technological environment.

Technology has developed to that extent like a revolution. Academic Librarians in collaboration with faculties should initiate action to improve state of the art technology in the lecture halls. In addition to infrastructure facilities students' personalized facility with information such as laptops, PDAs and online resources should be developed. Investment in physical facilities should be given highest priority.

Developing a web page for each course will help the Net generation to learn effectively. This type of Course Management system is adopted in many universities in USA. The web component contains course materials such as notes, slides, a webliography and other pertinent multimedia. The web page should not be static instead of interactive and engaging.

Blogging is another method that allows students to interact and become engaged in learning Blog is a web-log which allows students to contribute to and comment on the entries in the blog. Learners can research their information and provide their learning through the blog. Dynamic web page that helps learners interact with content, instructor and other learners will be more effective to this generation.

Using chat rooms, audio or video conferencing will allow students to learn in a collaborative workspace. E-books, e-journals and Multimedia based information sources should be developed.

8. CONCLUSION

It is important to note that the faculties have to revise the teaching strategies in order to align with the learning styles and expectations of net generation. There is no doubt that the Net Generation has entered into the university and higher education system even they are from developed countries or developing countries. Every where the influence of ICT is observed. We should understand the students, their expectations and their learning needs. Faculties should accommodate these learners considering various strategies to adapt in teaching.

"The greatest discovery of my generation is that human beings can alter their lives by altering their attitudes of mind." - William James

BIBLIOGRAPHY

- Clarke,T.& Clarke, E.(2009), Born didital? Pedagogy and computer-assisted learning, Education + Training Vol.51(5/6) pp 396-407 *http://www.emeraldinsght.com* [Accessed on 12th December, 2010]
- Doiron, R. and Asselin, M.(2011), Exploring a new learning landscape in tertiary education. New Library World, Vol.112 (5/6), pp.225-235464 *http://www.emeraldinsght.com* [Accessed on 12th August, 2011]
- Feiertag,J.and Berge, Z.L.(2008) Training Generation N: how educators should approach the Net Generation.Education + Training Vol.50(6), pp.457-464 *http://www.emeraldinsght.com* [Accessed on 12th August, 2011]
- Kennedy, G. et al (2006). Questioning the net generation: a collaborative project in Australian higher education. Proceedings of the 23rd annual ascillte conference: Who's learning? Whose technology *http://docs.google.com* [Accessed on 15th of January, 2011]
- Robinson, M.(2007) Digital nature and digital nurture: libraries, learning and the digital native. Library Management Vol.20 (1/2), pp.67-76 464 *http://www.emeraldinsght.com* [Accessed on 20th December, 2010]
- Mi. Jia & Nesta, F. (2006) Marketing library services to the Net generation. Library Management Vol.27 (6/7), pOblinger, D. (2003) Boomers and Gen-Xers, Millennials: understanding the new students. Educause Available at *www.educause.edu*
- Oblinger, D. (2003) Boomers and Gen-Xers, Millennials: understanding the new students. Educause Available at *www.educause.edu* [Accessed on 10th August, 2010]
- Oblinger, D. G.and Oblinger J.L.eds. (2005). Educating the Net generation. Educause available electronically at *www.educause.edu/educatingthenetgen/*
- Lippincott, J.K. (2010) Information commons: meeting millennials' needs. Journal of Library Administration, Vol.50(1) January 2010
- Scharber, C. et al (2009), Online book clubs for preteens and teens,

Library Review, Vol.58 (3), pp.176-195 *http://www.emeraldinsght.com* [Accessed on 28th December, 2010]

- Shaw,S.and Fairhurst D.(2008), Engaging a new generation of graduates, Education + Training Vol.50(5), pp 366-378 *http://www.emeraldinsght.com* [Accessed on 28th December, 2010]
- Skiba, J.D.and Barton, J.A.(2006). Adapting your teaching to accommodate the Net Generation of Learners. OJIN: The Online journal of Issues Nursing,Vol. 11(2)
- Kvavik, R. (2005), convenience, communications and control: how students use technology, In Oblinger, D. G.and Oblinger J.L.eds. (2005). Educating the Net generation. Educause available electronically at *www.educause.edu/educatingthenetgen*
- Prensky (2001) in Robinson, M.(2007) Digital nature and digital nurture: libraries, learning and the digital native. Library Management Vol.20 (1/2),pp.67-76 464 *http://www.emeraldinsght.com* [Accessed on 20th December, 2010]

UNIT 2

INFORMATION COMMUNICATION TECHNOLOGY

6

Use of Web 2.0 Tools in Higher Education: Analysing the Perceptions of Media Students at University of Kashmir

Dr. Sumeer Gul

**Assistant Professor, Department of Library and Information Science, University of Kashmir, India*

Tariq Ahmad Shah

Research Scholar, Department of Library and Information, University of Kashmir, India

ABSTRACT

Purpose : The study presents an overall view of the Web 2.0 awareness and usage by the Media Education Research Centre (MERC) students at University of Kashmir.

Design/Methodology : Survey method was employed, assisted by questionnaire as a tool.

Findings : The exposure level of MERC students to Web 2.0 is satisfactory. Though some of the students are not aware of Web 2.0 concept, yet they make use of tools and technologies associated with it.

Research Implications/Limitations : Further study can be done at an extensive level to compare Web 2.0 awareness among students and faculties of diverse departments at University of Kashmir. Analysing the web logs from local servers of the academia at University of Kashmir can also be helpful in analyzing their information seeking patterns on the interactive web platform.

Originality/Value : The study is first of its kind and it can help as a useful tool to familiarise the students of MERC about the potentialities of Web 2.0.

Keywords: *World Wide Web; Web 2.0; Communication Technologies; Interactivity Technologies*

INTRODUCTION

The concept of interactivity has helped to cross all the boundaries that society earlier had. Web resources, rivulets crossing all the borders, what **Gul (2007)** perceived about them have now become a gushing stream via Web 2.0 which has enhanced the wisdom of crowds, openness and information sharing **(Aharony, 2009)**.The term Web 2.0, that made its debut in 2004 **(O'Reilly, 2007)** has become the jugular vein of global information community. Information market is becoming passionate about Web 2.0. Though scholars have raised queries on the existence of Web 2.0 (Berners-Lee **as cited in Aharony, 2009; Miller, 2006)** but still it has not lost its charm. Web 2.0, in addition to recreational and social uses has made its significant place in academic lives also. It has become a tool supplementing the traditional, conservative and un-interactive classroom environment.

The young students are different from their older counterparts in seeking information. Web 2.0 has redefined their role and the way they seek information. They are no more clinched to those age-old ways of un-democratic medium of expressing themselves or sharing information. A democratic set-up in the form of Web 2.0 has helped to overcome the barriers to communication and the distance between the users **(Stuart, 2010)**. Web 2.0 allows users to create, describe, post, search, collaborate, share and communicate online content in various forms **(Macaskill& Owen, 2006; Virkus, 2008)** thus giving a more democratic set up to them.

Web 2.0 concepts have led to the development of social networks, wikis, blogs, folksonomies, photo sharing sites etc. A large scale change has been witnessed by the emergence of Web 2.0 technologies and time is not far when academic sector will be highly dependent on this miraculous technology. The Utopian Educational Philosophy of Thomas More **(Halpin, 2003)**, based on democratization and non-hierarchy has seen a real existence due to incorporation of Web 2.0. It has become a democratic platform where hope and possibility exist.

LITERATURE REVIEW

Macaskill & Owen, 2006; Stuart, 2010; O'Reilly, 2007 have witnessed Web 2.0 as an interactive, context rich and, easy to use platform. Web 2.0 represents an emerging suite of applications that hold immense potential in enriching communication, enabling collaboration and fostering innovation **(Chua & Goh, 2010)**.Web 2.0 can be seen as a shift both in technology and usage paradigms. The key technological properties of Web 2.0 includea focus on data-based services rather than on software, the provision of a large number of small channels to consumers rather than small numbers of big ones, and an inherent scalability **(Clarke, 2008)**. **McDermott (2007)** has laid a seven category platform for Web 2.0 tools and application, though they have exceeded the number and are mushrooming day by day.

Social Networking Sites, one of the facets of Web 2.0 have become one of the latest examples of communication technologies that have been widely adopted by students **(Roblyer, McDaniel ,Webb, Herman&Witty, 2010)**. **(Ahmed, 2011)** feels that Web 2.0 services and applications like social and professional networking systems, wikis, and blogs can facilitate in fostering discussion, improving online interaction, and enhancing collaboration among stakeholders of Higher Education Institutions in developing countries. Kashmir, being part of a developing nation, India can also reap the countless benefits out of this global service. Predicting the future of education, **Yamamoto and Karaman (2011)**, have renamed and redefined the conservative educational system as Education 2.0 because of the incorporation of Web 2.0 deeper in the roots of education. They feel that Education 2.0 system is unique in the ways it influences the individuals.

PROBLEM

Web 2.0 is evolving as a central topic in the information world. The study, keeping in view the growing popularity of Web 2.0 examines its level of awareness and use by the student community.

OBJECTIVES

The objectives of the study are to identify the levels of awareness and purpose of use of Web 2.0 tools by the Post Graduate students of Media Education Research Centre (MERC), University of Kashmir.

METHODOLOGY

The study is based on the data collected through a predefined close-ended 21 – item questionnaire, which was distributed among the students currently enrolled in the P.G department of Media Education and Research Centre

(MERC), University of Kashmir. Each year, the department enrolls 39 students for its two-year P.G programme, which is completed in four semesters. Out of the 65 enrolled students in the department, 38 were from the 1st semester and 27 from 3rd Semester. To achieve better results, proportionate stratified random sampling was employed in which 70% students of each semester were selected. The questionnaire was distributed in the first week of May 2011 among 46 students, i.e., 27 student of 1st semester and 19 students of 3rd semester. Responses were collected up to third week of May 2011. However, only 37 students (21 students from 1st semester and 16 from 3rd semester) responded back achieving a response rate of about 80 per cent. Data thus collected was tabulated in Microsoft Excel for further analysis.

SCOPE

Scope of the study is confined to the students of Media Education Research Centre (MERC), University of Kashmir.

ANALYSIS

Web 2.0 Familiarity

When the students were enquired of their familiarity with the concept of Web 2.0, majority of them (25, 67.56%) were found to be familiar, while one-third (12, 32.43%) reported ignorance. A follow-up question enlisted 10 different Web 2.0 tools (*Social Networking sites, Wikis, blogs, Photo Sharing, Instant Messaging, Youtube, RSS, News Group, Podcasts and Social Bookmarking*), and the students were asked to mark the tools used by them. All the students were found to be aware of one or more of them. Thus, suggesting that they may not be acquainted with the term "*Web 2.0*" but in practice, they make use of its tools.

Registration with Social Networking Sites and preference

Registration with different social networks and the preference over the use of them reveal that all the students have account in *Facebook,* while 32.43 per cent are registered with *Twitter* and 16.21 per cent with *LinkedIn* **(Fig. 1)**. Besides, majority (34, 91.89%) of the students prefer *Facebook* over other social networking tools **(Fig. 2)**.

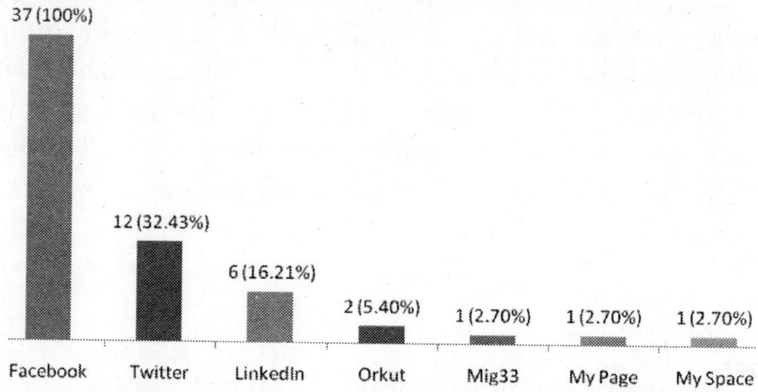

Fig. 1: Registration with Social Networking sites

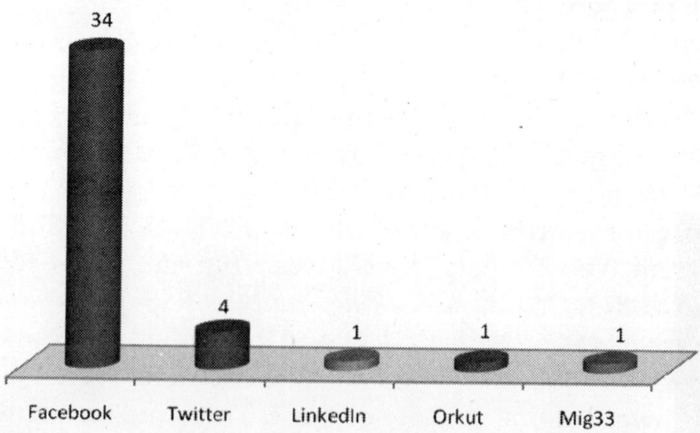

Fig 2: Preference among Social networking Sites

Purpose of using SNS

Purpose of the use of Social Networking sites was asked with five options. 81.08 per cent of students cited to remain in touch with friends, 35.13 cent use them for sharing *news items* and *events* each. While one-fourth (24.32%) post photos and videos via SNS **(Fig. 3).**

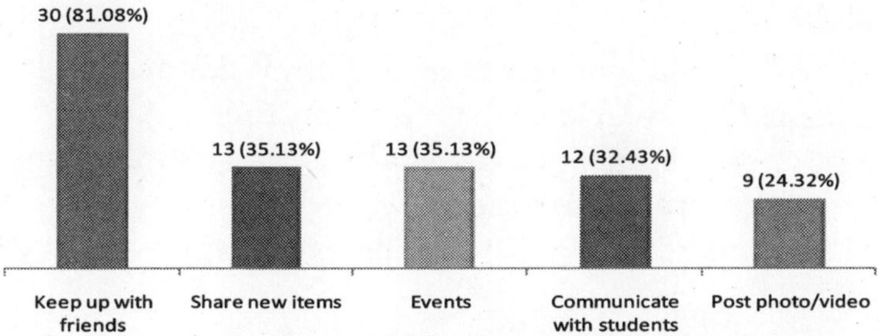

Fig. 3: Purpose of using SNS

Blogs

About 98 per cent (36) of the students are familiar with blogs and 59.46 per cent (22) do make use of them while 18.91 per cent (7) maintain their own blog. Regarding the purpose of use, 32.43 per cent (12) reported their use for General News and 29.72 per cent (11) for Knowledge Sharing. Only 8.10 per cent (3) use them for Learning and Teaching purposes.

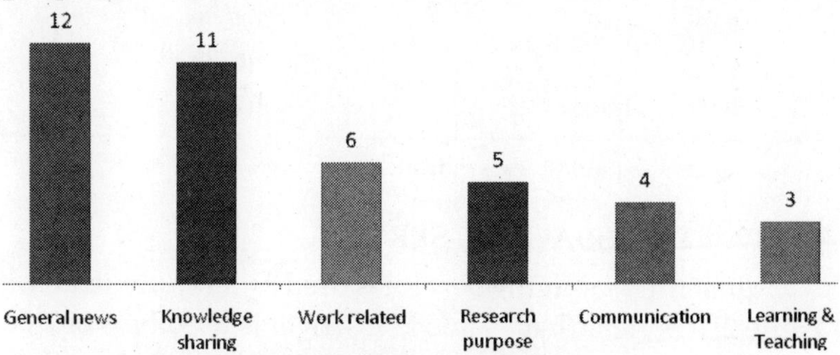

Fig. 4: Purpose of using Blogs

RSS & ATOM

When the respondents were asked about their awareness regarding RSS & ATOM, 37.85 per cent (14) showed familiarity with RSS while all reported ignorance about ATOM. Furthermore, only 16.22 per cent (6) do make use of RSS.

WIKIS

All the students are familiar with Wikis and about 90 per cent (33) search information on them. About their purpose of use, most of the students (56.75%, 21) consult them for general information followed respectively for class assignments (51.35%, 19) and research related activities (35.13%, 24).

VIDEO SHARING WEBSITES

80.96 per cent reported familiarity about video sharing websites. Regarding the purpose of use, 48.69 per cent watch entertainment videos, 43.24 per cent videos related to social issues and 2.70 per cent videos pertaining to news and religious issues **(Table 1)**.

Table 1. Type of videos being watched

Entertainment	18(48.64)
Social Issue	16(43.24)
Study related	17(45.95)
News	1(2.70)
Religious Issues	1(2.70)

Figures in parentheses indicate percentage

INSTANT MESSAGING SERVICE

Instant Messaging Service is used by 24 students. From **Table 2**, it is clear that Yahoo Messenger is used by 66.67 per cent (16), followed by Google talk and E-buddy by 41.67 per cent and 33.33 per cent respectively. Mig33 attracted least no. of students (4.17 per cent, 1 student). Further, when the respondents were asked about the purpose of use, about 80 per cent use them for social networking, 66.67 per cent for communication and a meager per cent of 8.33 for file sharing **(Table 3).**

Table 2. IM service used (n = 24)

Yahoo Messenger	16 (66.67)
Google talk	10 (41.67)
E-buddy	8 (33.33)
MSN	4 (16.67)
Skype	2 (8.33)
Mig33	1 (4.17)

Figures in parentheses indicate percentage

Table 3. Purpose of using IM (n = 24)

Social Networking	19 (79.17)
Communication	16 (66.67)
Information Sharing	6 (25)
Learning & teaching	3 (12.5)
File sharing	2 (8.33)

Figures in parentheses indicate percentage

PODCASTING SERVICE

Podcasts, which are audio recording (usually in mp3 format) of talks, interviews and lectures and listened online or by using MP3 devices, are used by 37.84 per cent of students (14) while the rest of students (23) have yet to get benefit from them.

SOCIAL BOOKMARKING

About 96 per cent of students (35) are aware and make use of Social Bookmarking while the rest (2 students) did not respond at all.

USEFUL TOOL FOR STUDENT

When asked about the tool/s, majority of students (25, 67.56%) recommended wikis as useful tools for other students. RSS and Blogs follow the list with 40.54 and 32.43 per cent respectively. On the other extreme, Social Bookmarking and Instant Messaging were least proposed **(Table 4)**.

Table 4. Useful tools for students (n = 37)

Rank	*Tool*	*Frequency*
1	Wikis	25(67.56)
2	RSS	15(40.54)
3	Blogs	12 (32.43)
4	Newsgroups/Forums	10 (27.02)
5	Social Networks	9(24.32)
6	Podcasts/Webcasts	5(13.51)
7	Online Video	3(8.10)
8	Social Bookmarking	2(5.40)
9	Instant Messaging	1(2.70)

Figures in parentheses indicate percentage

STUDENTS USAGE RATING OF WEB 2.0 TOOLS

Usefulness of any Web 2.0 tools cannot be justified with user's familiarity or awareness and without taking into account user's expertise over them. About 50 per cent of students (19) have good command over the use of Web 2.0 tools, 32.44 percent (12) average and an equal proportion of 5.41 per cent have excellent (2) and poor (2) proficiency over them.

Table 5: Student's usage rating of web 2.0 tools (n = 37)

Excellent	2(5.40)
Good	19(51.36)
Average	12(32.44)
Below Average	2(5.40)
Poor 2(5.40)	

Figures in parentheses indicate percent

NECESSITY OF WEB 2.0 TOOLS FOR EDUCATION

56.76 per cent of students (21) strongly agree with the statement that Web 2.0 tools have become a necessity for education, 35.14 per cent agree (13) while 8.1 per cent disagree (3).

DISCUSSION

Web 2.0, that has enhanced the global communication is also improving the networking in the academic sector and improving knowledge sharing in a number of ways **(Cheuk, 2007)**. From the study, it is evident that Facebook finds greater fondness while as preferential status of MySpace is very less. The reason can be that, MySpace has received a significant amount of negative attention from the media and many concerned adults, who point to several isolated incidents where predators have contacted, become involved with the people making use of MySpace **(Patchin and Hinduja, 2010)**. Facebook, on the other hand constitutes a rich site for researchers interested in the affordances of social networks due to its heavy usage patterns and technological capacities that bridge online and offline connections **(Ellison, Steinfield & Lampe, 2007)**. The results are further supported out by the study carried out by **Livingstone (2008)** and **Connell (2009)**.

Use of Social Networking Sites as a possible source of news items and events can be highly contributed to the political disturbance in Kashmir. In the times of conflict with 2008, 2009 and 2010 the peak years, Social Networking sites remained the only communication medium to keep up with friends and for sharing the news on a democratic platform. They remained the political engagement platforms between friends as also opined by **Baumgartner and Morris (2010); Boyd & Ellison, 2007; Lampe, Ellison & Steinfield, 2006.** However, communicating with students using Social Networking Sites is very less and yet the achievement of

Thomas More's Utopian Educational System has to be given a serious thought. Even blogs remain a priority for students to be in touch with the latest news. Blogs are used for work related and research activities also.

RSS, Podcast and ATOM, though wonderful tools, remain on a lower side. Wikis on the other hand are preferred by a larger rate of respondents. The reason may be the market value of Wikipedia which has facilitated the wiki awareness.

Entertainment videos remain the priority with the students. Since the leisure time needs to be spent smoothly, entertainment videos support the student community which is really the need of hour in a politically simmering area like Kashmir. Even a good score utilizes video sharing sites for studies also. Yahoo Messenger and Google Talk remain prime Instant Messaging Service. Social Bookmarking is also used by majority of students. Web 2.0 tools are rated good and a necessity for education by majority of users, with wikis as a suggested tool for other students to achieve academic excellence.

REFERENCES

Aharony, Noa. (2009). The influence of LIS students' personality characteristics on their perceptions towards Web 2.0 use. *Journal of Librarianship and Information Science*41,pp. 227. doi: 10.1177/0961000609345088

Ahmed, Malik. Aleem. (2011). Social media for higher education in developing countries - An intercultural perspective. In Charles Wankel (Ed.) *Educating Educators with Social Media: Cutting-edge Technologies in Higher Education, V.1 (pp.59-80)*. U.K: Emerald Group Publishing. doi: 10.1108/S2044-9968(2011)0000001006

Alton Y.K., & Goh, Dion. H. (2010).A study of Web 2.0 applications in library websites.*Library & Information Science Research*. 32, pp. 203-211. doi: 10.1016/j.lisr.2010.01.002

Baumgartner, Jody C., & Morris, Jonathan S. (2010). MyFace Tube Politics: Social Networking Web Sites and Political Engagement of Young Adults. *Social Science Computer Review*. 28 (1), 24-44. doi: 10.1177/0894439309334325

Boyd, D. M., & Ellison, N. B. (2007). Social network sites: Definition, history, and scholarship. *Journal of Computer-Mediated Communication*, 13(1), article 11. Retrieved from http://jcmc.indiana.edu/vol13/issue1/boyd.ellison.html

Cheuk, Bonnie. (2007). Social Networking Analysis : Its application to facilitate knowledge transfer. *Business Information Review*, 24(3), 170-176. doi: 10.1177/0266382107081612

Chua, Alton. Y.K., & Goh, Dion. H. A study of web 2.0 applications in library websites. *Library and Information Science Research*. 32 (3), 203-211. doi: 10.1016/j.lisr.2010.01.002

Clarke, R. (2008). Web 2.0 as syndication.*Journal of Theoretical and Applied Electronic Commerce Research*, 3(2), 30"43.

Connell, Ruth, Sara. (2009). Academic Libraries, Facebook and MySpace, and Student Outreach: A Survey of Student Opinion. *portal: Libraries and the Academy*, 9(1), 25-36. doi: 10.1353/pla.0.0036

Ellison, Nicole. B., Steinfield, Charles., & Lampe, Cliff. (2007). The Benefits of Facebook "Friends:" Social Capital and College Students' Use of Online Social Network Sites. *Journal of computer mediated communication*, 12, pp. 1143-1168. doi: 10.1111/j.1083-6101.2007.00367.x

Gul, Sumeer. (2007). Web Resources: Online Journals, Online Books and Electronic Theses and Dissertations - A Wave of the Future. *KnowGenesis: International Journal for Technical Communication (IJTC)*, 2 (1). Retrieved from *http://www.knowgenesis.com/journal/*

Halpin, David. (2003). Utopianism and education: The legacy of Thomas More. *Hope and Education: The role of Utopian Imagination (p. 45)*. New York: Rotledge Falmer.

Lampe, C., Ellison, N., & Steinfield, C . (2006). A Face (book) in the crowd: Social searching vs. social browsing. In *Proceedings of the 2006 20th Anniversary Conference on Computer Supported Cooperative Work (pp. 167-170)*. New York: ACM Press.

Livingstone, Sonia. (2008). Taking risky opportunities in youthful content creation: teenagers' use of social networking sites for intimacy, privacy and self expression. *New media and society*, 10 (3), 393-411. doi: 10.1177/1461444808089415

Macaskill, W., & Owen, D. (2006).Web 2.0 to go.*Proceedings of LIANZA Conference 2006*, Wellington.

McDermott, I. E. (2007). All A-Twitter about Web 2.0: What does it offer libraries.*Searcher*, 15(9), 34"39.

Miller, P. (2006). Web. 2: Building the New Library Gang. Recorded

Telephone Conference. Retrieved from http://talk.talis.com/archives/2006/02/introducing_the.html

O'Reilly, T. (2007). What is Web 2.0: Design patterns and business models for the nextgeneration of software.*Communications and Strategies*, 65, pp. 17"37.

Patchin, Justin. W. (2010). Trends in online social networking: adolescent use of MySpace over time. *New media and society*. 12 (2), 197-216. doi: 10.1177/1461444809341857

Roblyer, M.D., McDaniel,Michelle.,Webb,Marsena., Herman, James., &Witty, James Vince. (2010). Findings on Facebook in higher education: A comparison of college faculty andstudent uses and perceptions of social networking sites. *Internet and Higher Education*. 13, pp.134-140. doi: 10.1016/j.iheduc.2010.03.002

Stuart, D. (2010). What are libraries doing on Twitter? ExploringTechnology Resources for Information Professionals, 34(1),45-47, Retrieved from http://www.infotoday.com/Online/jan10/index.shtml

Virkus, Sirje. (2008). Use of web 2.0 technologies in LIS education: experiences at Tallinn university, Estonia. *Program: electronic library and information systems*. 42 (3), 262- 274. doi: 10.1108/00330330810892677

Yamamoto, Gonca. Telli., & Karaman, Faruk. (2011). Education 2.0. *On the horizon*. 19(2), 109-doi: 117. 10.1108/10748121111138308.

7

Reading Versus Surfing: Battle For Supremacy

Fayaz Ahmad Loan
Documentation Officer,
Centre of Central Asian Studies,
University of Kashmir, Srinagar (J&K), India

ABSTRACT

Purpose : The present study aims to identify how far surfing has affected the traditional reading culture of the net generation college students.

Design/methodology/approach : The stratified random sampling technique was employed for selection of students and questionnaire was used as a data collection tool. The data was analysed using the different quantitative and statistical techniques besides presented in the appropriate tabular formats. The Chi-square test was applied for the testing and verification of hypothesis.

Findings : The results reveal that reading and surfing have become the strong competitors in attracting attention of the 21st century students. Surfing has challenged reading in many ways as the preferences of students are growing for surfing very quickly. Majority of the students find surfing more informative, more attractive and more interesting but physically more harmful than reading. However, majority of the students disagree that surfing is perfect substitute to reading.

Research limitations/implications : The limitation of the study is that it is based on self reporting by students and it evaluates their own preferences between reading and surfing.

Practical implications : In general, the findings of the study should update the academicians, publishers, web designers, and library and information managers about the changing preferences of the students.

Originality/value : The surfing is one of the recent activities adopted by the net generation students. This study attempts to provide a clear picture how it has affected preferences of readers.

Keywords : Reading Habits; Surfing Habits; College Students; Kashmir

1. INTRODUCTION

Reading has been passion of the greatest personalities of all times. Humans have been reading since ages and thus words of knowledge have been passed on through generations. One of the first documentary sources for reading was manuscript, however, accessible to only creamy layer of society. Later, the arrival of Gutenberg printing press ended such discrimination by making the printed word available to all. The Gutenberg printing press brought drastic changes to the fundamentally oral society of the day. It was certainly a great jump in humanity's onward match and the beginning of transformation from oral to the reading society. Today, the emergence of the electronic media has created an extraordinary change in all spheres of the society including education, research, communication, entertainment, health, business, social relations, and other walks of life. The Internet is the most dominant electronic technology that changed the social, political and educational lifestyles of the global users.

Initially developed for scientific research community by the Department of Defence, United States of America **(Cheung & Huang, 2005)**, the Internet is now used by more than 1.7 billion world population. In the first four years, the number of Internet users reached 50 million and, in contrast, it took radio 38 years, television 13 years and the computers 16 years to reach the same milestone **(Lallana, 2003)**. The adoption of various information technologies, including Wi-Fi connectivity, RSS feeds, blog authoring and podcasts, drive Internet usage worldwide (**Burns, 2006)**. Now the emergence of the web 2.0 services especially social networking services (SNS) like facebook, twitter, MySpace, Orkut, hi5, etc. increases population of the Internet users across the globe at a rapid pace. Although very difficult to measure accurately, according to **Internet World Stats (2010)**, the population of worldwide Internet users is 1,733,993,741, almost covering 25.6% of the total world population. Interestingly, a significant proportion of the youth especially the college students uses the Internet and is potentially the largest group of the Internet users. **Williamson (2008)** reports that out of 18.0 million college students 17.1 million (95.0%) go online at least once in a month during 2007 and out of 18.2 million, 17.4 million (95.7%) use the Internet once in a month during 2008 in the United States of America (USA). The Internet has fixed deep roots in the lives of the net generation students **(Roberts and Foehr, 2004)**. This close association of students and the Internet posses a great threat to their traditional reading habits as more and more students are busy with surfing the Internet. Surfing the Internet has become a daily routine of the new generation. The researchers discover millions of people surfing the Internet at a time. Surfing means looking around or browsing the Internet. It is closely allied to browsing and sometimes the terms are used synonymously. The term "Surfing of Internet" was first used by Jean Armour Polly in 1992 **(Polly, 1992)** and defined it as "browsing the Internet while going from one page to another". According to **Comer (1999)**, "Surfing the Internet is a slang phrase that means using the Internet service to browse information". Thus, the comprehensive definition of Surfing is "using the Internet to search and browse the information in a hypertext/hypermedia environment like the World Wide Web". The Web is a worldwide hypertext/ hypermedia system that interconnects millions of documents. The connections are made through links, which can be textual or graphical. A link is a hot spot which, when selected, triggers the object of the link. Progressively clicking through the Web by triggering links that interest a user is known as Surfing. Surfing is considered synonymous to browsing (online reading) and is a new way of reading. Surfing enables to navigate a world full of interconnected information, discover new websites, read new information, meet new readers and authors and download information of interest. Today, millions of people especially students are now surfing on daily basis; therefore, there is a great competition between traditional reading and surfing in attracting students attention. Therefore, there is pressing need to identify how far this new activity has affected the traditional reading culture of students.

1.1. Internet facilities in Kashmir

The Internet services were introduced in Kashmir during 1994-95 by Bharat Sanchar Nigam Limited (BSNL). With the passage of time, three more privately owned ISPs- IPEAKS, SLICNET and INFONET were registered but only IPEAKS was operational **(Chawla, 2003)**. Presently, six ISPs namely BSNL, AIRTEL, AIRCEL, Tata Indicom, Reliance and Vodafone are operational in the Valley **(Loan, 2010)**. The Commercial Cyber Cafes are also available in all the major towns of the Valley. There are more than 100 Cybercafés in Srinagar city only **(Loan, 2009)**. Besides, 57 Community Information Centres (CICs) are available in Kashmir to access the online information **(Loan, 2010)**.

1.2. Internet facility Institutions

The Internet service isn't available to the whole

academic community in Kashmir valley. Most of the higher institutions like University of Kashmir, Srinagar and National Institute of Technology, Srinagar have started to provide these facilities to the academic community from last decade. The University of Kashmir has played a leading role in initiating the process. It established the Internet access centres in the library premises separately for students, scholars and teachers in 2002 and on December 4, 2008 established an "E-resource Centre" and a browsing centre in the Central Library which remained open round the clock and named it "24X7". Now almost more than 200 computers are available in the library for browsing the online information. Besides the services in the central library of the university, the Internet access centres are available in all the departments including the Wi-Fi system covers the whole campus. Initiated by the universities, most of the degree colleges also established browsing centres for their academic communities to overcome their social isolation and enhance their academic performance. The noteworthy colleges are Islamia College of Science & Commerce, Srinagar; Women's College, Srinagar; Amar Singh College, Srinagar; Govt. Degree College for Boys, Anantnag; Govt. Degree College for Boys, Baramulla etc. In addition, the many students have the Internet facilities in their homes and some access from their handsets devices like mobile phones **(Loan 2011)**.

2. RELATED LITERATURE

The emergence of the new media especially the Internet has also attracted many researchers all over the world to conduct research on its use and impact on other media. With the growing amount of digital information available, people particularly young adults are found spending more time reading electronic materials **(Ramirez, 2003; Liu, 2005)**. **CopperWiki (2008)** reports that reading habits among children are on the decline and the reasons for decline in reading habits among children are offshoots of technological advancements which have brought about overall changes in family, social and economic conditions. **Pivec (1998)** investigated teenagers about their surfing habits and reports that that the main rivals for attracting interest of teenagers are television and the Internet. **Korzenny & Korzenny (2007)** conducted a study on media use in five cultural groups and report that each of these five groups enjoy old as well as new media and spend close to 20 hours a week on television, and yet another 20 hours on surfing the Internet. **Hastings & Henry (2006)** depict that 85% of children prefer watching Television over reading. **Bookseller (2004)** reports that non-book-buyers prefer CDs and videos to books and non-readers prefer Television to books. **Gentile & Walsh (2002)** report that children in low income families watch more Television, watch more movies, play more video games, listen to the Radio and CDs more, read less, and use the computer less than children in higher-income families. **Graham & Kingsley (2005)** estimates that on average, young people spend 3:51 a day watching TV and videos, 1:44 listening to music, 1:02 using computers (0:48 online, 0:14 offline), 0:49 playing video games, 0:43 reading, and 0:25 watching movies. **Noll (2001)** reports that undergraduate students watch 2:0 hours of Television, 1:5 hours of videos, listen to 1:2 hours of Radio, and almost 1 hour of music each day. The total time spends watching and listening to entertainment for undergraduate students is 5:4 hours per day. The **Canadian Newspaper Association (2006)** study *Reading Between the Lines* shows that the time youth spend on surfing surpass the time they spend watching Television, listening to the radio or reading magazines and newspapers. According to this national report, youth spend 3:5 hours surfing the Internet, 3:1 hours watching Television, 2:4 hours listening to the Radio, 1:5 hour reading a book, 0:7 hours reading a newspaper, and 0:6 hours reading a magazine per week. **Ghimire (n.d.)** collected the information from teachers, intellectuals and guardians of the students about the effects of multi-media on children's reading habits. The findings brings out that 56.25% of the persons ranked it a 50% to 75% decrease and 43.75% of them reckoned between 15%-50%. **Majid & Tan (2007)** find that 57.6% of the children prefer playing on computer or surfing the Internet whereas only 44.1% prefers reading as their leisure time activity.

3. RESEARCH DESIGN

3.1. Research objectives

The current study focuses on the following research objectives:

- To identify the preferences of the net generation students between surfing and reading; and
- To examine how preferences between reading and surfing vary among students of different genders and regions.

3.2. Scope of the Study

The scope of the present study is limited geographically to the Kashmir Valley. The Valley is the major province of Jammu & Kashmir state consists of ten (10) districts. Academically, the study is limited to the academic college students of the Kashmir Valley. The student population belongs to the faculties of General Science, Computer Science, Business & Commerce, Social Sciences and Humanities covering the youth age group (18-25 years).

3.3. Hypothesis

In the present research study, a null hypothesis is formulated regarding preferences of the net generation students between surfing and reading with alternative hypothesis.

H_0 = Reading and surfing is preferred by the net generation students equally.

H_1 = Reading is preferred over surfing by the net generation students.

3.4. Methodology

The population of the universe was large and heterogeneous. Therefore, to obtain the appropriate sample size, the statistical sampling formula was used.

$$n = \frac{Z^2Npq}{Ne^2 + Z^2pq}$$

Where,

Z = Probability given under 96.5% reliability

N = Population or universe

E = Sampling error

pq = Proportion of the total population

The population of the undergraduate students in the academic colleges of the Kashmir Valley was 54,191. The value of the proportion of the total population (pq) was obtained from rural and urban ratio. Further, to ensure an optimal sample size, the 96.5% confidence level was pre-assigned and a small sampling error (0.04) was fixed.

$$n = \frac{Z^2Npq}{Ne^2 + Z^2pq}$$

$$= \frac{(2.1)^2\,(54191)\,(0.54)\,(0.46)}{(54191)\,(0.04)^2 + (2.1)^2\,(0.54)\,(0.46)}$$

$$n = 676.11 = 676$$

Using the stratified sampling technique, 676 college students were selected from the degree colleges of the Kashmir Valley with respect to three demographics of the students *i.e.* gender, region and faculty using population allocation method as:

$$n_i = n \frac{N_i}{N}$$

$i = 1, 2, 3, 4$

$n = 676$ (total Sample size)

N_i = total number of students in the Category

N = Total population from which sample is taken.

The data was collected using the questionnaire method. Before drafting the questionnaire, the relevant literature was reviewed and analysed which provided some directions in drafting questionnaire. After the survey questionnaire was drafted, it was pre-tested with 30 students. The questionnaire was then modified according to the result of the pre-test. Later, the data was collected from the students during classes. However, out of 676 only 302 were Internet users. The questionnaires of the self described Internet users (302) were analysed to complete the present study.

3.5. Analyses

The data was analysed using different statistical quantitative techniques and presented in the appropriate tabular formats. Besides, *the Chi-square* test was applied for the testing and verification of hypothesis.

4. RESULTS & DISCUSSION

4.1. Students preference in Surfing and Reading

Majority of students (55.63%) prefer reading (academic and non-academic) to surfing and little less like Internet surfing to reading (44.37%). The classification of data shows that the Internet surfing is more preferred by males (46.15%) than females (40.43%) and by urban (46.99%) than rural (40.34%). The overall trend depicts that below 50% of students prefer surfing over reading (Table 1).

Table 1. Students preference in Surfing and Reading (Gender & Region wise)

Students prefer	*Total*	*Male*	*Female*	*Rural*	*Urban*
Surfing	134/302 (44.37)	96/208 (46.15)	38/94 (40.43)	48/119 (40.34)	86/183 (46.99)
Reading	168/302 (55.63)	112/208 (53.85)	56/94 (59.57)	71/119 (59.66)	97/183 (53.01)

Note: Figures in parenthesis indicate Percentage

The testing of hypothesis using *chi square* proves this difference insignificant. The tabulated value of chi-square at 1 degree level of freedom and 5% level of significance (á=0.05) is 3.841. Since, the calculated value (3.828) of *Chi-square* is less than the tabulated value (3.841) at 5% level of significance. Therefore, the null hypothesis (H_0) is accepted and alternative hypothesis (H_1) is rejected. Thus, the inference can be drawn from the testing and verification of hypothesis that surfing and reading is preferred by the net generation students equally. It is a matter of concern that what students are doing while surfing? Surfing can be a blessing for reading as it enables to navigate a world full of interconnected information, discover new sites, read up-to-date information, and download things of interest and at the same time, it can be counter-productive when students use it only as an entertaining media and view inappropriate websites (pornographic etc.), download music, view videos, play video games and do online chatting all the time. Therefore, the students should avoid surfing unintended directions like unwanted websites, and clicking blinking pictures, attractive screen savers, irrelevant headings, etc. and be focused while surfing to serve the purpose and save time.

4.2. Comparison of Surfing & Reading Features

The females find surfing compared to reading time

saving, more informative, more expensive, more interesting and more useful than the male counterparts whereas males find surfing more attractive and more harmful than females. On the other hand urban students find surfing more informative, more interesting and physically more harmful than rural counterparts whereas rural students find surfing time saving, more expensive, more attractive and more useful than reading. The overall picture depicts that 91.72% students find surfing more informative, 73.84% more attractive, 72.85% more interesting and 70.20% physically more harmful than reading (Table 2). The students like most of the features of surfing to reading but at the same time claim that surfing is more expensive and physically more harmful than reading. The need is to bring down the surfing charges and design user friendly screens to overcome these problems.

Table 2. Comparison of surfing and reading features (Gender & Region wise)

Surfing as compared to Reading is	*Total*	*Male*	*Female*	*Rural*	*Urban*
Time Saving	208/302 (68.87)	141/208 (67.79)	67/94 (71.28)	93/119 (78.15)	115/183 (62.84)
More Informative	277/302 (91.72)	187/208 (89.90)	90/94 (95.74)	109/119 (91.60)	168/183 (91.80)
More Expensive	175/302 (57.95)	116/208 (55.77)	59/94 (62.77)	79/119 (66.39)	96/183 (52.46)
More Interesting	220/302 (72.85)	151/208 (72.60)	69/94 (73.40)	83/119 (69.75)	137/183 (74.86)
More Attractive	223/302 (73.84)	160/208 (76.92)	63/94 (67.02)	92/119 (77.31)	131/183 (71.58)
More Useful	169/302 (55.96)	112/208 (53.85)	57/94 (60.64)	81/119 (68.07)	88/183 (48.09)
More Harmful	212/302 (70.20)	149/208 (71.63)	63/94 (67.02)	77/119 (64.71)	135/183 (73.77)

Note: Figures in parenthesis indicate Percentage

4.3. Change of Hobby from Reading to Surfing

Above 45% students agree/strongly agree that the Internet surfing replaces reading as their hobby in which male students are slightly more than females and urban slightly more than rural students (Table 3). The surfing presents a challenge for reading for survival as preferences of students are growing for surfing as well. For the survival of traditional reading culture the students should always spend its share on academic and non-academic reading without any fall. The students can also set limits on the amount of media allowed, the types of content allowed, or the context within which media consumption may take place. Teachers and parents can play an important role in educating students how to keep balance in their day-to-day activities including reading and surfing.

Table 3. Change of hobby from reading to Surfing (Gender & Region wise)

Surfing replaces reading as my hobby	*Total*	*Male*	*Female*	*Rural*	*Urban*
Strongly agree	52/302 (17.22)	38/208 (18.27)	14/94 (14.89)	20/119 (16.81)	32/183 (17.49)
Agree	84/302 (27.81)	59/208 (28.37)	25/94 (26.60)	31/119 (26.05)	53/183 (28.96)
Disagree	92/302 (30.46)	59/208 (28.37)	33/94 (35.11)	38/119 (31.93)	54/183 (29.51)
Strongly disagree	74/302 (24.50)	52/208 (25.00)	22/94 (23.40)	30/119 (25.21)	44/183 (24.04)

Note: Figures in parenthesis is Percentage

4.4. Surfing as Substitute for Reading

The glance on data shows that irrespective of gender and regional differences, majority of the students (63.34%) believe that the Internet surfing is not a perfect substitute for reading (Table 4). The respondents highlight many reasons. The prominent reason is that reading is very essential for educational achievements, actual consumption of information and gaining knowledge. The respondents further argue that surfing is highly suitable for entertainment purpose and daily update of news and information and not so effective in academic achievements.

Table 4. Surfing as substitute for reading (Gender & Region wise)

Surfing as substitute for reading	*Total*	*Male*	*Female*	*Rural*	*Urban*
Strongly agree	35/302 (11.59)	20/208 (9.62)	15/94 (15.96)	12/119 (10.08)	23/183 (12.57)
Agree	76/302 (25.17)	54/208 (25.96)	22/94 (23.40)	31/119 (26.05)	45/183 (24.59)
Disagree	135/302 (44.70)	98/208 (47.12)	37/94 (39.36)	56/119 (47.06)	79/183 (43.17)
Strongly disagree	56/302 (18.54)	36/208 (17.31)	20/94 (21.28)	20/119 (16.81)	36/183 (19.67)

Note: Figures in parenthesis is Percentage

5. CONCLUSION

Reading and surfing have become the strong competitors in attracting time and attention of the 21st century students. Surfing has challenged reading habits of students in many ways as the preferences of students are growing for surfing day by day and in a very short span of time it has replaced reading as a hobby of some students. However, surfing is not considered as a perfect substitute for reading. Reading is considered very essential for educational achievements, actual consumption of information and gaining knowledge. It guarantees that reading has a future and will survive in all times to come. Therefore, it can be concluded that the Internet surfing is complimentary to reading and not substitute of reading.

ACKNOWLEDGEMENT

The author is greatly indebted to his praiseworthy teacher and supervisor, Prof. S. M. Shafi, Head, Department of Library & Information Science, University of Kashmir, J&K (India) for his enthusiastic guidance, constructive criticism, sound advices and valuable suggestions during the accomplishment of the present study.

REFERENCES

- Bookseller (2004). *Books face challenge to win new readers.* Retrieved June 15, 2010 from http://www.literacytrust.org.uk/Database/Mori.html
- Burns, E. (2006). Global internet adoption slows while involvement deepens. Retrieved June 15, 2010 from
- www.clickz.com/stats/sectors/demographics/article.php/3596131#table1
- Canadian Newspaper Association (2006). *Reading between the Lines.* Retrieved June 15, 2010 from
- http://www.cnaacj.ca/Client/CNA/cna.nsf/object/d_Codereport/$file/DCODE-FINAL.pdf
- Chawla, R. (2003). *Report of Information and Communication Technologies (ICTs) in Kashmir.* Retrieved June 15, 2010 from www.gipi.org.in/ict/kashmir
- Cheung, W. and Huang, W. (2005). Proposing a framework to assess Internet usage in university education: an empirical investigation from a student's perspective. *British Journal of Educational Technology,* 36(2), 237-253.
- Comer, D. E. (1999). *The Internet Book: everything you need to know about computer networking and how the Internet works* (p. 340) (2nd ed.), New Delhi: Prentice- Hall.
- CopperWiki (2008). *Reading habits in children.* Retrieved June 15, 2010 from http://www.copperwiki.org/index.php/Reading_Habits_in_Children
- Gentile, D. A. & Walsh, D. A. (2002). A normative study of family media habits. *Applied Developmental Psychology,* 23, pp.157-178. Retrieved June 15, 2010 from http://www.mediafamily.org/research/report_g_w2002.pdf
- Ghimire, B. (n.d.). Impact of multimedia on children of Nepal. *Asian*

Book Development, 30(2). Retrieved June 15, 2010 from http://www.accu.or.jp/appreb/report/abd/abd3021.html

- Graham, R. & Kingsley, S. W. (2005). *Media multi-tasking changing the amount and nature of young people's media use: Bedrooms have become multi-media centers.* Retrieved June 15, 2010 from
- http://www.kff.org/entmedia/entmedia030905nr.cfm
- Hastings, C. & Henry, J. (2006). *Reading is a closed book to today's children. Telegraph.* Retrieved June 25, 2010 from
- http://www.telegraph.co.uk/news/1524595/Reading-is-a-closed-book-to-today's-children.html
- Internet World Stats, (2010). *The Internet big picture world Internet users and population stats.* Retrieved June 15, 2010 from
- http://www.internetworldstats.com/stats.htm
- Korzenny, F. & Korzenny, B. A. (2007). *Old and new media use.* Retrieved June 15, 2010 from hmc.comm.fsu.edu/OldandNewMedia091307.pdf
- Lallana, E. C. (2003). *The information age.* Malaysia: UNDP. Retrieved June 15, 2010 from http://www.apdip.net/publications/iespprimers/eprimer-infoage.pdf
- Loan, F. A. (2009). *Growth and development of Internet in India with special reference to Kashmir Valley*, in National Convention Knowledge Resources in India with Special Reference to J&K State. Srinagar: University of Kashmir, from 11-13 May, 2009.
- Loan, F. A. (2010). Internet usage habits of second generation college students. In S. Kataria, , J. Poul, and S. Ram, (Eds.) Proceedings of International Symposium on Emerging Trends and technologies in Library & Information Services 2010. Himachal Pradesh: pp.192-196.
- Loan, F. A. (2011). Internet use by the college students across disciplines: a study. *Annals of Library and Information Studies*, 58(2), 118-127. Retrieved July 20, 2011 from
- http://nopr.niscair.res.in/bitstream/123456789/12183/1/ALIS%2058(2)%20118-127.pdf
- Liu, Z. (2005). Reading behaviour in the digital environment: Changes in reading behaviour over the past 10 years. *Journal of Documentation*, 61(6), 700-712.
- Majid, S. & Tan, V. (2007). Understanding the reading habits of children in Singapore. *Journal of Education Media & Library Sciences*, 45(2), 187-198. Retrieved June 15, 2010 from http://joemls.tku.edu.tw/45/45-2/187-198.pdf

- Noll, A.M., (2001). *Voice vs. data: Estimates of media usage and network traffic*. Retrieved October 25, 2010 from http:/www.arxiv.org/pdf/cs.cy/0109007
- Polly, J. A. (1992). Surfing the Internet: An introduction, *Wilson Library Bulletin*, 66(10), 38-42.
- Pivec, F. (1998). Surfing through the Internet-The new content of teenagers spare time. *ASLIB Proceedings*. 50(4), 88-92.
- Ramirez, E. (2003). The impact of the Internet on the reading practices of a university community: the case of UNAM", *Proceedings of the 69th IFLA General Conference and Council*, Retrieved June 15, 2010 from
- http://www.ifla.org/IV/ifla69/papers/019e-Ramirez.pdf
- Roberts, D. F., & Foehr, U. G. (2008). Trends in media use. *Future of Children*. 18 (1), 11-37.
- Williamson, D. A. (2008). College students online: Driving change in Internet and mobile usage. *eMarketer*, September 2008. Retrieved June 15, 2010 from www.emarketer.com/Report.aspx? emarketer_2000524

8

Social Networking With Special Reference to Facebook: Implications for Libraries

Dr. Nabi Hasan

Deputy Librarian, Indian Institute of Technology Delhi, New Delhi-110016

ABSTRACT

The paper describes the concept and the current environment of social networking. The need and features of social networking with emphasis on emerging trends in its usage is elaborated. The paper comprehensively covers opportunities and practical aspects in social networking usage. The scenario in India is explained with regard to the use of social networking sites with special reference libraries. Use of Social Networking by libraries and information centres is explained giving examples. The most popular social networking site, facebook has been covered in detail with its use and implications on libraries and librarians.

Keywords: Social Networking, Online community, Blogs, Facebook, Library web page

1. INTRODUCTION

Today, as the use of mobile devices like iPhones and BlackBerry is increasing on the job, so does easy access to social networking sites, such as Facebook, Twitter, LinkedIn, etc. A social network service is an online service, platform, or site that focuses on building and reflecting of social networks or social relations among people who share interests and/or activities. These are websites that provide a virtual community in which people with a shared interest may communicate.

A social network service essentially consists of a representation of each user (often a profile), his/her social links, and a variety of additional services. Most social network services are web based and provide means for users to interact over the Internet, such as e-mail and instant messaging. Social networking sites allow users to share ideas, activities, events and interests within their individual networks.

Social Networking is the way; the 21st century communicates today and is the grouping of individuals into specific groups.

2. NEED AND FEATURES

Through **social networking,** people can use networks of online friends and group memberships to keep in touch with current friends, reconnect with old friends or create real-life friendships through similar interests or groups. Besides establishing important social relationships; social networking members can share their interests with other like-minded members by joining groups and forums. Some networking can also help members find a job or establish business contacts.

Most social networking websites also offer additional features. In addition to blogs and forums; members can express themselves by designing their profile page to reflect their personality. They present freedom of expression by offering the ability to upload photos, music and videos. Each site also offers customized profile pages using varying themes, making homepage design a quick and simple process. Another shared quality is the ability to search for new friends with common interests or the option to search for existing friends by simply entering their name or e-mail address.

3. OPPORTUNITIES AND USAGE ISSUES

As the increase in popularity of social networking is on a constant rise, new uses for the technology are constantly being observed. The forefront of emerging trends in social networking sites is the concept of "real time" and "location based." Real time allows users to contribute contents, which is then broadcasted as it is being uploaded - the concept is similar to live television broadcasts. Twitter set the trend for "real time" services, where users can broadcast to the world what they are doing, or what is on their minds within a character limit. Facebook followed suit with their "Live Feed" where users' activities are streamed as soon as it happens. While Twitter focuses on words, Clixtr, another real time service, focuses on group photo sharing where users can update their photo streams with photos while at an event. In the location based social networking space, Foursquare gained popularity as it is allowed for users to "check-in" to places that they are frequenting at that moment. Gowalla is another such service which functions in much the same way that Foursquare does, leveraging the GPS in phones to create a location based user experience. Clixtr, though in the real time space, is also a location based social networking site since events created by users are automatically geotagged, and users can view events occurring nearby through the Clixtr iPhone application.

One popular use for this new technology is social networking between businesses. Companies have found that social networking sites such as Facebook and Twitter are great ways to build their brand image. These companies are able to drive traffic to their own online sites while encouraging their consumers and clients to have discussions on how to improve or change products or services.

Social networks are also being used by teachers and students as a communication tool. Because many students are already using a wide-range of social networking sites; teachers have begun to familiarize themselves with this trend and are now using it to their advantage. Teachers are doing everything from creating chat-room forums and groups to extend classroom discussion to posting assignments, tests and quizzes, to assisting with homework outside of the classroom setting. Social networks are also being used to foster teacher-parent communication. These sites make it possible and more convenient for parents to ask questions and voice concerns without having to meet face-to-face. Social networks are also being used by activists as a means of low-cost grassroots organizing.

Social network services are increasingly being used in legal and *criminal investigations*. Information posted on sites such as MySpace and Facebook is being used by police (*forensic profiling*), probation, and university officials to prosecute users of said sites. In some situations, contents posted on MySpace have been used in courts. Facebook is increasingly being used by school administrations and law enforcement agencies as a source of evidence against student users.

On large social networking services; there have been growing concerns about users giving out too much personal information and the threat of sexual predators. Users of these services also need to be aware of data theft or viruses. However, large services, such as MySpace and Netlog, often work with law enforcement to try to prevent such incidents.

In addition, there is a perceived privacy threat in relation to placing too much personal information in the hands of large corporations or governmental bodies, allowing a profile to be produced on an individual's behavior on which decisions, detrimental to an individual, may be taken.

A common misuse of social networking sites such as Facebook is that it is occasionally used to emotionally abuse individuals. Such actions are often referred to as trolling. It is not rare for confrontations in the real world to be translated online. Online bullying (Cyber-bullying) is a relatively common occurrence and it can often result in emotional trauma for the victim.

Interpersonal communication has been a growing issue as more and more people have turned to social networking as a means of communication. Further, social networking sites have become popular sites for youth culture to explore them, for relationships and to share cultural artifacts. Many teens and social networking users may be harming their interpersonal communication by using sites such as Facebook and MySpace.

Almost every industry has seen the influence of social networking, and capital markets are no different. Traders use social networks to share trading information, investors use them to share tips and companies are creating internal social networks to increase employee productivity. In other words, social networking in financial services is useful and it's here to stay.

4. SOCIAL NETWORKING SCENARIO IN INDIA

The social networking phenomenon continues to gain steam worldwide, and India represents one of the fastest growing markets at the moment. Though Facebook has tripled its audience in the last couple of years; several other social networking sites have posted their own sizeable gains. India now ranks as the seventh largest market worldwide for social networking, after the U.S., China, Germany, Russian Federation, Brazil and the UK. The total Indian social networking audience grew 43 percent in the last year, more than tripling the rate of growth of the total Internet audience in India.

Facebook is the best social networking site at present and the second most visited site in the world after Google. In India it got the third Rank based on Alexa Ranking and this is on the top of the ranking list. Facebook is already most visited social networking website in many countries.

Top Social Networking sites used in India in 2011 are: Facebook, LinkedIn, Orkut, Ibibo, BharatStudent, Myspace, Hi5, Fropper, Bigadda and Perfsopt[12].

5. LIBRARY APPLICATIONS OF SOCIAL NETWORKING IN GENERAL

If a librarian wish to ignore the social networking trend in libraries; it would be difficult to do so. Nearly every library homepage has links to its presence on Facebook, Twitter, Flickr, and other social networks. The Library of Congress has acknowledged the cultural significance of social networking with its announcement that Twitter has donated its entire tweet archive to the library. Librarian of Congress, James H. Billington described the value of the donation by saying, "The Twitter digital archive has extraordinary potential for research into our contemporary way of life"[13].

The use of online social networks by libraries is an increasingly prevalent and growing tool that is being used to communicate with more potential library users, as well as extending the services provided by individual libraries. A final rise in social network use is being driven by college students using the services to network with professionals for internship and job opportunities.

Social networking is rapidly infiltrating the information environment, and it is essential that librarians understand how best to use these sites and tools with their work to better serve their users and reach people who have never before used the library. The sites like; MySpace, Facebook, and others help as a way to expand and improve crucial library functions like instructions, outreach, service delivery and marketing.

Social Networking has changed the way we all work and play online, leading us into an age of participation. It is also opening up new opportunities for reaching out to patrons, providing library services and transforming our websites from static sources of information to vibrant and interactive virtual branches. Facebook's ability as a communication tool is wide-reaching. Facebook was used to reach out to students and providing library information in an innovative manner in a community where students already were. Twitter's rapid growth has pushed the concepts of mobility and brevity to the forefront of library discourse, revolutionizing the way we interact with each other and with information. Libraries are using Twitter to enhance and expand library services and collections, and to prepare for its long term impacts on library operations. A year ago; the Young Adult Library Services Association (YALSA) division of the American Library Association launched the *30 days of positive uses of social networking* project. Every day throughout October (2010), three YALSA bloggers use to post ideas and information about using social networking in the school and public library[10].

Blog is a great way for us to offer value and content for your library and it has become the standard for libraries to have one. The library needs to offer valuable contents that one's patrons will read and appreciate. Social networking also helps in planning to accomplish objectives of the library with social networking. One can share resources of the library through social networking. The Social Networking for the libraries may also be used for; youth outreach; creation of online groups to support library; lead into catalog, highlight collections, provide online reference through messaging; promote events; staff development & communication/ professional networking; create Facebook applications for searching library resources, keeping up with library news, etc.

6. FACEBOOK APPLICATIONS BY LIBRARIES AND INFORMATION CENTRES

On February 4, 2004, Zuckerberg launched "Thefacebook", originally located at thefacebook.com and it was founded to link students at Harvard University. The membership was initially restricted to students of Harvard College only. The website's name stems from the colloquial name of books given at the start of the academic year by university administration with the intention of helping students to get to know each other better.

As of July 2011, Facebook has more than 750 million active users. Users may create a personal profile, add other users as friends, and exchange messages, including automatic notifications when they update their profile. Additionally, users may join common-interest user groups, organized by workplace, school, college, subject or other characteristics[5].

Some of the uses and applications offered with reference to libraries and librarians have been narrated below:

1) Facebook provides opportunities for meaningful interactions between the librarian and patrons. It is one of those trends of our users that we just can not ignore. Libraries in particular have been eager to capitalize on Facebook's potential for building and maintaining relationships with students. Libraries have created search bar applications (e.g., for JSTOR),

communication tools, and more comprehensive virtual library service applications. Research on Facebook use in libraries has encouraged librarians and other library staff members to create their own profiles and join Facebook groups as a way of sharing information amongst colleagues and with patrons.

2) "Friending" students from instruction sessions and customizing profiles to highlight library resources are other recommended methods of library Facebook use. Users may be more inclined to "friend" a librarian if that librarian's area of expertise (or the resources on his or her profile) were tailored to the student's own interests and needs. These librarians use their profiles to share research tips, display library applications, and emphasize their availability to their student "friends."

3) Facebook offers an effective means of sending targeted messages to students or other patron groups like, "Librarian is Your Friend" campaign, "Your Librarian is Your Friend" campaign.

4) Individual librarians might do some outreach in Facebook like to search the catalogue, databases, ask questions, collect and answer reference questions, search online public access catalogs, host multimedia collections, still images, short tutorials, issue instructions, self-organizing groups of users, consultations via Facebook, as mail forums and more.

5) Most libraries with a Facebook presence use it for promotional purposes and for hosting research applications and as chat reference and communication forums, to market the library, push out announcements to library users and have a presence in the social network. These libraries feel positive about the future success of their Facebook presence. You also have to add new contents to it in order to keep it fresh and keep your fans coming back. Facebook is used for

course assignments, missed lecture notes, paper due dates, assignment guidelines, to discuss academic interests, etc.

6) Reach users who don't visit the library, libraries' core skill is not delivering information ... libraries are about learning and building communities" , upload photos, share links and videos, professional interest groups, can be put onto blogs and websites.

Some of the important libraries of the globe using the Facebook applications include: George Washington University, Yarra Plenty Public Library, National Library of Australia, Deakin University, University of Adelaide, Edith Cowan University, etc.

7. CONCLUSION

Online social networking offers people great convenience of easy socializing. It allows people to keep in touch with friends, patrons, reconnect with old friends or acquaintances, meet new people, and even conduct business with the click of a few buttons. You can find people with similar interests and get to know them better, even if they are in a different country without having to worry about an enormous phone bill or going over the restricted minutes on a phone card. These features of the Social Networking with special reference to most popular social networking sites like Facebook offers great features to libraries and librarians in reaching to its patrons, market their resources and services and help them to use the same.

However other side of the Social Networking is that the more time spent on online communities and chatting means less time spent socializing with real people. People slowly become disembodied with real life and believe they live in a virtual world with virtual friends. As they begin to lose touch with other people, they increasingly isolate themselves. Therefore, even though it has its benefits in the virtual world, the real world is greatly impeded by the increasing use of online social networking. It is therefore some people feel that socializing and having real friends in the real world is much better than living in a virtual world.

REFERENCES

- A to Z of Social Networking for Libraries *http:// socialnetworkinglibrarian.com* /2010/01/22/ a-to-z-of-social-networking-for-libraries/ [Accessed on July 21, 2011].
- Archive for the Social Networking for Libraries Category - http:// socialnetworking librarian. com/category/social-networking-for-libraries/ [Accessed on July 21, 2011].
- Breeding, Marshall. 2007. Librarians Face Online Social Networks. *Computers in Libraries.* 27(8): 30-32.
- Clap, Sharon. Social Networking sites and libraries- *http:// www.slideshare.net* /sbclapp/social-networking-libraries [Accessed on July 21, 2011].
- http://www.facebook.com [Accessed on July 21, 2011].
- Huwe, Terence. 2007. Surfing the Library 2.0 Wave. *Computers in Libraries.* 27(1): 36-38.
- Online community - http://en.wikipedia.org/wiki/ Online_community [Accessed on July 21, 2011].
- Prabhudesa, Aruni. The power of Blogging and Social Networking - http://trak.in/Tags/Business/2007/08/25/indian-power-blogging-social-networking-secret/ [Accessed on July 21, 2011].
- Social Networking- A site comparison - http:// www.searchenginejournal.com/social-networking-a-site-comparison/332/#ixzz0qDcZ9LRQ [Accessed on July 21, 2011].
- Social Networking and DOPA - http://www.ala.org/ala/aboutala/ offices/oif/ifissues/positive_uses.pdf [Accessed on July 23, 2011].
- Social networking service - http://en.wikipedia.org/wiki/ Social_networking_service [Accessed on July 21, 2011].
- Top 10 Most Popular Social Networking Sites in India in 2011 - Source: http://www.blogdefined.com/2011/01/top-most-popular-social-networking-sites-in-india/#ixzz1StsJdKio [Accessed on July 23, 2011].
- Twitter Donates Entire Tweet Archive to Library of Congress - http:/ /www.prweb.com/releases/Library_of_Congress/tweet_archive/ prweb3881504.htm [Accessed on July 23, 2011].

UNIT 3

INTELLECTUAL PROPERTY

9

Intellectual Property Right

Shelke S. M.
Librarian, Shri Bhagwan Homoeopathic Medical College,
N-6, CIDCO, Aurangabad.

Dr. (Mrs.) Khaparde V. S.
Associate Professor & Head, Dept.of Lib & I Sc.
Dr. Babasaheb Ambedkar Marathwada University,
Aurangabad (MS) India.

Ad. Kalbande S. S.
Assistant Professor, Mastyodari Law College,
Jalna. (MS) India.

ABSTRACT

The goal of this article is to familiarize with the concept of intellectual property. Property is an asset that can be owned. There are two broad types of property. The first type of property is tangible. Tangible property includes items that can be seen and touched. Tangible property includes what we commonly associate with property, real estate, cars, jewelry and clothing. Another type of property is intangible. Intangible property is what cannot be seen. Examples of intangible property include the ideas contained in books, journals, or music. It also includes the coding for computer software. These intangible forms of property are often called intellectual property. This article is focuses on the topics of

Intellectual property and branches of related rights i.e. **INDUSTRIAL PROPRTY** (Patent, Industrial Design, Trademarks, Service mark, Layout of design of Integrated Circuit, Geographical Indication, Utility Models) & **COPYRIGHT** [Books, Music, Paintings, Sculpture, Films, Technology based works(databases & softwares)].

Keywords: Intellectual Property Right, Industrial Property Right, Copy right, WIPO (World Intellectual Property Organization), Berne Convention, Internet.

1. INTRODUCTION

The term Intellectual Property (IP) reflects the idea that its subject matter is the product of the mind or the intellect. These new solutions are ideas, and protected as such; protection of inventions under patent law does not require that the invention be represented in a physical embodiment. The protection accorded to inventors is, against any use of the invention without the authorization of the owner. Even a person who later makes the same invention independently, without copying or even being aware of the first inventor's work, must obtain authorization before he can exploit it. The law can be - and in most countries is - simply declaratory, i.e., the law may state that the author of an original work has the right to prevent other persons from copying or otherwise using his work. So a created work is considered protected as soon as it exists, and a public register of copyright protected works is not necessary.

Intellectual property, like real property is an asset. However, unlike real property, is not something your can feel, smell, or touch. In order for intellectual property to exist, of course an idea must first come into existence. It must then have some form of instantiation. This is the concrete expression of the idea. An example of instantiation occurs when an author envisions a story and then puts his/her idea on paper. Without this concrete expression, the idea is not intellectual property (Hefter & Litwitz, 1999). Like real property, intellectual property comes with a bundle of rights.

Ownership allows one to restrict access to intellectual property. This called a negative right. Negative rights allow one to prohibit certain actions. Because access can be limited, it is possible to create value if others are interested in acquiring the idea. Ownership allows intellectual property to be bought and/or sold (positive rights.) It can also be temporarily rented out. For example, some computer software programs require the user to pay a periodic fee to maintain usage rights.

2. HISTORY

The development of intellectual property rights began during the European Enlightenment of the 17th and 18th centuries. Two British authors, John Locke and Edward Young were particularly influential in nurturing this concept. In 1690, John Locke published his *Second Treatise*. It discussed natural property rights that include the ownership of a person's creations and ideas. Locke stated, "Every Man has a Property to his own Person" (Hesse, 2002). Locke also argued that knowledge was the product of the senses' interpretation of nature. Several decades later, Edward Young's *Conjectures on Original Composition* (1759) discussed how authors inject their personality into their works. Young believed that authorship constituted a higher form of labor. Thus, he argued that authors should have a perpetual right to their work. He differentiated between products of the mind and machines. Young believed that property protections for machines should be time limited (Hesse, 2002). French contributors such as Diderot argued that authors could own and sell intellectual property rights. A German, Johann Gottlieb Fichte brilliantly differentiated between copies of a work and its original manifestation. He held that the ideas contained in a work belong to society. However, the original unique expression of an idea belonged to its author (Hesse, 2002). Another pillar of support for intellectual property rights exists within utilitarian philosophy (Hesse, 2002; Moore & Unsworth, 2005). Utilitarian philosophy addresses the relationship between the social benefits and social costs of an action. When social benefits outweigh the social costs, then the action should be encouraged. It is argued that intellectual property rights promote the greater good. Property protections provide incentives for the creation of new ideas and inventions (Moore & Unsworth, 2005).

Some people argue that the spread of knowledge is a greater social good than the author's right to restrict its use. For instance, one could argue that photocopying and distributing booklets containing vital information on cancer prevention is more important than the author's right to be paid for his/her effort. The counter argument is that the booklet is less likely to be written if the author's right is not preserved. This enumerated power provides authorization for copyright and patent laws in the United States. Natural property rights and social utilitarianism provide the philosophical underpinning of intellectual property laws.

Intellectual property relates to items of information or knowledge, which can be incorporated in tangible objects at the same time in an unlimited number of copies at different locations anywhere in the world. The property is not in those copies but in the information or knowledge reflected in them. Intellectual property rights are also characterized by certain limitations, such as limited duration in the case of copyright and patents.

The importance of protecting intellectual property was first recognized in the *Paris Convention for the Protection of Industrial Property* in 1883 and the *Berne Convention for the Protection of Literary and Artistic Works* in 1886. Both treaties are administered by the World Intellectual Property Organization (WIPO).

3. BRANCHES OF INTELLECTUAL PROPERTY

Intellectual property is usually divided into two branches, namely **industrial property** (which broadly speaking protects inventions) and **copyright** (which protects literary and artistic works).

Industrial Proprty	*Copyright*
Patent	Books
Industrial Design	Music
Trademarks	Paintings
Service mark	Sculpture
Layout of design of Integrated Circuit	Films
Geographical Indication	Technology based works (databases & softwares)
Utility Models	

3.1. Industrial Property

A separate WIPO booklet, Understanding Industrial Property, offers an equivalent introduction to the subject of industrial property, including patents for invention, industrial designs, trademarks and geographical indications.

3.1.1 Patent

3.1.1.1. History

In 500 BC, in the Greek city of *Sybaris* (located in now southern Italy), "encouragement was held out to all who should discover any new refinement in luxury, the profits arising from which were secured to the inventor by patent for the space of a year." The *Florentine* architect *Filippo Brunelleschi* received a three-year patent for a barge with *hoisting* gear, that carried marble along the *Arno River* in 1421.*[6]* In 1449, King Henry VI granted the first patent with a license of 20 years to *John of Utynam* for introducing the making of colored glass to England.

Patents in the modern sense originated in 1474, when the *Republic of Venice* enacted a decree that new and inventive devices, once put into practice, had to be communicated to the Republic to obtain the right to prevent others from using them. England followed with the *Statute of Monopolies* in 1623 under King *James I*, which declared that patents could only be granted for "projects of new invention." During the reign of *Queen Anne* (1702–14), the lawyers of the English Court developed the requirement that a written description of the invention must be submitted. The patent system in many other countries, including Australia, is based on British law and can be traced back to the Statute of Monopolies. In 1641, *Samuel Winslow* was granted the first patent in North America by the *Massachusetts General Court* for a new process for making salt. In France, patents were granted by the monarchy and by other institutions like the "Maison du Roi". The *Academy* examined novelty. Examinations were generally done in secret with no requirement to publish a description of the invention. Actual use of the invention was deemed adequate disclosure to the public. The modern French patent system was created during the Revolution in 1791. Patents were granted without examination since inventor's right was considered as a natural one. In the United States, during the so-called colonial period and *Articles of Confederation* years (1778–89), several states adopted patent systems of their own. The first Congress adopted a *Patent Act*, in 1790, and the first patent was issued under this Act on *July 31, 1790* (to *Samuel Hopkins* of Vermont for a *potash* production technique).

3.1.1.2. Concept

The word *patent* originates from the *Latin patere*, which means "to lay open" (i.e., to make available for public inspection), and more directly as a shortened version of the term *letters patent*, which originally denoted an open for public reading *royal decree* granting exclusive rights to a person.

The term *patent* usually refers to an exclusive right granted to anyone who invents any new, useful, and non-obvious process, machine, article of manufacture, or composition of matter, or any new and useful improvement thereof, and claims that right in a formal patent application. The additional qualification *utility patent* is used in the United States to distinguish it from other types of patents (e.g. *design patents*) but should not be confused with *utility models* granted by other countries. Examples of particular species of patents for inventions include *biological patents, business method patents, chemical patents* and *software patents.* Some other types of intellectual property rights are referred to as *patents* in some jurisdictions: *industrial design rights* are called *design patents* in some jurisdictions (they protect the visual design of objects that are not purely utilitarian), *plant breeders' rights* are sometimes called *plant patents,* and utility models or *Gebrauchsmuster* are sometimes called *petty patents* or *innovation patents.* Certain grants made by the monarch in pursuance of the royal prerogative were sometimes called *letters patent,* which was a government notice to the public of a grant of an exclusive right to ownership and possession. These were often grants of a patent-like monopoly and predate the modern origins of the patent system. For other uses of the term *patent* see notably *land patents,* which were land grants by early state governments in the USA, and *printing patent,* a precursor of modern copyright. These meanings reflect the original meaning of *letters patent* that had a broader scope than current usage.

A patent is a set of *exclusive rights* granted by a *state* (national government) to an inventor or their assignee for a *limited period of time* in exchange for the public disclosure of an *invention.*

The procedure for granting patents, the requirements placed on the patentee, and the extent of the exclusive rights vary widely between countries according to national laws and international agreements. Typically, however, a patent application must include one or more *claims* defining the invention which must be *new, non-obvious,* and *useful* or *industrially applicable*. In many countries, certain *subject areas* are excluded from patents, such as *business methods,* treatment of the human body, and mental acts. The exclusive right granted to a patentee in most countries is the right to prevent others from making, using, selling, or distributing the patented invention without permission. It is essentially a right to exclude others who are not licensed. A patent does not give the proprietor of the patent the right to *use* the patented invention, should it fall within the scope of an earlier patent.

Under the *World Trade Organization*'s (WTO) *Agreement on Trade-Related Aspects of Intellectual Property Rights,* patents should be available in WTO member states for any inventions, in all fields of technology, and the term of protection available should be a minimum of twenty years.*[3]* Different types of patents may have varying *patent terms* (i.e., durations).

3.1.2. Industrial designs / 3.1.3. Trademarks / 3.1.4. Service marks /3.1.5. Commercial names & designations

In trademark treatises, it is usually reported that blacksmiths who made swords in the *Roman Empire* are thought of as being the first users of trademarks. Other notable trademarks that have been used for a long time include *Löwenbräu,* which claims use of its lion mark since 1383, and *Stella Artois,* which claims use since 1366.

Trademark or service mark is recognition of *brand,* product or service *name*. Trademarks can be text, stylized text, design, color, or combination. Includes names, slogans, and logos. Trade or business name can be considered trademark or service mark only if used to identify goods or services. Trade name filing is not trademark protection unless separately protected as trademark. Domain name registration is separate from trademark or service mark. Use of domain name, even if registered, can be found to be trademark infringement.

Trademarks and service marks are effective upon first use and only in areas of use. Registration effective upon filing or actual use in commerce, whichever is first.

Registered trademarks involve registering the trademark with the government. The oldest registered trademarks in various countries include:

- *United Kingdom*: 1876 – The *Bass* Red Triangle was the first trademark to be registered under the Trade Mark Registration Act 1875.
- *United States*: Picture of Samson wrestling a lion, to Samson Rope in 1884.

A trademark, trade mark, or trade-mark is a distinctive *sign* or indicator used by an individual, *business organization*, or other *legal entity* to identify that the *products* or *services* to *consumers* with which the trademark appears originate from a unique source, and to distinguish its products or services from those of other entities.

A trademark may be designated by the following symbols:

- TM (for an *unregistered trade mark*, that is, a mark used to promote or brand goods)
- ! (for an unregistered *service mark*, that is, a mark used to promote or brand services)
- ® (for a registered trademark)

A trademark is typically a name, word, phrase, *logo*, *symbol*, design, image, or a combination of these elements. There is also a range of *non-conventional trademarks* comprising marks which do not fall into these standard categories, such as those based on color, smell, or sound.

The owner of a registered trademark may commence *legal proceedings* for *trademark infringement* to prevent unauthorized use of that trademark. However, registration is not required. The owner of a common law trademark may also file suit, but an unregistered mark may be protectable only within the geographical area within which it has been used or in geographical areas into which it may be reasonably expected to expand.

The term trademark is also used informally to refer to any distinguishing attribute by which an individual is readily identified, such as the well-known characteristics of celebrities. When a trademark is used in relation to services rather than products, it may sometimes be called a *service mark,* particularly in the *United States.*

The essential function of a trademark is to exclusively identify the commercial source or origin of products or services, such that a trademark, properly called, indicates source or serves as a badge of origin. In other words, trademarks serve to identify a particular business as the source of goods or services. The use of a trademark in this way is known as trademark use. Certain *exclusive rights* attach to a registered mark, which can be enforced by way of an *action* for *trademark infringement,* while unregistered trademark rights may be enforced pursuant to the common law *tort* of *passing off.*

It should be noted that trademark rights generally arise out of the use or to maintain exclusive rights over that sign in relation to certain products or services, assuming there are no other trademark objections.

Different goods and services have been classified by the *International (Nice) Classification of Goods and Services* into 45 *Trademark Classes* (1 to 34 cover goods, and 35 to 45 services). The idea of this system is to specify and limit the extension of the intellectual property right by determining which goods or services are covered by the mark, and to unify classification systems around the world.

3.1.6. Layout-Designs of Integrated Circuits / Mask Works

Three-dimensional computer *chip designs,* also called integrated circuit designs. WHEN EFFECTIVE; Upon filing of application for protection with the U.S. Copyright Office, but only if filed within 2 years after date of first commercial exploitation of the mask work. DURATION OF PROTECTION; Until the end of the 10th calendar year after the earlier of the date of registration or the date of first commercial exploitation. HOW TO PROTECT; Give notice of mask work rights by using 1) the words "mask work", the symbol *M*, or the symbol M in a circle and 2) the name or abbreviation of the name of the owner of the rights on the mask work or chip. File civil lawsuit to protect mask work registration rights. LAW GOVERNING; Semiconductor Chip Protection Act (SCPA) of 1984, 17 U.S. Code §901 and following. INTERNATIONAL CONSIDERATIONS; World Trade Organization (WTO) members and other countries such as Australia, Canada, Japan, Switzerland and European Community Members are eligible for mask work protection in the United States. Canada, Australia, Hong Kong, and possibly other countries give equivalent protection. Some protection is afforded by the Agreement on Trade-Related Aspects of Intellectual Property Rights (TRIPs Agreement) of the WTO, which requires member countries to protect mask works.

3.1.7. Geographical Indications (GI)

Governments have been protecting *trade names* and *trademarks* used in relation to food products identified with a particular region since at least the end of the nineteenth century, using *laws* against false trade descriptions or *passing off,* which generally protect against suggestions that a product has a certain origin, quality or association when it does not.

In such cases, the limitation on competitive freedoms which results from the grant of a monopoly of use over a geographical indication is justified by governments either by consumer protection benefits or by producer protection benefits.

A GI is a name or sign used on certain products which corresponds to a specific geographical location or origin (e.g. a town, region, or country). The use of a GI may act as a certification that the product possesses certain qualities, is made according to traditional methods, or enjoys a certain reputation, due to its geographical origin.

One of the first GI systems is the one used in *France* from the early part of the twentieth century known as *appellation d'origine contrôlée* (AOC). Items that meet geographical origin and quality standards may be endorsed with a government-issued stamp which acts as official certification of the origins and standards of the product to the consumer. Examples of products that have such 'appellations of origin' include *Gruyère cheese* and many *French wines.*

Geographical indications have long been associated with the concept of *terroir* and with *Europe* as an entity, where there is a tradition of associating certain food products with particular regions. Under *European Union Law*, the *protected designation of origin* framework which came into effect in 1992 regulates the following systems of geographical indications: *Protected designation of origin* (PDO), *protected geographical indication* (PGI) and *Traditional Speciality Guaranteed* (TSG).

3.1.8. Utility Model

A utility model is an *intellectual property* right to protect *inventions.* This right is available in a number of national *statutes,* as described below. It is very similar to the *patent,* but usually has a shorter *term* (often 6 to 15 years) and less stringent *patentability* requirements.

The *German* and *Austrian* utility model is called the "*Gebrauchsmuster*", which influenced some other countries such as in Japan. In Indonesia the utility model is called a "Petty Patent".

A utility model is a statutory monopoly granted for a limited time in exchange for an inventor providing sufficient teaching of his or her invention to permit a person of ordinary skill in the relevant art to perform the invention. The rights conferred by utility model laws are very similar to those granted by patent laws, but are more suited to what may be considered as "incremental inventions". Terms such as "petty patent", "innovation patent", "minor patent", and "small patent" may also be considered to fall within the definition of "utility model". A "utility innovation" is available in Malaysia.

3.1.9. Department of Industrial Policy & Promotion (DIPP) & Intellectual Property Rights (IPRS)

DIPP is concerned with legislations relating to Patents, Trade Marks, Designs and Geographical Indications. These are administered through the *Office of the Controller General of Patents, Designs and Trade Marks* (CGPDTM), subordinate office, with headquarters at Mumbai, as under:

1. The Patents Act, 1970 (amended in *1999, 2002* and *2005*) through the Patent Offices at Kolkata (HQ), Mumbai, Chennai and Delhi.
2. The *Designs Act, 2000* through the Patent Offices at Kolkata (HQ), Mumbai, Chennai and Delhi.
3. The *Trade Marks Act, 1999* through the Trade Marks Registry at Mumbai (HQ) Chennai, Delhi, Kolkata and Ahmedabad.
4. The *Geographical Indications of Goods (Registration & Protection) Act, 1999* through the Geographical Indications Registry at Chennai.

The Controller General of Patents, Designs and Trade Marks (CGPDTM) is also in-charge of the Office of the Patent Information System, Nagpur and the Intellectual Property Training Institute, Nagpur. The office has 446 personnel in the patents and designs Offices and 291 personnel in trademarks and geographical indication Offices. Necessary safeguards have been built into the IP laws, in particular in the Patents law, for protection of public interest including public health.

Along with the legislation, rules have also been amended to install a user-friendly system for processing of IP applications. All rules and forms are available on the website: *http://www.ipindia.nic.in*

3.2. Copyright

Copyright relates to artistic creations, such as **books, music, paintings** and **sculptures, films** and **technology-based works** (such as computer programs and electronic databases). Copyright legislation is part of the wider body of law known as intellectual property. In most European languages other than English, copyright is known as author's rights. The expression copyright refers to the main act which, in respect of literary and artistic creations, may be made only by the author or with his authorization. That act is the making of copies of the work. The expression author's rights refers to the creator of the artistic work, its author. It thus underlines the fact, recognized in most laws, that the author has certain specific rights in his creation which only he can exercise (such as the right to prevent a distorted reproduction). Other rights (such as the right to make copies) can be exercised by other persons, for example, a publisher who has obtained a license from the author.

While other types of intellectual property also exist, it is helpful for present purposes to explore the distinction between industrial property and copyright in terms of the basic difference between inventions and literary and artistic works. Inventions may be defined in a non-legal sense as new solutions to technical problems. Unlike protection of inventions, copyright law protects only the form of expression of ideas, not the ideas themselves. The creativity protected by copyright law is creativity in the choice and arrangement of words, musical notes, colors and shapes. So copyright law protects the owner of property rights against those who copy or otherwise take and use the form in which the original work was expressed by the author.

From this basic difference between inventions and literary and artistic works, it follows that the legal protection provided to each also differs. Since protection for inventions gives a monopoly right to exploit an idea, such protection is short in duration- usually about 20 years. The fact that the invention is protected must also be made known to the public. There must be an official notification that a specific, fully described invention is the property of a specific owner for a fixed number of years; in other words, the protected invention must be disclosed publicly in an official register.

Since the legal protection of literary and artistic works under copyright, by contrast, prevents only unauthorized use of the expressions of ideas, the duration of protection can be much longer than in the case of the protection of ideas themselves, without damage to the public interest.

3.2.1. *Copyright and Plagiarism*

Copyright is a form of protection provided by the laws of the United States (title 17, U.S. Code) to the authors of "original works of authorship" including literary, dramatic, musical, artistic, architectural and certain other intellectual works. This protection is available to both published and unpublished works. Material in the "public domain" is intellectual property that does not come under copyright laws. Nearly all work before the 20th C. is not copyrighted.

Plagiarism is the act of stealing and passing off the ideas, words, or other intellectual property produced by another as one's own. For example, using someone else's words in a research paper without citing the source, is an act of plagiarism.

3.2.2. History of Copyright

- First law enacted 1790.
- 1976 copyright law followed international law, extending copyright for 50 years after death of the author/creator.
- On October 27, 1998, President Clinton signed into law the "Sonny Bono Copyright Extension Act," which extends the terms of almost all existing copyrights by 20 years, to provide copyrights in the United States the same protection afforded in Europe. The basic term of copyright protection, the life of the creator plus 50 years, has been increased to life plus 70 years. The term for "work for hire" has been extended from 75 to 95 years.

3.2.3. How long does copyright last?

- Works created on or after Jan 1978 - life of author + 70
- Work for hire 95 years

3.2.4. The OWNER/manufacturer/creator [but not always the creator] of the work CAN

- Copy the work.
- Create derivative works based upon the work.
- Sell, rent, lease, and lend copies of the work.
- Publicly perform literary, musical, dramatic, motion picture and other audiovisual works.
- Publicly perform sound recordings.

It is not necessary to have a notice of copyright (i.e.: ©

1997 Jane Doe) for material to be copyright protected in the U.S. Once something tangible is produced, text, graphics, music, video, etc., it is automatically copyrighted. Sound recordings and some other property use other copyright symbols. Anyone can use the copyright symbol on her or his original work.

3.2.6. *Works Protected by Copyright*

For the purposes of copyright protection, the term "literary and artistic works" is understood to include every original work of authorship, irrespective of its literary or artistic merit. The ideas in the work do not need to be original, but the form of expression must be an original creation of the author. The *Berne Convention for the Protection of Literary and Artistic Works* (Article 2) states: "The expression 'literary and artistic works' shall include every production in the literary, scientific and artistic domain, whatever may be the mode or form of its expression". The Convention goes on to list the following examples of such works:

1. Books, pamphlets and other writings;
2. Lectures, addresses, sermons;
3. Dramatic or dramatico-musical works;
4. Choreographic works and entertainments in dumb show;
5. Musical compositions with or without words;
6. Cinematographic works to which are assimilated works expressed by a process analogous to cinematography;
7. Works of drawing, painting, architecture, sculpture, engraving and lithography;
8. Photographic works, to which are assimilated works expressed by a process analogous to photography;
9. Works of applied art; illustrations, maps, plans, sketches and three-dimensional works relative to

geography, topography, architecture or science;

10. "Translations, adaptations, arrangements of music and other alterations of a literary or artistic work, which are to be protected as original works without prejudice to the copyright in the original work..
11. Collections of literary or artistic works such as encyclopedias and anthologies which, by reason of the selection and arrangement of their contents, constitute intellectual creations, are to be protected as such, without prejudice to the copyright in each of the works forming part of such collections."

Member countries of the Berne Union, and many other countries, provide protection under their copyright laws for the above categories of works. The list, however, is not intended to be exhaustive. Copyright laws also protect other modes or forms of expression of works in the literary, scientific and artistic domain, which are not included in the list.

Computer programs are a good example of a type of work which is not included in the list in the *Berne Convention*, but which is undoubtedly included in the notion of a production in the literary, scientific and artistic domain within the meaning of Article 2. Indeed, computer programs are protected under the copyright laws of a number of countries, as well as under the *WIPO Copyright Treaty* (1996). A computer program is a set of instructions, which controls the operations of a computer in order to enable it to perform a specific task, such as the storage and retrieval of information. The program is produced by one or more human authors, but in its final "mode or form of expression," it can be understood directly only by a machine (the computer), not by humans.

Multimedia productions are another example of a type of work not listed in the Berne Convention, but which clearly comes within the notion of creations in the literary, scientific and artistic domain. While no acceptable legal definition has been developed, there is a consensus that the combination of sound, text and images in a digital format, which is made accessible by a computer program, embodies an original expression of authorship sufficient to justify the protection of multimedia productions under the umbrella of copyright.

3.2.7. Rights Protected

The most important feature of any kind of property is that the owner may use it exclusively, i.e., as he wishes, and that nobody else can lawfully use it without his authorization. This does not, of course, mean that he can use it regardless of the legally recognized rights and interests of other members of society. Similarly the owner of copyright in a protected work may use the work as he wishes, and may prevent others from using it without his authorization. The rights granted under national laws to the owner of copyright in a protected work are normally exclusive rights to authorize a third party to use the work, subject to the legally recognized rights and interests of others.

There are two types of rights under copyright. **Economic rights** allow the rights owner to derive financial reward from the use of his works by others. **Moral rights** allow the author to take certain actions to preserve the personal link between him and the work.

Moral rights The *Berne Convention* (Article 6bis) requires Member countries to grant to authors: (i) the right to claim authorship of the work (sometimes called the right of paternity); and (ii) the right to object to any distortion or modification of the work, or other derogatory action in relation to the work, which would be prejudicial to the author's honor or reputation (sometimes called the right of integrity).These rights are generally known as the moral rights of authors. The Convention requires them to be independent of the author's economic rights, and to remain with the author even after he has transferred his economic rights. It is worth noting that moral rights are only accorded to individual authors. Thus even when, for example, a film producer or a publisher owns the economic rights in a work, it is only the individual creator who has moral interests at stake.Moral rights are *rights* of creators of *copyrighted* works generally recognized in *civil law* jurisdictions and, to a lesser extent, in some *common law* jurisdictions. They include the right of *attribution*, the right to have a work published *anonymously* or *pseudonymously*, and the right to the integrity of the work. The preserving of the integrity of the work bars the work from alteration, distortion, or mutilation. Anything else that may detract from the artist's relationship with the work even after it leaves the artist's possession or ownership may bring these moral rights into play. Moral rights are distinct from any economic rights tied to copyrights. Even if an artist has assigned his or her copyright rights to a work to a third party, he or she still maintains the moral rights to the work.Moral rights were first recognized in *France* and *Germany*, before they were included in the *Berne Convention for the Protection of Literary and Artistic Works* in 1928. *Canada* recognizes moral rights in its Copyright Act, although the French translation of the phrase used in the legislation is "droits moraux", not "droit d'auteur" (the latter refers to copyright as a whole). While the *United States* became a signatory to the convention in 1988, it still does not completely recognize moral rights as part of *copyright law*, but rather as part of other bodies of law, such as defamation or unfair competition.Some jurisdictions allow for the *waiver* of moral rights. In the United States, the *Visual Artists Rights Act* of 1990 (VARA) recognizes moral rights, but applies only to works of *visual art*.

Most copyright laws state that the author or rights owner has the right to authorize or prevent certain acts in relation to a work. The rights owner of a work can **prohibit or authorize**:

- its reproduction in various forms, such as printed publications or sound recordings;
- the distribution of copies;
- its public performance;
- its broadcasting or other communication to the public;
- its translation into other languages;
- its adaptation, such as a novel into a screenplay.

These rights are explained in more detail in the following paragraphs.**Reproduction, distribution and related rights**: The right of the copyright owner to prevent others from making copies of his works without his authorization is the most basic right protected by copyright legislation. The right to control the act of reproduction – be it the reproduction of books by a publisher, or the manufacture by a record producer of compact discs containing recorded performances of musical works - is the legal basis for many forms of exploitation of protected works.Other rights are recognized in national laws in order to ensure that this basic right of reproduction is respected. Many laws include a right specifically to authorize **distribution** of copies of works. Obviously, the right of reproduction would be of little economic value if the owner of copyright could not authorize the distribution of the copies made with his consent. The right of distribution usually terminates upon first sale or transfer of ownership of a particular copy. This means, for example, that when the copyright owner of a book sells or otherwise transfers ownership of a copy of the book, the owner of that copy may give the book away or even resell it without the copyright owner's further permission.Another right which is achieving increasingly wide recognition, and is included in the WIPO Copyright Treaty, is the right to authorize **rental** of copies of certain categories of works, such as musical works in sound recordings, audiovisual works, and computer programs. This became necessary in order to prevent abuse of the copyright owner's right of reproduction when technological advances made it easy for rental shop customers to copy such works.Finally, some copyright laws include a right to control **importation** of copies as a means to prevent erosion of the principle of territoriality of copyright; that is, the legitimate economic interests of the copyright owner would be endangered if he could not exercise the rights of reproduction and distribution on a territorial basis.Certain forms of reproduction of a work are exceptions to the general rule, because they do not require the authorization of the rights owner. These exceptions are known as limitations on rights (see page...). An area of current debate relates to the scope of one particular limitation traditionally present in copyright laws, which allows individuals to make single copies of works for private, personal and non-commercial purposes. The continued justification for such a limitation on the right of reproduction is being questioned now that digital technology has made it possible to produce high-quality, unauthorized copies of works, which are virtually indistinguishable from the source - and thus a perfect substitute for the purchase of authorized copies.**Rights of public performance, broadcasting and communication to the public, and making available to the public:** A public performance is considered under many national laws to include any performance of a work at a place where the public is or can be present; or at a place not open to the public, but where a substantial number of persons outside the normal circle of a family and its close acquaintances is present. The right of public performance entitles the author or other copyright owner to authorize live performances of a work, such as a play in a theater, or an orchestra performance of a symphony in a concert hall. Public performance also includes performance by means of recordings. Thus a musical work is considered publicly performed when a sound recording of that work, or phonogram, is played over amplification equipment, for example in a discotheque, airplane, or shopping mall.The right of **broadcasting** covers the transmission for public reception of sounds, or of images and sounds, by wireless means, whether by radio, television, or satellite. When a work is **communicated to the public**, a signal is distributed by wire or wireless means, which can be received only by persons who possess the equipment necessary to decode the signal. Cable transmission is an example of communication to the public.Under the Berne Convention, authors have the exclusive right to authorize public performance, broadcasting and communication of their works to the public. Under some national laws, the exclusive right of the author or other rights owner to authorize broadcasting is replaced, in certain circumstances, by a right to **equitable remuneration**, although this sort of limitation on the broadcasting right is less and less common.In recent years, the rights of broadcasting, public performance and communication to the public have been the subject of much discussion. New questions have arisen as a result of technological developments, in particular digital technology, which has introduced interactive communications, whereby the user selects which works he wishes to have delivered to his computer. Opinions diverge as to which right should be applied to this activity. The WIPO Copyright Treaty (WCT) (article 8) clarifies that it should be covered by an exclusive right, which the Treaty describes as the authors' right to authorize making their works available to the public "in such a way that members of the public can access these works from a place and at a time individually chosen by them". Most national laws implement this right as a part of the right of communication to the public, although some do so as part of the right of distribution.

3.2.8. Translation and adaptation rights

The acts of translating or adapting a work protected by copyright also require authorization from the rights owner. Translation means the expression of a work in a language other than that of the original version. Adaptation is generally understood as the modification of a work to create another work, for example adapting a novel to make a film; or the modification of a work for different conditions of exploitation, e.g., by adapting a textbook originally written for university students to make it suitable for a lower level.

Translations and adaptations are themselves works protected by copyright. So in order to publish a translation or adaptation, authorization must be obtained both from the owner of the copyright in the original work and from the owner of copyright in the translation or adaptation.

The scope of the right of adaptation has been the subject of significant discussion in recent years because of the greatly increased possibilities for adapting and transforming works which are embodied in digital format. With digital technology, manipulation of text, sound and images by the user is quick and easy. Discussions have focused on the appropriate balance between the rights of the author to control the integrity of the work by authorizing modifications, and the rights of users to make changes which seem to be part of a normal use of works in digital format.

3.2.9. Limitations on Rights

1. The exclusion from copyright protection of **certain categories of works**. In some countries, works are excluded from protection if they are not fixed in tangible form. For example, a work of choreography would only be protected once the movements were written down in dance notation or recorded on

videotape. In certain countries, the texts of laws, court and administrative decisions are excluded from copyright protection.

2. Acts of exploitation, normally requiring the authorization of the rights owner, which may, under circumstances specified in the law, be carried out without authorization. There are two basic types of limitations in this category: (a) **free use**, which carries no obligation to compensate the rights owner for the use of his work without authorization; and (b) **non-voluntary licenses,** which do require that compensation be paid to the rights owner for non-authorized exploitation.

Examples of free use include: a) quoting from a protected work, provided that the source of the quotation and the name of the author is mentioned, and that the extent of the quotation is compatible with fair practice; b) use of works by way of illustration for teaching purposes; and c) use of works for the purpose of news reporting.In respect of **free use for reproduction**, the *Berne Convention* contains a general rule, rather than an explicit limitation. Article 9(2) states that Member States may provide for free reproduction in special cases where the acts do not conflict with normal exploitation of the work and do not unreasonably prejudice the legitimate interests of the author. As noted above, many laws allow for individuals to reproduce a work exclusively for their **personal, private and non-commercial use**. However, the ease and quality of individual copying made possible by recent technology has led some countries to narrow the scope of such provisions, including through systems which allow certain copying, but incorporate a mechanism for payment to rights owners for the prejudice to their economic interests resulting from the copying.In addition to the specific categories of free use set out in national laws, the laws of some countries recognize the concept known as **fair use** or **fair dealing**. This allows use of works without the authorization of the rights owner, taking into account factors such as the nature and purpose of the use, including whether it is for commercial purposes; the nature of the work used; the amount of the work used in relation to the work as a whole; and the likely effect of the use on the potential commercial value of the work.**Non-voluntary licenses** allow use of works in certain circumstances without the authorization of the owner of rights, but require that compensation be paid in respect of the use. Such licenses are called non-voluntary because they are allowed in the law, and do not result from the exercise of the exclusive right of the copyright owner to authorize particular acts. Non-voluntary licenses were usually created in circumstances where a new technology for the dissemination of works to the public had emerged, and where the national legislator feared that rights owners would prevent the development of the new technology by refusing to authorize use of works. This was true of two non-voluntary licenses recognized in the *Berne Convention*, which allow the mechanical reproduction of musical works and broadcasting. The justification for non-voluntary licenses is, however, increasingly called into question, since effective alternatives now exist for making works available to the public based on authorizations given by the rights owners, including in the form of collective administration of rights.

3.2.10. Duration of Copyright

Copyright does not continue indefinitely. The law provides for a period of time during which the rights of the copyright owner exist. The period or duration of copyright begins from the moment when the work has been created, or, under some national laws, when it has been expressed in a tangible form. It continues, in general, until some time after the death of the author. The purpose of this provision in the law is to enable the author's successors to benefit economically from exploitation of the work after the author's death.

In countries party to the *Berne Convention,* and in many other countries, the duration of copyright provided for by national law is as a general rule the life of the author plus not less than 50 years after his death. The Berne Convention also establishes periods of protection for works such as anonymous, posthumous and cinematographic works, where it is not possible to base duration on the life of an individual author. There is a trend in a number of countries toward lengthening the duration of copyright. The European Union, the United States of America and several others have extended the term of copyright to 70 years after the death of the author.

3.2.11. Ownership, Exercise and Transfer of Copyright

The owner of copyright in a work is generally, at least in the first instance, the person who created the work, i.e. the author of the work. But this is not always the case. The *Berne Convention* (Article 14bis) contains rules for determining initial ownership of rights in cinematographic works. Certain national laws also provide that, when a work is created by an author who is employed for the purpose of creating that work, then the employer, not the author, is the owner of the copyright in the work. As noted above, however, moral rights always belong to the individual author of the work, whoever the owner of economic rights may be.

The laws of many countries provide that the initial rights owner in a work may transfer all economic rights to a third party. (Moral rights, being personal to the author, can never be transferred). Authors may sell the rights to their works to individuals or companies best able to market the works, in return for payment. These payments are often made dependent on the actual use of the work, and are then referred to as **royalties**. Transfers of copyright may take one of two forms: assignments and licenses.

Under an **assignment**, the rights owner transfers the right to authorize or prohibit certain acts covered by one, several, or all rights under copyright. An assignment is a transfer of a property right. So if all rights are assigned, the person to whom the rights were assigned becomes the new owner of copyright.

In some countries, an assignment of copyright is not legally possible, and only **licensing** is allowed. Licensing means that the owner of the copyright retains ownership but authorizes a third party to carry out certain acts covered by his economic rights, generally for a specific period of time and for a specific purpose. For example, the author of a novel may grant a license to a publisher to make and distribute copies of his work. At the same time, he may grant a license to a film producer to make a film based on the novel. Licenses may be exclusive, where the copyright owner agrees not to authorize any other party to carry out the licensed acts; or non-exclusive, which means that the copyright owner may authorize others to carry out the same acts. A license, unlike an assignment, does not generally convey the right to authorize others to carry out acts covered by economic rights.

Licensing may also take the form of **collective administration of rights**. Under collective administration, authors and other rights owners grant exclusive licenses to a single entity, which acts on their behalf to grant authorizations, to collect and distribute remuneration, to prevent and detect infringement of rights, and to seek remedies for infringement. An advantage for authors in collective administration lies in the fact that, with multiple possibilities for unauthorized use of works resulting from new technologies, a single body can ensure that mass uses take place on the basis of authorizations which are easily obtainable from a central source.

A rights owner may also **abandon the exercise of the rights**, wholly or partially. The owner may, for example, post copyright protected material on the Internet and leave it free for anybody to use, or may restrict the abandonment to noncommercial use. Some very impressive cooperation projects have been organized on a model where contributors abandon certain rights as described in the licensing terms adopted for the project, such as the General Public License (GPL). They thereby leave their contributions free for others to use and to adapt, but with the condition that the subsequent users also adhere to the terms of the license. Such projects, including the open source movement, which specializes in creating computer programs, also build their business models on the existence of copyright protection, because otherwise they could not impose an obligation on subsequent users.

3.2.12. *Enforcement of Rights*

The *Berne Convention* contains very few provisions concerning enforcement of rights, but the evolution of new national and international enforcement standards has been dramatic in recent years due to two principal factors. The first concerns advances in the technological means for creation and use (both authorized and unauthorized) of protected material. Digital technology in particular makes it easy to transmit and make perfect copies of any information existing in digital form, including copyright-protected works. The second factor is the increasing economic importance in the realm of international trade of the movement of goods and services protected by intellectual property rights. Simply put, trade in products embodying intellectual property rights is now a booming, worldwide business. This is acknowledged in the *WIPO Copyright Treaty* (WCT), which requires Contracting Parties to ensure that enforcement procedures are available under their law so as to permit effective action against any infringement of rights covered by the Treaty, including remedies to prevent or deter further infringements.

The Agreement on Trade-Related Aspects of Intellectual Property Rights (TRIPS), which contains more detailed provisions on the enforcement of rights, is ample evidence of this new link between intellectual property and trade. The following paragraphs identify and summarize some of the enforcement provisions found in recent national legislation. They may be divided into the following categories: conservatory or provisional measures; civil remedies; criminal sanctions; measures to be taken at the border; and measures, remedies and sanctions against abuses in respect of technical devices.

Conservatory or provisional measures have two purposes: first, to prevent infringements from occurring, in particular to prevent the entry of infringing goods into the channels of commerce, including entry of imported goods after clearance by customs; and second, to preserve relevant evidence in regard to an alleged infringement. Thus, judicial authorities may have the authority to order that provisional measures be enacted without advance notice to the alleged infringer. In this way, the alleged infringer is prevented from relocating the goods to avoid detection. The most common provisional measure is a search of the premises of the alleged infringer and seizure of suspected infringing goods, the equipment used to manufacture them, and all relevant documents and other records of the alleged infringing business activities.

Civil remedies compensate the rights owner for economic injury suffered because of the infringement, usually in the form of pecuniary damages, and create an effective deterrent to further infringement. This is often in the form of a judicial order to destroy the infringing goods and the materials which have been predominantly used for producing them. If there is a danger that infringing acts may be continued, the court may also issue injunctions against such acts, failure to comply with which would subject the infringer to payment of a fine.

Criminal sanctions are intended to punish those who willfully commit acts of piracy on a commercial scale and, as in the case of civil remedies, to deter further infringement. The purpose of punishment is served by substantial fines, and by prison sentences consistent with the level of penalties applied for crimes of corresponding seriousness, particularly for repeat offenses. The purpose of deterrence is served by orders for the seizure and destruction of infringing goods, and of the materials and equipment used predominantly to commit the offense.

Measures to be taken at the border are different from the enforcement measures described so far, in that they involve action by the customs authorities rather than by the judicial authorities. Border measures allow the rights owner to request that customs authorities suspend the release into circulation of goods that are suspected of infringing copyright. This is intended to give the rights owner a reasonable time to commence judicial proceedings against the suspected infringer, without the risk that the alleged infringing goods will disappear into circulation after customs clearance. The rights owner must (a) satisfy the customs authorities that there is prima facie evidence of infringement, (b) provide a detailed description of the goods so that they can be recognized and (c) provide a security to indemnify the importer, the owner of the goods, and the customs authorities in case the goods turn out to be non-infringing.

The final category of enforcement provisions, which has achieved greater importance since the advent of digital technology, includes measures, remedies and sanctions against **abuses in respect of technical means**. In certain cases, the only practical means of preventing copying is through so-called copy-protection or copy-management systems. These use technical devices, which either entirely prevent copying, or make the quality of the copies so poor as to be unusable. Technical means are also used to prevent the reception of encrypted commercial television programs except with use of decoders. However, it is technically possible to manufacture devices to circumvent such copy-protection and encryption systems. The enforcement provisions are intended to prevent the manufacture, importation and distribution of such devices. Provisions to this effect are included in the WCT. So too are provisions to prevent the unauthorized removal or alteration of electronic rights management information, and the dissemination of copies of works from which such information has been removed. Such information may identify the author or rights owner, or contain information about the terms and conditions of use of the work. Removing it may result in the distortion of computerized rights management or fee-distribution systems.

3.2.13. The Internet and Copyright

"The Internet has been characterized as the largest threat to copyright since its inception. The Internet is awash in information, a lot of it with varying degrees of copyright protection. Copyrighted works on the Net include new s stories, software, novels, screenplays, graphics, pictures, Usenet messages and even email. In fact, the frightening reality is that almost everything on the Net is protected by copyright law. That can pose problems for the hapless surfer." (*"The Copyright Web site" http://www.benedict.com/*)

3.2.14. What is protected on the WWW?

The unique underlying design of a Web page and its contents, including:

- links

- original text
- graphics
- audio
- video
- html, vrml, other unique markup language sequences
- List of Web sites compiled by an individual or organization
- and all other unique elements that make up the original nature of the material.

3.2.15. *When creating a Web page, you CAN:*

- Link to other Web sites. [However, some individuals and organizations have specific requirements when you link to their Web material. Check a site carefully to find such restrictions. It is wise to ask permission. You need to cite source, as you are required to do in a research paper, when quoting or paraphrasing material from other sources. How much you quote is limited.]
- Use **free** graphics on your Web page. If the graphics are not advertised as "free" they should not be copied without permission.

3.2.16. *When creating a Web page, you CANNOT*

- Put the contents of another person's or organizations web site on your Web page
- Copy and paste information together from various Internet sources to create "your own" document. [You CAN quote or paraphrase limited amounts, if you give credit to the original source and the location of the source. This same principle applies to print sources, of course.]
- Incorporate other people's electronic material, such as e-mail, in your own document, without permission.

- Forward someone's e-mail to another recipient without permission
- Change the context of or edit someone else's digital correspondence in a way which changes the meaning
- Copy and paste others' lists of resources on your own web page
- Copy and paste logos, icons, and other graphics from other web sites to your web page (unless it is clearly advertised as "freeware." Shareware is **not** free). Some organizations are happy to let you use their logos, with permission - it is free advertising. But they want to know who is using it. They might not approve of all sites who want to use their logo.

Many aspects of the issue of copyright and the Internet are still not resolved. This information, however, should serve as a useful guide to help you avoid violation of copyright rules and the pitfalls of unknowingly plagiarizing someone else's material. When in doubt, please consult the *official copyright rules and guidelines*.

Authors' rights Authors' rights are a part of *copyright* law. The term is a direct translation of the *French* term ***droit d'auteur*** (also *German Urheberrecht*), and is generally used in relation to the copyright laws of *civil law* countries and in *European Union law*. Authors' rights are internationally protected by the *Berne Convention for the Protection of Literary and Artistic Works* and by other similar treaties. "Author" is used in a very wide sense, and includes composers, artists, sculptors and even architects: in general, the author is the person whose creativity led to the protected work being created, although the exact definition varies from country to country.Authors' rights have two distinct components: the economic rights in the work and the *moral rights* of the author. The economic rights are a *property right* which is limited in time and which may be transferred by the author to other people in the same way as any other property (although many countries require that the transfer must be in the form of a written *contract*). They are intended to allow the author or their holder to profit financially from his or her creation, and include the right to authorize the reproduction of the work in any form (Article 9, Berne Convention)*[1]*. The authors of *dramatic works* (plays, etc.) also have the right to authorize the public performance of their works (Article 11, Berne Convention).The protection of the moral rights of an author is based on the view that a creative work is in some way an expression of the author's personality: the moral rights are therefore personal to the author, and cannot be transferred to another person except by *testament* when the author dies.*[2]* The moral rights regime differs greatly between countries, but typically includes the right to be identified as the author of the work and the right to object to any distortion or mutilation of the work which would be prejudicial to his or her honour or reputation (Article 6bis, Berne Convention). In many countries, the moral rights of an author are perpetual.***Distinction between common law copyright and civil law authors' rights***It is common to draw a distinction in the treatment of authors and other interested parties between common law jurisdictions and civil law systems. Although there are certainly differences between national laws, the differences in effective protection should not be overstated. Both copyright and authors' rights arose in the eighteenth century to address identical problems: the inequality in relations between authors and publishers (and between publishers themselves) if *intellectual property* is not recognised and protected, and the need to provide an income for authors other than *patronage*. Both systems provide for a *monopoly* right granted to the author for a limited term which can be transferred to another person, which was initially the right to copy or otherwise reproduce the work (hence "copyright") but has since been expanded to take account of technological developments.It is an essential feature of authors' rights and of many copyright laws that the object which is protected must arise from the creativity of the author rather than from his or her simple effort or investment (see *Feist v. Rural* in the *United States*): both *French* and *German copyright laws* protect "works of the mind" (*oeuvres de l'esprit*). This has led civil law systems to adopt a strong link between the rights (at least initially) and the person of the author: the initial ownership rights by a *corporation* are severely restricted or even impossible (as in *Germany[3]*). Common law jurisdictions are more willing to accept corporate ownership of copyright, as in the U.S. *work for hire* principle. Although the following comparison is simplistic and dependent on the exact laws of individual countries, it is difficult to see an effective difference in the two situations:

- **Common law:** employer owns the copyright in work created by employees
- **Civil law:** employer enjoys an exclusive licence to the economic rights in work created by employees

Civil law systems have also been forceful in protecting the moral rights of authors, arguing that their creativity deserves protection as an integral part of their personality. The protection of the personality in common law jurisdiction has for long been separate from the law of copyright, embodied in such *torts* as *defamation* (also *passing off* and *malicious falsehood*). Moral rights were not, therefore, explicitly mentioned in *UK copyright law* until 1988,*[4]* over a century after the United Kingdom signed the Berne Convention.*[5]* The difference runs both ways: UK and Irish copyright laws protect the privacy of the subject of certain photographs and films as a moral right under copyright law,*[6]* while civil law systems treat this as a separate *portrait right*. The different protections of *industrial design rights* cut across the divide between the two systems of law.

4. INTERNATIONAL ORGANIZATIONS & TREATIES

A UN agency, namely, *World Intellectual Property Organization* (WIPO) based in Geneva administers treaties in the field of intellectual property. India is a member of WIPO.

Department of Industrial Policy & Promotion is the nodal Department in the Government of India for all matters concerning WIPO.

India is also member of 2 major treaties, namely, Paris Convention for the Protection of Industrial Property (relating to patents, trademarks, designs, etc.) of 1883 and the Berne Convention for the Protection of Literary and Artistic Works (relating to copyright) of 1886. Apart from these, India is also a member of the Patent Cooperation Treaty (PCT) which facilitates obtaining of patents in several countries by filing a single application.

India is also a member of the World Trade Organization (WTO). The WTO agreement, *inter-alia,* contains an agreement on IP, namely, the Agreement on Trade Related Aspects of Intellectual Property (TRIPS). This Agreement made protection of intellectual property an enforceable obligation of the Member States. TRIPS Agreement sets out minimum standards of intellectual property protection for Member States.

India has complied with the obligations contained in the TRIPS Agreement and amended/enacted IP laws.

5. INTELLECTUAL PROPERTY APPELLATE BOARD (IPAB)

An Intellectual Property Appellate Board (*IPAB*) has been set up at Chennai to hear appeals against the decisions of Registrar of Trademarks, Geographical Indications and the Controller of Patents.

6. OTHER IP LEGISLATIONS

- Copyright is protected through *Copyright Act, 1957*, as amended in 1999 - administered by the Department of Higher Education.
- Layout of transistors and other circuitry elements is protected through the *Semi-conductor Integrated Circuits Layout-Design Act, 2000* - administered by the Department of Information Technology.
- New varieties of plants are protected through the *Protection of Plant Varieties and Farmers' Rights Act, 2001* - administered by the Department of Agriculture and Cooperation.
- Article 39 of the TRIPs Agreement mandates protection of test data submitted to regulatory authorities for obtaining marketing approvals against unfair commercial use. A Committee under the chairmanship of Secretary, Department of Chemicals and Petro-chemicals has examined this issue and submitted its *Report* to the Government.

7. MODERNISATION OF IP ADMINISTRATION

To complement the legislative initiatives, modernisation of IP infrastructure has also been undertaken and new integrated offices have been established in Delhi, Kolkata, Chennai and Mumbai. A programme costing Rs.153 crore has been implemented in the 10th Five Year Plan. The programme focused on: Infrastructure development; computerisation; human resource development; training and awareness.

E-filing facility for patent and trademark applications has been introduced on 20.7.2007.

8. INTERNATIONAL COOPERATION

Bilateral cooperation agreements (MoUs) have been

entered into with UK, France, USA, European Patent Office and Japan. These focus on human resources development, capacity building and awareness and outreach activities.

Multilateral Cooperation: India has an active cooperation programme in intellectual property matters with WIPO. These, inter alia, include organization of joint seminars and workshops and study programmes besides technical assistance by WIPO experts.

9. ENFORCEMENT OF INTELLECTUAL PROPERTY

Civil and criminal provisions exist in various laws for dealing with counterfeiting and piracy. The Department of IPP has set up an Inter-ministerial Committee to coordinate IP enforcement issues.

10. IMPACT OF MODERNIZATION

10.1. Patents

The filing of patent applications has increased from 4824 in the year 1999-2000 to 28,882 applications in the year 2006-2007. The number of applications examined has gone up to 14,119 in 2006-07 against the figure of 2824 in the year 1999-2000.

10.2. Trademarks

The backlog of unexamined applications of approximately 5 lacks cases brought down to zero. Renewal of Trademarks certificates being done instantaneously in clear cases and new applications are examined within one week. As against only 8,010 registrations in 1999-2000, 13 times more TMs were registered in 2006-07, that is, 109,361. 3.38 lacks trademark certificates were issued during the last 3 years whereas only 1.65 lacks marks were registered in 64 years (since 1940 to 2004).

10.3. Geographical Indications

39 Geographical Indications products have been registered since September, 2003. These include Darjeeling Tea, Chanderi Saree, Pochanpally Ikat, Solapur Chaddar, Mysore Silk, Kullu Shawl, Bidriware, etc.

10.4. Designs

The filing of applications for Design has increased from 2874 in 1999-2000 to 5372 in 2006-07. The number of applications examined has also gone up to 5179 in 2006-07 against the figure of 2067 in 1999-2000. The number of Designs registered has also increased from 1382 in 1999-2000 to 4431 in 2006-07.

11. CURRENT ISSUES

A. Establishment of NIIPM

The Government has approved a proposal for establishment of a National Institute for Intellectual Property Management (NIIPM) at Nagpur. The Institute will perform training, education, research and think tank functions.

B. Modernisation of IP Offices

Further modernisation of IP Offices to provide additional human resources, higher level of computerisation to support on-line processing, strengthening of data-base and novelty search facilities, awareness generation activities, accession to international treaties/conventions is being taken up in 11th Five Year Plan.

C. Madrid Protocol on Trademarks

Madrid Protocol, administered by WIPO, is a simple, facilitative and cost effective system for registration of International Trademarks. India's membership of Madrid Protocol will help Indian companies to register their trademarks in the member countries of the Protocol through a single application. An exercise to amend the Trade Marks Act is underway to enable joining the Madrid Protocol.

D. ISA and IPEA

A proposal is under consideration to seek recognition for the Indian Patent Office as an International Searching Authority (ISA) and International Preliminary Examining Authority (IPEA) under the Patent Co-operation Treaty. ISA and IPEAs provide search reports on novelty and examination reports on patentability of inventions.

E. Mashelkar Committee

Government has set up a technical expert group under the chairmanship of former Director General of CSIR (Dr. R.A. Mashelkar) to examine the following two patent law issues: (a) whether it would be TRIPS compatible to limit the grant of patent for pharmaceutical substance to new chemical entity or to new medical entity involving one or more inventive steps; and (b) whether it would be TRIPS compatible to exclude micro-organisms from patenting. The Report of the Group is available at http://ipindia.nic.in/ipr/patent/mashelkar_committee_report.doc

12. THE ROLE OF WIPO

The World Intellectual Property Organization (WIPO) is an international organization dedicated to ensuring that the rights of creators and owners of intellectual property are protected worldwide, and that inventors and authors are thus recognized and rewarded for their ingenuity.

As a specialized agency of the United Nations, WIPO exists as a forum for its Member States to create and harmonize **rules and practices** to protect intellectual property rights. Most industrialized nations have protection systems that are centuries old. Many new and developing countries, however, are now building up their patent, trademark and copyright laws and systems. With the rapid globalization of trade during the last decade, WIPO plays a key role in helping these new systems to evolve through treaty negotiation, legal and technical assistance, and training in various forms, including in the area of enforcement of intellectual property rights.

The field of copyright and related rights has expanded dramatically as technological developments have brought new ways of disseminating creations worldwide through such forms of communication as satellite broadcasting, compact discs, DVDs and the Internet. WIPO is closely involved in the on-going international debate to shape new standards for copyright protection in cyberspace.

WIPO administers the following **international treaties on copyright and related rights**:

- *Berne Convention* for the Protection of Literary and Artistic Works
- *Brussels Convention* Relating to the Distribution of Program-Carrying Signals Transmitted by Satellite
- *Geneva Convention* for the Protection of Producers of Phonograms Against Unauthorized Duplication of Their Phonograms
- *Rome Convention* for the Protection of Performers, Producers of Phonograms and Broadcasting Organizations
- *WIPO Copyright Treaty* (WCT)
- *WIPO Performances and Phonograms Treaty* (WPPT)

WIPO also provides an *Arbitration and Mediation Center*, which offers services for the resolution of international commercial disputes between private parties involving intellectual property. The subject matter of these proceedings includes both contractual disputes (such as patent and software licenses, trademark coexistence agreements, and research and development agreements) and non-contractual disputes (such as patent infringement).

The Center is also now recognized as the leading dispute resolution service provider for disputes arising out of the abusive registration and use of Internet domain names.

13. CONCLUSION

Intellectual property is a complex topic. Its complexity is driven by two factors. The first factor is the intangible nature of ideas. Second, there are the sometimes competing, sometimes complementary philosophical traditions of natural law and utilitarianism. The legal system attempts to balance these forces by providing ownership rights to authors and inventors. However, the legal framework also provides important limitations on ownership such as the fair use doctrine and time limitations. Because academia is based on the creation and dissemination of ideas, it is vital that scholars understand the ethics, law and regulations surrounding intellectual property. This article provided a brief overview of these areas. However, it is important to monitor the evolution of this field throughout your career. Additionally, since regulations differ among academic institutions and employers, you should familiarize yourself with the regulations which apply to you.

Countries generally have laws to protect intellectual property for two main reasons. One is to give statutory expression to the moral and economic rights of creators in their creations and to the rights of the public in accessing those creations. The second is to promote creativity, and the dissemination and application of its results, and to encourage fair trade, which would contribute to economic and social development.

14. REFERENCES

- Anderson, R. Low-Cost Computers for the People, Benton Foundation, (27 August 2001), *http://www.digitaldividenetwork.org/content/stories/index.cfm?key=178*
- Barlow, J. Selling Wine Without Bottles: The Economy of Mind on the Global Net., WIRED MAGAZINE, (1994).
- Benkler, Y. .Coase.s Penguin, or Linix and the Nature of the Firm., Unpublished paper presented at .The Public Bridges.org, .Spanning the Digital Divide - Understanding and Tackling the Issues., (May 2001), *http://www.bridges.org/spanning/*
- Business Software Alliance, Eight Annual BSA Global Software Piracy Study., (June 2003), *http://global.bsa.org/globalstudy/2003_GSPS.pdf.*
- Business Software Alliance, .Global Software Piracy Study- Asia/Pacific, 2002., *http://global.bsa.org/globalstudy/asia/*
- Festa, P. Governments push open-source software., CNET NEWS, (29 August 2001), *http://news.cnet.com/news/0-1003-200-6996393.html?tag=tp_pr*
- Fokkena, L. Like Breast Milk and Goat Poop: The Case for Using Open Source Software in the Third World., Kite Inc., (2001), *http://www.kiteinc.org/Goats*
- Gervais, D.J. .The TRIPS Agreement- Interpretation and Implementation. EUROPEAN INTELLECTUAL PROPERTY REVIEW 156, (1999).
- Ghosh, R.A. Licence fees and GDP per capita: the case for open source in developing countries, FIRST MONDAY, Vol.12, No. 8 (December 2003).
- Hefter, L. & Litwitz, R. (1999). Protecting intellectual property. *Prosperity Paper Series*. U.S. Department of State, Bureau of International Information Programs. Retrieved May 22, 2006 from http://usinfo.state.gov/products/pubs/archive/prosper/prosper7.htm
- Kretschmer, M. .Piracy Revisited., Issue paper for the Social Sciences Research Council conference on Intellectual Property, Markets and Cultural Flows, (24-25 October 2003).
- Lerner, J. and Tirole, J. .The Simple Economics of Open Source., National Bureau of Economics Research Working Paper 7600, (March 2000).
- Menell, P.S. .The Challenges of Reforming Intellectual Property

Protection for Computer Software. 94 COLUMBIA LAW REVIEW 2644, (1994).

- Mies, Maria, .Gender and Global Capitalism., in L. Sklair, ed. CAPITALISM AND DEVELOPMENT, 107, (1994).
- Moore, A. & Unsworth, K. (2005). Information ethics: An introduction. In Moore, A. (Ed.), *Information ethics: Privacy, property, and power*. Seattle WA: University of Washington Press.
- Oddi, S. .The International Patent System and Third World Development; Reality or Myth., DUKE LAW JOURNAL 831, (1987).
- Orlowski, A. .Open Source thieves stealing my American code . SCO boss., THE REGISTER, (22 January 2004).
- Osorio, C.A. .Illegal Copying and Diffusion of Software in Developing Countries: Empirical and analytical evidence on the conquer of emerging markets. software markets., (2003), (Unpublished paper on file with the author).
- Otter, A. .NGO launches long-term open source research., Tectonic-the source for open source, (17 January 2003).
- Panos.org.uk, .The Internet and the South: Superhighway or Dirt-Track?., Panos Media Briefing No. 16, (October 1995), http://www.oneworld.org/panos/briefing/internet.htm.
- Peeling, N. and Satchell, J. .Analysis of the Impact of Open Source Software., (October 2001)
- Primo Braga, C.A. and Fink, C. .The Economic Justification for the Grant of Intellectual Property Rights: Patterns of Convergence and Conflict., 72 CHICAGO-KENT LAW REVIEW, 439, (1996).
- Rebelo, P..Brazil Counting on a Net Gain., WIRED, (23 February 2001), http://www.wired.com/news/ culture/ 0,1284,41785,00.html.
- U.S. Code, Title 17-Copyright. http://www.access.gpo.gov/uscode/title17/title17.html
- U.S. Copyright Office. (2004). Works made for hire under the 1976 Copyright Act. Retrieved May 20, 2006 from http://www.copyright.gov/circs/circ09.pdf
- U.S. Copyright Office. http://www.copyright.gov
- U.S. Department of State, Bureau of International Information Programs. (2006). Field, T. *Focus on Intellectual Property*. Retrieved May 22, 2006 from http://usinfo.state.gov/products/pubs/intelprp/
- U.S. Patent and Trademark Office. (2005). *General information*

concerning patents. Retrieved January 14, 2006 from http://www.uspto.gov/web/offices/pac/doc/general/index.html#ptsc

- U.S. Patent and Trademark Office. http://www.uspto.gov
- World Intellectual Property Organization. (2004). *World intellectual property handbook: Policy, law and use*: WIPO publication no.489(e). Retrieved January 14, 2006, from http://www.wipo.int/about-ip/en/iprm/index.htm
- World Intellectual Property Organization. http://www.wipo.int/index.html.en

UNIT 4

LIBRARY AND INFORMATION MANAGEMENT

10
Total Quality Management in Libraries

Dr. Vaishali Khaparde
Associate Professor & Head, Dept.of Library & Information Science, Dr. Babasaheb Ambedkar Marathwada , University, Aurangabad, (MS), India

ABSTRACT

The concept of quality management originated in Japan and later moved into the USA and other countries industry. Since then, the theory of quality management has been growing fast. TQM was initially applied as a management philosophy in the manufacturing sector. Following its enormous success, this philosophy is increasingly being applied in the service sector, including libraries. The purpose of this paper is to present an overview of total quality management (TQM) in the library and information sectors. Focusing on TQM implementation in the library and information sectors

Keywords: Total Quality Management ,Libraries, Information,

INTRODUCTION

Since the early 1980s, TQM has proved the most persisting management theory in industries and businesses.

The total quality concept and the term "total quality management" was first introduced to the western business world by Armand Feigenbaum in 1957, in the first edition of his book "Total Quality Control". Some of the most famous "quality gurus" are Phillip Crosby, Joseph Juran and W. Edwards Deming. Crosby is known for his work on the cost implication of poor quality and his book "Quality is Free". Juran emphasised that quality is a continuous process and introduced the "pareto principle" or "85/15 rule". Deming is often referred to as the father of quality control in Japan, he is known for his "14 points for quality improvement" (Slack, et al., 1995 and Varnadoe, 1996).

WHAT IS TQM?

- TQM is "a system of continuous improvement employing participative management and centered on the needs of customers" (Jurow & Barnard, 1993).
- Total Quality Management is a management system for a customer focused organization that involves all employees in continual improvement of all aspects of the organization.

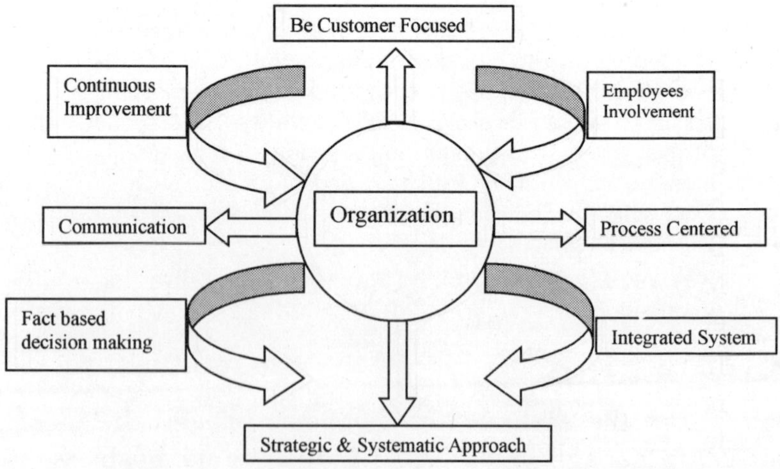

- A total Quality Management concept is integrative systems that use strategy data, and effective communication to integrate the quality principles into the culture and activities of organization.

WHAT IS QUALITY?

- Quality is customer satisfaction through product or by service. The customer in the academic Library is the user/reader/student which is a part of the Academic community?
- As a response of this challenge of quality, India's University Grants Commission (UGC-www.ugc.ac.in/) has set up NAAC (www.naac-india.com/index.asp/), the National Accreditation and Assessment Council. NAAC conducts audits and inspections on the quality of service provided by educational institutions, including library service. Grants are linked to the outcomes of these strategies for managing quality.
- The primary purpose of an academic library is to support the teaching, research, and other academic programs of its parent organization. An academic library is part of a service organization which delivers products personally to the customer.
- In the 1950s, the Japanese asked W. Edwards Deming, an American statistician and management theorist, to help them to improve their war torn economy.
- By implementing Deming's principles of Total Quality Management (TQM), Japan experienced dramatic economic growth.
- In the 1980s, when the United States began to see a reduction in its own world market share in relation to Japan, American business rediscovered Deming.
- Quality management experts, Joseph Juran and Philip

Crosby, also contributed to the development of TQM theories, models, and tools.

- TQM is now practiced in business as well as in government, the military, education, and in non-profit organizations including libraries (Jurow & Barnard, 1993).

KEY COMPONENTS OF TQM

- Key components of TQM are employee involvement and training, problem- solving teams, statistical methods, long-term goals and thinking, and recognition that the system, not people, produces inefficiencies. Libraries can benefit from TQM in three ways:
- Breaking down interdepartmental barriers;
- Redefining the beneficiaries of library services as internal customers (staff) and
- External customers (patrons), and reaching a state of continuous improvement (Jurow & Barnard, 1993).

Quality Control

The term control in the context of management is the function where by performance is measured against the set objectives, and in case of deficiency, necessary remedial measures are taken to ensure the achievement of the stipulated objectives

It involves

- Setting up of quality targets
- Appraisal of conformance
- Taking corrective action where any deviation is noticed
- Planning for improvement in quality

Measuring Quality

When a service or product surpasses our/user

expectations we consider that as quality

- Quality is some what of an intangible perception and it can be quantified as follows

  Q= P/F

  Where Q= Quality
  P= Performance
  E=Expectations

Dimensions of Quality

Performance	Primary product characteristics, such as the brightness of the picture
Features	Secondary characteristics, added features such as remote control
Conformance	Meeting specifications or industry standards, workmanship
Reliability	Consistency of performance overtime, average time of the unit to fail
Durability	Useful life, includes repair
Service	Resolution of problems and complaints, case of repair
Response	Human-to Human interface, such as the courtesy of the dealer
Aesthetics	Sensory characteristics, such as exterior finish
Reputation	Past performance and other intangibles such as being ranked first

Quality Council

In order to build quality in to the culture of organisation , a quality council should be established to provide overall direction . It is the driver of the TQM engine

CEO (Chief executive officer)

↓

Coordinator
Build two way trust

↓

Teams

General duties of the Quality Council

1. Develop core values, vision ,statement, mission statement, and quality policy statement
2. Develop strategies for long term plan with goals and annual quality improvement programs with objectives
3. Create total education and training plan
4. Determine and continually monitor the cost of poor quality
5. Determine the performance measures for the organisation
6. Continually determine the projects that improve the process es which affect the external and internal user satisfaction
7. Establish multifunctional and workgroup teams and monitor their progress
8. Establish and revise the recognition and reward system

Quality Statements

Vision Statement

The vision statement is a declaration of what an organization should look like five to ten years in the future. It is a realistic picture of what it wants to become and what is possible. This statement is short and consists of few sentences.

Mission Statement

The mission Statement answers the following questions

Who we are?

Who are our clientele?

What do we do?

And how we do it?

Quality Policy Statement

The *Quality Policy Statement* is a guide for everyone in the organization as to how they should provide products and services to their customers. It should be written by CEO with feedback from the whole work force and be approved by the quality council.

The common characteristics are:

- Quality is first among equals
- Meet the needs of the internal and external customers
- Exceed the competition
- Continuously improve the quality
- Include business and production process
- Utilize the entire work force

Strategic Planning

- Now a days many organizations find that strategic quality plans and business plans are inseparable.
- The time horizon for strategic planning is three to ten years and short term planning is one year.
- Both types of planning require goals and objectives

Seven Steps for Strategic Quality planning

The process starts with the principle that quality and customer satisfaction are the centre of an organisation's future. It brings together all stakeholders

- Customer needs(user needs)
- Customer positioning: Does the organisation wants to retain, reduce, or expand the customer base?
- Predict the future
- Gap analysis
- Closing the gap
- Alignment

- Implementation

Customer (User) Satisfaction

TQM implies an organisational obsession with meeting or exceeding customer expectations to the point that the customers are delighted

Understanding the user's needs and expectations is essential to winning new avenues for growth and sustaining in the competitive environment

For E.g.; a library has to provide its users a quality product/service that meets their needs, a reasonable price, on time delivery, and out standing service

5. LIBRARY SERVICE QUALITY DIMENSIONS

Zeithmal, Parusurama and Berry (1990) identified the following dimensions for service quality:

Reliability : delivery of promised service dependably and accurately

Responsiveness : readiness and timeliness of library staff to provide service and information

Assurance : knowledge and courtesy of library staff and their ability to covey confidence

Access : sufficient number of staff, equipment and hours of operation

Communication : keeping the customers informed in the language they can understand and listening to them

Security : freedom from danger and risk or doubt, physical safety.

6. SERVICE WITH TQM

Harvard College Library

Created a task force which rewrote the library's vision statement, and considered changes that would have to be made in order to develop a new organization culture

Harvard learned about TQM, and found that its principles of service excellence, teamwork, ongoing training and skill building, process/system focus, continuous improvement, and co-operation across boundaries could help them to make the changes they need.

The Oregon State University

The Oregon State University Libraries also decided to test TQM. Two small teams, the shelving Team from the stack maintains unit, and the Documents Team from the government publications unit worked with outside facilitators. Each team surveyed users and staff and found that some issues, perceived as critical by staff, were not perceived as critical by customers and therefore needed rethinking in terms of TQM.

7. ISO 9001 CERTIFICATION FOR INDIAN LIBRARIES

1. Asiatic Society of Mumbai

- The Asiatic Society of Mumbai has been awarded ISO certification- The first library in India to get it.
- Although the library is 204 years olds, its managing committee felt the need to get international standardization to meet growing competition from the Internet.
- To get new ISO-9001 certification under the American National Accreditation Board, every employee underwent training under the Toyota Production System method, which helps streamlining processes-for better organizing the catalogue with colored tags to create a calendar for housekeeping.

2. IIT Madras Chennai Library

- Dr. Harish Chandra librarian of IIT Madras and his team worked to establish quality services in IIT Madras

Library and IIT Madras Library has ISO-9000 certification

8. ISO-9000

ISO-9000 is a family of standards for quality management systems.

ISO-9000 is maintained by ISO, the International Standards Organization and is administered by accreditation and certification bodies.

Some of the requirements in ISO 9001 (which is one of the standards in the ISO-9000 family) include:

- A set of procedures that cover all key processes in the business;
- Monitoring processes to ensure they are effective;
- Keeping adequate records;
- Checking output for defects, with appropriate and corrective action where necessary;
- Regularly reviewing individual processes and the quality system itself for effectiveness; and
- Facilitating continual improvement

9. ISO-9001:2000 CERTIFICATION

- Although the standards originated in manufacturing, they are now employed across several types of organizations.
- A 'Product', in ISO vocabulary, can mean a physical object, service, or software.
- In fact, according to ISO in 2004, "service sectors now account by far for the highest number of ISO-9001:2000 certificates - about 31% of the total".

10. ISO-9000 FAMILY

- ISO-9000:2000, Quality management system-

Fundamental and vocabulary: - Covers the basics of what quality management systems are and also contains the core languages of the ISO-9000 series of standards. A guidance document; not used for certification purpose.

- ISO-9001:2000 Quality management system:- Requirements is intended for use in any organization which designs, develops, manufactures, installs and/ or services any product or provides any form of service.
- It provides a number of requirements which an organization needs to fulfill if it is to achieve customer satisfaction through consistent products and services which meet customer expectations.
- It includes a requirement for the continual (i.e. planned) improvement of the Quality Management System.

11. ISO-9004:2000 QUALITY MANAGEMENT SYSTEMS - GUIDELINES FOR PERFORMANCE IMPROVEMENTS

Covers Continual Improvement

- This gives you advice on what you could do to enhance a mature system. This standard very specifically states that it is not intended as a guide to implementation.
- ISO-9001:2000 combines the three standards 9001, 9002 and 9003 into one called 9001. Design and development procedures are required only if a company does in fact engage in the creation of new products Expectations of continual process improvement and tracking customer satisfaction were made explicit
- ISO-9001:2008 only introduces clarifications to the existing requirements of ISO-9001:2000 and some changes intended to improve consistency with ISO-14001:2004. There are no new requirements. A quality management system being upgraded just needs to be

checked to see if it is following the clarifications introduced in the amended version

- The ISO 9000 standard is continually being revised by standing technical communities and advisory groups, who received feedback from those professionals who are implementing the standard.
- ISO does not itself certify organizations. Many countries have formed accreditation bodies to authorize certification bodies, which audit organizations applying for ISO 9001 compliance certification.
- Although commonly referred to as ISO 9000:2000 certifications, the actual standard to which an organizations quality management can be certified is ISO 9001:2000.
- Both the accreditation bodies and the certification bodies charge fees for their services.
- The various accreditation bodies have mutual agreements with each other to ensure that certificates issued by one of the accredited certification body (CB) are accepted worldwide.

12. ADVANTAGES OF IMPLEMENTING ISO-9000

1. Create a more efficient, effective operation.
2. Increase customer satisfaction and retention.
3. Reduce audits.
4. Enhance Marketing.
5. Improve employee motivation, awareness, and morale.
6. Promote international trade.
7. Increase profit.
8. Reduce waste and increases productivity.

13. SIRKIN (1993) SUGGESTED SOME WAYS LIBRARY MIGHT USE THE PRINCIPLES OF TQM TO ENHANCE LIBRARY SERVICES

- Create service brochures and information kits.
- Conduct a user survey about Library services.
- Improve Signage.
- Change hours of operation.
- Provide a more convenient material return.
- Simplify checkout of materials.
- Use flexibility in staff assignments.

14. 14 STEPS TO TOTAL QUALITY MANAGEMENT

Based on his work with Japanese managers and others, Deming (1986; Walton, 1986) outlined 14 steps that managers in any type of organization can take to implement a total quality management program.

1. Create constancy of purpose for improvement of product and service. Constancy of purpose requires innovation, investment in research and education, continues improvement of product and service, maintenance of equipment, furniture and fixtures, and new aids to production.
2. Adopt the new philosophy. Management must undergo a transformation and begin to believe in quality products and services.
3. Cease depends on mass inspection. Inspect products and services only enough to be able to identify ways to improve the process.
4. End the practice of awarding business on prize tag alone. The lowest priced goods are not always the highest quality; Choose a supplier based on its record of improvement and then make a long- term commitment to it.

5. Improve constantly and forever the system of product and service. Improvement is not a one-time effort; management is responsible for leading the organization in to the practice of continual improvement in quality and productivity.
6. Institute training and retraining. Workers need to know how to do their Jobs correctly even if they need to learn new skills.
7. Institute leadership. Leadership is the job of management. Managers have the responsibility to discover the barriers that prevent staff from taking pride in what they do. The staff will know what those barriers are.
8. Drive out fear. People often fear reprisal if they "Make waves" at work. Managers need to create an environment where workers can express concerns with confidence.
9. Break down barriers between staff areas. Managers should promote team work by helping staff in different areas/Departments work together. Fostering interrelationship among departments encourages higher quality decision-making.
10. Eliminate slogans, exhortations, and targets for the workforce. Using slogans alone, without an investigation into the processes of the workplace can be offensive to workers because they imply that a better job could be done. Managers need to learn real ways of motivating people in their organizations.
11. Eliminate numerical quotas. Quotas impede quality more than any other working condition; they leave no room for improvement. Workers need the flexibility to give customers the level of service they need.
12. Remove barriers to pride of workmanship. Give workers respect and feedback about how they doing are doing their jobs.

13. Institute a vigorous program of education and retraining. With continuous improvement, job descriptions will change. As a result employees need to be educated and retrained so they will be successful at new job responsibilities.
14. Take action to accomplish the transformation. Management must work as a team to carry out the previous 13 steps.

15. HUMAN FACTORS IN QUALITY MANAGEMENT

- Attitude of Top management
- Cooperation of other Functional groups
- Attitude of Operating staff
- Operating Staff's Responsibility for quality

16. CAUSES FOR STAFF'S ERRORS

- Incompetence
- Lack of awareness
- Lack of Interest

17. CONCLUSION

Libraries are ideal places to implement TQM. They are service organizations dedicated to their customers, the patrons. By formulating a strategic plan and following it with a commitment to continuous quality improvement, library managers can transform and improve their organizations.

REFERENCES

Bavakutty, M. and Majeed, K.C. Abdul. (2005) Methods for Measuring Quality of Libraries. New Delhi: Ess Ess Publications.

Johannsen, C.G. (1992). The use of quality control principles and methods in library and information science: theory and practice. Libri 42 (4): 283–95.

Johannsen, C.G. (1992). The use of quality control principles and methods in library and information science: theory and practice. Libri 42 (4):

283–95

Johannsen, C.G. (1996). ISO 9000-managerial approach. Library Management 17 (5): 14–24.

Johannsen, C.G. (1996). Quality management and innovation: findings of a Nordic quality management survey. Libri 45 (September/ December; 3/4): 131–44.

Juran, J.M. and F. M. Gryna. (1993). Quality Planning and Analysis. New York: McGraw-Hill.

Juran, J.M. (1989). Quality Control Handbook. New York: McGraw-Hill.

Jurow, S. (1993). Tools for measuring and improving performance. Journal of Library Administration 18 (1/2): 113–26.

Jurow, S. and S. B. Barnard, ed. (1993). Integrating total quality management in a library setting. New York: Haworth Press.

Kackar, R.N. (1988). Quality planning for service industries. Quality Progress, 21 (8): 39–42.

King, C.A. (1987). A framework for a service quality assurance system. Quality Progress 20 (9): 27–32.

Kingman-Brundage, J. (1989). The ABCs of service system blueprinting. In Designing a Winning Service Strategy. Chicago: American Marketing Association.

Lam, K. and X. Zhao. (1998). An application of quality function deployment to improve the quality of teaching. International Journal of Quality & Reliability Management 15 (4): 389–413.

Mitra, A. (1993). Fundamentals of Quality Control and Improvement. New York: Macmillan.

11

Social Sciences Open Repositories: Reflections

Dr. Muzamil Shafi

Professional Assistant,

College of Teacher Education (CET),

Maulana Azad National Urdu University (MANUU),

Srinagar

ABSTRACT

Purpose: The research paper provides a picture of open access repositories in the field of Social Sciences. Their present status and growth are reflected vividly through the study carried out.

Methodology: The growth and development of Social Sciences open repositories with a multitude of parameters like subject, source type, software used, geographical distribution, language usage and collection strength is carried out using Open DOAR as a base.

Findings: The growth of Social Science repositories is very slow. They have gear up to evolve up with an open social platform.

Originality: The paper provides a richer experience of whole host of developmental diversity of Social Science Open Repositories. It also addresses to those wishing to be informed of the latest developments regarding open access repositories in the field of Social Sciences.

Keywords: Open Access; Open Access Repositories; Open Source Softwares; Scholarly Communication; Social Sciences.

INTRODUCTION

Repositories increasingly play a pivotal role in the evolving scholarly information environment of open access research outputs and scholarly collections. They have opened new roads to e scholarship where an open mode enhancing the open scholarship can be achieved. Open repositories attempt to create an opportunity to explore the challenges faced by user communities and others in today's economy based world where money hindered the users many a times of the information needed by them. Many repository platforms available today are changing the nature of scholarly communication. Institutions such as universities, research laboratories, publishers, and libraries are creating innovative repository-based systems that address the entire lifecycle of information-from supporting the creation and management of digital content, to enabling use, re-use, and interconnection of information, to ultimately ensuring long-term preservation and archiving as envisioned by **International Conference on Open Repositories (OR 2010)**. Majority of repositories are designed for Natural Sciences, Engineering, and Medical Sciences. Certainly there is also a good score of repositories for Social Sciences **(Wani, Gul & Rah, 2009)** yet they have to evolve up as a promising platform. The popular perception is that the Social Sciences do not have an urgent need for rapid data exchange as the Natural Sciences do. Similarly, the perception is that research results in the Social Sciences do not have immediate impacts on contemporary research activities. Some believe that "the culture of information use in the various disciplines" determines the demand for a digital repository **(Lawal, 2002)**.

Yet, "discipline culture" cannot completely be the determining factor the development of repositories.

Actually, some attempts have already been made to promote the development of digital repositories in the Social Sciences **(Wani, Gul & Rah, 2009)**. It is unfortunate that most of the attempts have not gained ground as was originally anticipated . The causes are many. The operational status of a repository is one of the main reasons. Such operational styles can include the strategies that "digital libraries use to ensure long-term sustainability for projects" **(McNeill-Harman, Roderick, Branschofsky, & Arms, 2002)**.

The invention of paper and Gutenberg printing press revolutionized the dissemination and preservation of knowledge in the past **(Wani, Gul & Rah, 2009)**. Similarly OA movement, especially the Open Access repositories, are going to set new standards for information sharing and management not only in Science, Technology or Medical disciplines but also in Social Sciences.

REVIEW OF LITERATURE

Lots of research has been carried out on different aspects of open access repositories. **Prosser (2004) and Chan (2004)** visualize open access repositories as a transformative revolution in the scholarly world. Supporting **Prosser (2004), Swan and Brown (2005)** studied the author perspectives towards open access repositories. **Chan (2004)** also looks upon open access repositories as a digital asset management system and **Eysenbach (2006)** visualises citation increase advantage for authors. He is of the view that author recognition through open access repositories has increased to a greater extent. The efficient and effective future of research in tough times is seen in open access repositories by **Dovey and Yeeles (2011)**.

Development and growth of repositories has been researched by a number of authors **(Vattulainen, 2004;**

Jacobs, Thomas & McGregor, 2008; Palmer, Teffeau & Newton, 2008; Wani, Gul & Rah, 2009; Robinson, 2009; Chan, 2009). The development of open access repositories is contributed to the rising cost of serial subscriptions, rapid changes in technology and document delivery **(Palmer, Teffeau & Newton, 2008)**

OBJECTIVES

The purpose of this paper is to review the open access repositories in the field of Social Sciences. An attempt has been made to understand the distribution and magnitude of Open Access Repositories (OARs) in different perspectives with the following objectives:

- To ascertain the geographical distribution of OAR's.
- To determine the subjective coverage.
- To find out the language diversity.
- To explore the core content types.
- To reveal various Softwares used for creation of OARs.
- To check the collection strength of each repository.

Scope/Limitations : The study is confined to the "Directory of Open Access Repositories," popularly known as OpenDOAR (*http://www.opendoar.org/*).

Methodology

OpenDOAR (a database that lists open access repositories from all over the globe) was selected as the source directory for tracing the development of OAR's in the field of Social Sciences. A total of 82 repositories were identified from OpenDOAR between February 9-10, 2010. The repositories identified were thoroughly analyzed for the necessary information as per the set objectives.

FINDINGS

Geographical Distribution

The study reveals that United States occupies the top position by contributing 21 (25.60%) repositories, followed by Germany (12, 14.63%) and United Kingdom (8, 9.75%). Some Countries like Spain, Ireland and Russia have contributed only 1 (1.21%) repository each. It shows that developed nations have jumped in the Open Repository market but developing nations need to pay a greater attention in terms of their repository development.

Table 1. Geographical Distribution

Country	*n*
United States	21 (25.60)
Germany	12 (14.63)
U.K	8 (9.75)
France	7 (8.53)
Netherlands	5 (6.09)
Belgium	3 (3.65)
Spain	2 (2.43)
New Zealand	2 (2.43)
Finland	2 (2.43)
Hungary	2 (2.43)
Australia	2 (2.43)
Portugal	2 (2.43)
Denmark	1 (1.21)
Italy	1 (1.21)
Estonia	1 (1.21)
Canada	1 (1.21)
Ecuador	1 (1.21)
Costa Rica	1 (1.21)
Brazil	1 (1.21)
Argentina	1 (1.21)
Chile	1 (1.21)

Columbia	1 (1.21)
Mexico	1 (1.21)
Spain	1 (1.21)
Ireland	1 (1.21)
Russia	1 (1.21)
Total	**82**

Figures in Parentheses Indicate %age

Software Usage

The study shows that D-space turns to be the most favorite software used by 14(17.073%) repositories, followed by E-prints (12, 14.634%) and SciELO (6, 7.3170 %). The reason for D-space to be the most prominent software used by the repository developers are the enormous features adhered to it **(Fig 1)**.

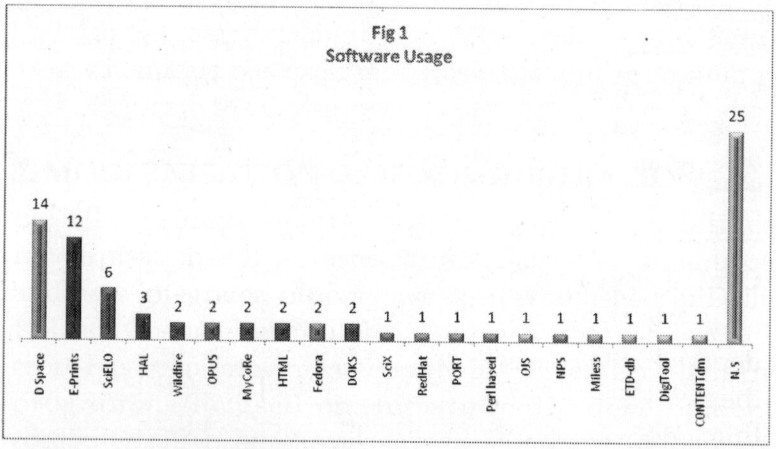

Lingual Behaviour

The study shows that a number of repositories use more than one language. At the same time it has been observed that English is the most favorite language used by 58 (70.73%) repositories, followed by German (16, 19.51%) and Spanish (12, 14.63%) **(Table 2)**.

Table 2. Lingual Behaviour

Language	*n*
English	58
German	16
Spanish	12
French	7
Dutch	5
Portuguese	4
Italian	3
Japanese	2
Danish	1
Estonian	1
Swedish	1
Hungarian	1
Chinese	1
Catalan	1
Finnish	1
Maori	1
Latin	1
Russian	1
Total	**117**

Content-Wise Distribution

The study shows the various content types are being deposited in different Social Science repositories. Most of the repositories hold *"Journal Articles"* (61). The second and third place is occupied by *unpublished reports* (45) and *Thesis and dissertation* (37) respectively.

Table 4. Content-Wise Distribution

Content Type	*n*
Journal Articles	61
Unpublished Reports	45
Theses & Dissertations	37
Conferences	30
Books	31
Multimedia	18
Special items	17
Learning Objects	18
Reference	17
Datasets	9
Softwares	3

Collection Strength

The study shows that 48 repositories have a collection size in the range of 0-5000 which sounds very low while as only one repository is rich in its content with size defined between 65,000-70,000.

Table 5. Collection Strength

Size	*n*
0-5000	48
5000-10000	8
10000-15000	0
15000-20000	2
20000-25000	0
25000-30000	0
30000-35000	0
35000-40000	1
40000-45000	0
45000-50000	1
50000-55000	0
55000-60000	0
60000-65000	0
65000-70000	1
Undefined	21
Total	**82**

CONCLUSION

Open Repositories, a catalyst in disseminating research output need to be taken care of by the Social Science institutes globally. The concept of repository and the benefits accrued through them have to be socialized in the academic institutes so that more repositories in Social Sciences will be seen in the future. Their open and flexible nature that has made them so popular in the developed nations should be discussed in developing and under developed states also. The acquisition of content is still the central issue for most repositories. The repository content needs an enhancement in terms of the type of material because a huge score of repositories in Social Sciences are under populated. Not only journal or research articles should be mounted on the repositories but scholarly works like theses and dissertations, books, monographs, patents; etc should find an agreeable score in the repositories. In order to increase the collection strength in the repositories their familiarity is of prime importance. Faculty and researchers at educational institutions should be made aware of the repository realities at practical grounds. Uploading a paper in the repositories and the benefits associated with the mounting of the content on repositories should be discussed at special workshops and training courses. Repository developers should evolve up with multilingual interface to their content in order to increase visibility to their content. For fostering the dissemination of the scholarly works, a shared objective in the form open access repositories should be framed out, no matter in Social Sciences it is in its infancy stage. But, a holistic community is required to support both the users of the systems (institutions) and the users of the resources within the systems (scholars). No matter the perception of repositories is yet juvenile but it is a rapidly surfacing part of the scholarship and the scholarly communication, and in the near future they will become well established campus infrastructure components. They will become a catalyst in the e-Social Sciences and e-research. However, the proliferation of Social Science repositories worldwide suggests that this open trend is technology-driven rather than demand-driven as opined by **Robinson (2009)**. Since Social Sciences are less magnetized towards technology, this can be one of the causes of their meager growth. People associated with them need get techno-literate in order to compete with other disciplines in terms of repository output. The Web, digital libraries and repositories are changing the way scientiûc knowledge is distributed and accessed, providing new opportunities for a more exhaustive and balanced coverage of the scholar literature **(Aguillo, Ortega, Ferna´ndez & Utril, 2010)**. It is a right time to stand on the digital forefront so that Social Sciences can also take a lead in the repository souk.

REFERENCES

Aguillo, Isidro. F., Ortega, Jose´. L. , Ferna´ndez, Mario., & Utrill, Ana. M. (2010). Indicators for a webometric ranking of open access Repositories. *Scientometrics,* 82 (3), 477–486. doi: 10.1007/s11192-010-0183-

Chan, Leslie. (2004). Supporting and Enhancing Scholarship in the Digital Age: The Role of Open Access Institutional Repository. *Canadian Journal of Communication,* 29 (3), 277-300. Retrieved from http://www.cjc-online.ca/index.php/journal/article/viewArticle/1455/1579

Chan, Diana. L.H. (2009). (2009). An Integrative View of the Institutional Repositories in Hong Kong: Strategies and Challenges. *Serials Review,* 35 (3), 119-124. doi: :10.1016/j.serrev.2009.04.00

Dovey, Mathews., & Yeeles, Nicola. (2010/ 2011. Dec/Jan). The future of research in tough times. *Research Information.* Retrieved from http://www.researchinformation.info/features/feature.php?feature_id=294

Eysenbach, Gunther. (2006). Citation Advantage of Open Access Articles. *PLOS Biology.* 4(5), e157. doi:10.1371/journal.pbio.0040157

International Conference on Open Repositories (OR 2010). *International Conference on Open Repositories (OR, 2010), 6 July 2010 to 09 July 2010.* Madrid, Spain. Retrieved from http://www.eblida.org/

index.php?mact=Calendar,cntnt01,default,0&cntnt01year=2011&cntnt01month=7&cntnt01event_id=232&cntnt01display=event&cntnt01lang=en_US&cntnt01detailpage=&cntnt01return_id=149&cntnt01returnid=149

Jacobs, Neil., Thomas, Amber., & McGregor, Andrew. (2008). Institutional Repositories in the UK: The JISC Approach. *Library Trends*, 57 (2), 124-141. doi: 10.1353/lib.0.0035

Lawal, I. (2002). Scholarly communication: the use and non-use of e-print archives for the dissemination of scientific information. *Issues in Science and Technology Librarianship. Retrieved from* www.istl.org/02-fall/article3.html

McNeill-Harman, K., Roderick, E., Branschofsky, M. and Arms, C. (2002), Foundations of digital libraries: Organizational & management issues. Sponsored by SIG DL, SIG MGT. *Proceedings of the American Society for Information Science and Technology*, 39, pp. 499–500. doi: 10.1002/meet.1450390182

Palmer, Carole. L., Teffeau, Lauren. C., & Newton, Mark. P. (2008). Strategies for Institutional Repository Development: A Case Study of Three Evolving Initiatives. *Library Trends*, 57 (2), 142-167. doi: 10.1353/lib.0.0033

Prosser, David.C. (2004). The next information revolution : how open access repositories and journals will transform scholarly communications. *Liber Quarterly*. 14(1). Retrieved from http://liber.library.uu.nl/cgi-bin/pw.cgi/articles/000047/article.pdf

Robinson, Michael. (2009). Promoting the Visibility of Educational Research through an Institutional Repository. *Serials Review*. 35 (3), 133-137. doi: 10.1016/j.serrev.2009.06.00

Swan, Alma., & Brown, Sheridan. (2005). *Open access self-archiving: An author study*. U.K: Key Perspectives Limited Retrieved from www.keyperspectives.co.uk

Vattulainen, Pentti. (2004). National repository initiatives in Europe. *Library Collections, Acquisitions, and Technical Services*, 28 (1). doi:10.1016/j.lcats.2003.11.00

Wani, Zahid Ashraf; Gul, Sumeer; & Rah, Javeed Ahmad. (2009). Open Access Repositories: A Global Perspective with an Emphasis on Asia. *Chinese Librarianship: an International Electronic Journal*, 27. Retrieved from http://www.iclc.us/cliej/cl27WGR.htm

12
A Glance on Manpower in Public Library System in Kenya

Dr. Henry D S Kinya
Senior Researcher, Africa Nazarene University, Nairobi, Kenya

ABSTRACT

Every public library in the community is unique and different in one way or the other by the community needs and services required by those it services, it should be reflected in distribution of manpower, also posting of the staff of the same job description and qualification is duplication of services and resources. Without diversifying and prioritizing services, duplication can deny users fundamental professional library information services like provision of subject analysis, statistical information and users' guidance. In assisting information users to access and use not only online information services but also access other websites services the role of public libraries within the information age context is changing from that of information provider to that of service provider and so is the roles of librarians; changing its old-age manual operations of print to print service to that of library networking to facilitate information sharing services and activities fundamentally requires the new dimension of trained manpower in ICT. In this paper manpower development, distribution and qualification in public libraries in Kenya has been discussed.

Keywords: public libraries, public library manpower development and library qualifications.

1. PREAMBLE

Productive contribution and the development of democracy depend on acceptable education as well as on free and unlimited access to thought, culture and information. As per UNESCO public library manifesto (UNESCO, 1994), the public library, the local gateway to information make available a basic condition for lifelong knowledge, sovereign decision-making and cultural development of the individual and social groups.

Manifesto declares UNESCO's belief in the public library as a breathing force for education, culture and information, and as an indispensable agent for the nurturing of peace and spiritual wellbeing through the minds of men and women. UNESCO therefore supports national and local governments to maintain and actively take part in the development of public libraries. The enormous amount of information produced per second worldwide front is a greatest challenges to library system more so the public libraries in the history of publication. With advancement of standards through IFLA/UNESCO public libraries are stirring from the conventional and conservative services to expansion of database and information sharing through network accessibility of resources.

Public libraries represent an indispensable link in the scientific system chain, a crucial role link in the development and maintenance of wide range and intensity of knowledge modernization and ideas in society and at individual level.

2. PROPOSED RESEARCH

Many information scientists have used different terms for public library system study. The recognition of public library first took place in western-Saxon countries. The term public library first appeared in Latin (bibliotheca publica) as a technical term in 17th century to distinguish the general university libraries of Oxford and Cambridge by then from those of endowed libraries. The historical combination of the growth of printing, public education, democratic institutions and urbanization during 19th century led to the establishment and development of public libraries in USA and UK. UNESCO stated that 'the public library is the principal means whereby the records of man's thoughts and ideas and the expression of his imagination are made freely available to all'

In 1977 D J Fosket describes the public library system as 'the central feature in the concept of whole entities, whose past are linked by specific pattern of relation; the system as a whole is greater than the mere sum of its parts by virtue of this pattern.

Kumar (2004) defined public library system as 'a A combination of people, activities, events and object resources working together to convert inputs to outputs'

Public libraries are libraries serving the community or region with multipurpose information- education –culture, agency in respect of information dissemination services, free of charge or at nominal fee (Thompson, 1974).

The term system has been incorporated in the public libraries in recent development to denote all segments of the library i.e. legislation, funding, manpower, collection, services, building and ICT. Although in practice all those segments are often inseparable in any public library

Public library system: it is the communication of ideas and information for any type of users for their inseparable utilization in the promotion of democratic development of education to raise their economy as a result of sincere participation. Mostly it takes a pyramidal structure in nature with, state central libraries, district central libraries and village libraries(Iyer , 1999).

Kenya national library services (KNLS): The Kenya National Library Service (KNLS) Board is a national corporation established by an Act of Parliament, Cap 225 of the Laws of Kenya in 1965 the Board commenced its mandated functions in 1967.

Board is empowered to develop public library services in Kenya to fill the vacuum that existed before and soon after independence regarding the provision of public library services hence bridge the level of literacy. The headquarters library in Nairobi opened its doors to the public in 1969. Currently, the Board is responsible for managing 8 libraries in 8 provinces and over 32 libraries spread throughout the country at district level.

3. OBJECTIVES OF THE STUDY

The fundamental principle of creating a national public library network is to provide information and library services to users. The basic purpose of the study was to evaluate the performance of KNLS manpower. The specific objectives of the study are:

1. To evaluate the performance of manpower in public library system in Kenya;
2. To suggest best policy on manpower development in public library system in Kenya.

4. HYPOTHESES

The researcher, initiated the process of investigation, and so it resorted to the following hypothesis for the study:

1. Cultural and social situation of the country has its impact on public library system;
2. Public libraries in Kenya are economically disadvantaged;

3. Manpower development in Public libraries in Kenya is in the developing stage;

5. SCOPE AND LIMITATIONS:

Scope of the study was limited to the manpower development in public library y system in Kenya e.g. KNLS.

6. RESEARCH METHODOLOGY

Present study used survey method as well as comparative method. A survey is one of the most effective and sensitive instrument of research which produces much needed knowledge.

7. TOTAL MANPOWER

Attempt was made to collect data on manpower in KNLS 32(100%) libraries which is presented in table 1.

Table 1. Total manpower

Name of library	*Number of staff*	*Percentage*
Nairobi	142	16.51%
Buruburu	14	1.63%
Mombasa	85	9.88%
Kwale	12	1.40%
Kilifi	15	1.74%
Voi	18	2.10%
Kisumu	45	5.23%
Kisii	34	3.96%
Ukwala	10	1.05%
Nyilima	18	2.10%
Awendo	8	0.93%
Embu	48	5.88%
Meru	13	1.51%
Mwingi	21	2.44%
Kithasyu	12	1.40%
Nakuru	36	4.19%

Eldoret	27	3.14%
Kabarnet	16	1.86%
Kericho	24	2.80%
Silibwet	20	2.33%
Kapsabet	14	1.63%
Laikipia	21	2.44%
Rumuruti	18	2.10%
Nyeri	45	5.23%
Thika	22	2.56%
Naivasha	18	2.10%
Karatina	15	1.74%
Olkalou	10	1.05%
Kakamega	43	5.00%
Garissa	24	2.80%
Wajir	6	0.70%
Mandera	6	0.70%
Total	**860**	**100.00%**

The table 1 shows total manpower distribution in KNLS 32(100%) libraries. It can be noted that the provincial libraries have a range of 5.00%- 16.51% manpower while district libraries have a range of 0.70%-4.88%. Further it was noted that out of the total 860 KNLS manpower women were 40% of the total staff while men were 60%. The researcher attempted to response on the professional distribution which was not disclosed by the librarians in charge, due to personal reasons, this necessitated to get information from KNLS Director who gave information as presented in table 1.2.The gender imbalance in KNLS is due to the cultural and social factor.

8. DESIGNATION, QUALIFICATION AND PAY SCALE OF MANPOWER

An attempt was made to collect data on manpower i.e. designation, qualification and pay scale in KNLS 32(100%)

libraries, which is presented in table 2.

Table 2. Man power in KNLS

Designation	*No of posts*	*Qualification*	*Pay scale(Ksh)*
Director	1(0.12%)	MLISc (Master in library & information sc)	450,000-550,000
Deputy Director	2(0.24%)	MLISc	150,000-200,000
Chief librarian	1(0.12%)	MLISc	120,000-150,000
Principle librarian	9(1.05%)	MIISc	90,000-120,000
Senior librarian	14(1.63%)	MLISc	70,000-90,000
Librarian I	28(3.26%)	MLISc	60,000-70,000
Librarian II	36(4.19%)	MLISc /bachelors/ Diploma in Library Sc	50,000-60,000
IT Officer	15(1.74%)	Degree in Computer Sc	50,000-60,000
Senior library assistant	126(14.65%)	Diploma in library sc/ certificate	20,000-60,000
Library assistant	178(20.69%)	Certificate in library Sc	10,000-20,000
Library clerk	201(23.37%)	12th class	10,000-20,000
Library attendant	146(16.98%)	12th class	7,000-10,000
Support staff	103(11.98%)	12th	7,000-10,000
Total	**860**		

The table 1.2 shows manpower presentation in KNLS in 32(100%) libraries. It can be noted that manpower in KNLS ranging from master degree and 12th class in the academic qualification. Further it was observed that manpower with a certificate to a master degree in library and information science in KNLS are 45.69% of the total manpower in KNLS, this representing 0.71% of total registered members, while those on the supporting staff are 54.31%. It can be observed that KNLS has over staffed on non-profession grades i.e. drivers, cleaners and clerks. The gap in the profession in KNLS has been attributed with lack of local institutions of higher learning offering the education in library and information science till 1990 when Moi University started the course. Most of the senior professionals are graduates from foreign countries. Also library science being a young profession in the country has not attracted many people to join it so is their pay scale it has not been fully recognized as a fully profession as lawyers and doctors.

On the refresher course offered to the KNLS staff it was observed from the librarian 32(100%) libraries confirmed to have received two refresher course in 2008; i.e. i) Performance contract ii) Supervisory skills, however, they stated that refresher course are done at the convenience of the management without prior consultation of the staff needs and knowledge gaps in the profession.

9. CONCLUSION

Manpower gender imbalance and professional storage be addressed from the policy level. KNLS has 860 total numbers of staff in the whole republic: of which 45% of these are professionals, being a national information service provider this picture (Table 1.1&1.2) is below recommended IFLA public library staffing, hence service provision is affected with this shortage. 40% of the total staff being ladies again this imbalance has impacted even the registered members of the library indirectly.(it is not books that lack in the public libraries of KNLS; it is the key to their effective employment- staff matters most. The individualities and attainments of librarians and their staffs are fundamental for better results to users). — —Less on books and more on educated staff, far better results would be obtained and KNLS goals and objective will be realized. The available manpower with library technical skills should be transformed to be having better communication skills, managerial skills, training skills and facilitation skills. These skills are acute and specific in enhancing better services to the users of KNLS in this era of technology. Staff will further acquire information analysis skills, repackaging, consolidation, technical reporting and downloading both structured and unstructured information available through internet for users.

REFERENCE

- Iyer , V.K(1999). Public library system in India. New Delhi: Rajat publication.
- Jackson, M. M (1970). Comparative and International Librarianship: Essays on Themes and Problems. Greenwood: Wingley.
- Jast, L.S (1939) .The library and the community. London: Clive Bingley press.
- Johnson, Elmer. D (1966). Communication: An introduction of history of writing, printing, books and Libraries. New York: The scarecrow press.
- Kawatra, P.S (1987). Comparative and international librarianship. New Delhi: Sterling Publisher private.
- Kelly, T. (1973). A history of public libraries in Great Britain. London: library association.
- KENET (Kenya National Education Network) 2008: Introduction Kenya / National Education Network. Available: http://www.kenet.org (12/09/08)
- KNLS(Kenya National Library Services)2008.>http://www.knls.org)05/07/2009
- Kenya (1986). The Kenya National Library Board Act (Cap225) / Republic of Kenya. Nairobi: Government Printer.
- Mangla, P.B (1986). Library legislation in India. New Delhi: Reliance publishing house.
- Martin, L A (1969). Library response to urban change. Chicago, USA: ALA
- McColvin, Lionel (1964). The British public library. London: Clive Bingley.

13

Public Libraries in The Service of Society

Md. Nurul Islam

Librarian, DNC College, Murshidabad, West Bengal

Dr. Nabi Hasan

Deputy Librarian, Indian Institute of Technology Delhi, New Delhi-16

ABSTRACT

The activity of Public Libraries reflects on society in social, cultural and educational needs. Public libraries inspire and help the people for better living in modern dynamic society. This paper throws light on modern civilizations and development of nations from where knowledge and information is disseminating to the society. UNESCO and other different library associations have an important role and support for establishment, promotion and advancement of public libraries for the progress of the society.

Keywords: *Public Libraries, society, civilization, UNESCO.*

INTRODUCTION

'Society `, this word is derived from the Latin word 'socius' which literally means a companion. Society is complex organism constituted by persons bound in willing allegiance to some common standards of psychological approach and outward behavior [10]. The story of libraries reflects the social, economical, cultural and educational needs to which libraries have responded. In preliterate society, human beings depended on live memory and the spoken words. By 2700 BC, the Sumerians had established private and government libraries for preserving their varied writings for use in the form of clay tablets. Ancient Egypt, from where writing was developed, produced some libraries which were composed of papyrus rolls [11]. So we can see, from the very initial stage of the society; books, papers, manuscripts, drawings, copper plates and other articles were being presented to it by various sources. We know that there is close relation between books and society. Healthy society is the creation of sound mind by books. Without sound mind, social progress can not be achieved properly. Every significant book may reflect distinct period of history. It is not essential to say that an author and his works can create new culture and lead to social changes. The books of authors of different countries in the world had /have a long influence on society [3].

In this present era, literature and knowledge is growing very fast and for their proper collection, preservation and to properly disseminate to people, we need public libraries. Society always depends on smooth growth and this growth is neither willful nor arbitrary[10]; it is consistent and systematic. For Smooth and systemic growth of society, the government of different countries and states in the world have established schools, colleges and universities. No doubt, the government, different organizations, industrialists have to give priority to drinking water, sanitation and other conveniences. On the other hand, to remove illiteracy or to educate the citizens/nations and to introduce the human beings with phenomenal explosion of knowledge and information, government and other reputed agencies have established and also are establishing public libraries whose services are great aspects of social and national progress and development.

SOCIAL DEVELOPMENT

Society is not static; it is dynamic, animated and vibrant. If society changes, the value system and culture necessarily gets changed. This change will be possible by proper education. Education is possible only in a society because education is impartation of knowledge and training from the accumulated store of the human race and the impartation of skills necessary for meaningful, creative and adjusted living in society. The people develops his/her potentialities through his/her life providing in general a common basis towards which all may move together towards mutual, national and international understanding. Public libraries are bringing 'social change' that change should be reflected in society in the world. A society must change for better. It is the duty of global public libraries to inspire the public with new ideas for better living and better thinking. The term 'social change' includes [10]:

(i) Change in social structure
(ii) Change in inter-group relationships and mobility
(iii) Change in living style
(iv) Change in value system
(v) Change in intellectual horizon
(vi) Change in educational clientele i.e. universal education
(vii) Change in total culture

The social changes are based on:

(i) Curriculum and instructional strategy
(ii) Learning requirements and learning style
(iii) Free from duplication of information
(iv) Provision for validation and tryout
(v) Maintenance and distribution, etc.

The role of public libraries in this present scenario of "social development" is very crucial and multifaceted. These facets may be: children education, adult literacy, community information, citizenship education, international studies, exhibitions, health information, sports society, coaching and guidance, job information, carrier counseling, publications, etc.

Public library is a social institution. It is the centre of modern civilization [7]. Public library grows and develops in response to social conditions and needs for equipping the people with necessary proportion of accumulated knowledge and preparing them for co-operative social life. Knowledge society and citizenship education are two faces. The citizenship education is based on the acquisition of knowledge. Actually, citizenship education is one of the goals of public libraries across the countries in the globe. It is seen that citizenship education depends on national educational policy of that particular country. Hence, it is urgently required to have universal public library system, which integrates the component of global citizenship education.

The world in the 21st century is a knowledge based society with multiple opportunities [9]. Knowledge and information are effective apparatus in society, which can play vital role in improving the quality of life of human beings. Now a days, information is one of the most important weapons, which analyzes past, present and future and predict in solving problem and decision-making and play a crucial role in the community for its socio-economic development. Public library gives information relating to different aspects to the people, which are very needful for community development. The new idea of Community Information Service (CIS) [3] has been added in public library services. It can be helpful to people for solving their problems in democratic way.

Public libraries should provide opportunities and take necessary steps for developing the personality of the readers so that they may achieve their full potential and involving them in different nation building activities on the one side, and broad basing of sports and achieving excellence at national and international level on the other. It is indispensable that government or sponsoring authority should formulate a leading principles and proper guidelines which will assist to make sports society of public libraries in that state.

In the 21st century, the challenging danger of the earth's environment scenario is climate change and global warming, due to excessive usage of fossil fuels [9]. A great number of people in our modern world are still not interested, indifferent and ignorant on the issue of global warming [8]. The learning society is the protector and architecture of future generations of our society. It is urgently needed to bring awareness about present situation for the international community. The public libraries can arrange seminars, discussions, about the most complex issue of climate change process. How it affects of our daily life, health, various resources, total environment system, etc. The public library can carry out crucial role to increase public awareness on climate change and global warming.

A public library is a cultural, recreational and educational institution and is need of the community. It is one of the important media for mass-communication which is essential not only for the continuance of the existing democratic institutions but also to encourage their growth and development in future. This is a distributing centre which provides facilities for mass-communication [1], necessary to the development of human personality. A public library can rightly be called an index to the human development [7] in the field of humanities, social, physical and biological activities. In fact, personal, social and emotional development of the human being can be a success by establishing public libraries.

In September1948, the international seminar was

organized by UNESCO in co-operation with IFLA in Manchester and London. The basic theme was public libraries with emphasis on their services to popular education and the promotion of international understanding [4].

Public libraries are way to progress and build a healthy society of a country. There is no necessity to say of the function of UNESCO in all kinds of library construction, enlargement and development, particularly public libraries in the world. The UNESCO public library Manifesto 1994 stated the following key missions which relate to information, literacy, education and culture and should be at the core of public library services [6]:

(i) Creating and strengthening reading habits in children at an early age

(ii) Supporting both individual and self conducted education as well formal education at all level

(iii) Providing opportunities for personal creative development

(iv) Stimulating the imagination and creativity of children and young people

(v) Promoting awareness of cultural heritage, appreciation of the arts

(vi) Supporting both individual and self conducted education as well as formal education at all level

(vii) Providing opportunities for personal creative development

(viii) Supporting the oral tradition

(ix) Ensuring access for citizens to all sorts of community information

(x) Providing adequate information services to local enterprises, associations and interest groups

(xi) Facilitating the development of information and computer literacy skills

(xii) Supporting and participating in literacy activities and programs for all age groups and initiating such activities if necessary

The UNESCO public library manifesto of 1994 (2nd revision) [6] also encourages growth of literacy through different programmes such as National Education Programme, National Literacy Mission, Total Literacy Campaign, Education for All Programme, etc. The public libraries in a developing society should preserve cultural heritage and provide access to all forms of cultural representation. The decision of the Member states of UNESCO to authorize the institution or organization to undertake a programme of public library development is of great significance in the history of public service. For this reason, the UNESCO has directed and promoted almost every public library project on the earth.

Role of Library Associations

Promotion and enlargement of public libraries and its services and duties is an important aspect of national advancement. In Western Europe and North America, public library system is an integral part of the social structure [4]. Every association has vital role in their respective subject field. Here, Library associations are not exception in their own subject field. The subject intellectuals and library professionals are supporting public library movement and the society gets benefits to developing socio-economical, socio- educational, socio-cultural life. The library associations of different countries have a unique role in education, research, literacy programmes and awareness programmes. The associations should support more schemes/ projects of NGOs, providing rural public library services. Many associations have started publishing journals, newsletters, bulletins for their members. The state level associations are really active in public libraries' growth and movement in their respective states.

There are many associations in the world, out of which some associations directly/indirectly assisting the public libraries [2],[5]:

(i) International Federation of Library Associations and Institutions (IFLA)-1927

(ii) Federation Internationale De Documentation (FID)-1937

(iii) Commonwealth Library Association (COMLA)-1972

(iv) American Library Association (ALA)-1876

(v) Library Association (LA) United Kingdom-1877

(vi) Indian Library Association (ILA)-1933

(vii) Indian Association of Special Libraries and Information Centers (IASLIC)-1955

(viii) Raja Ram Mohan Roy Library Foundation (RRRLF)-1972

(ix) Baroda Library Association (BLA)-1910

(x) Madras Library Association (MLA)-1927

(xi) Bengal Library Association (BLA)-1927, etc.

The objectives of the above mentioned associations are also in the direction of growth and progress of public libraries. Some of them are listed below: [1],[5]

(i) Promotion of library movement and to interact with the society

(ii) Promotion of library and information science education, research, new ideas of the subject

(iii) To encourage library professionals to participate in workshops, seminars, conferences and symposia

(iv) Bring out publication in the form of journals, newsletters, books, etc

(v) Establishment of libraries, documentation and

information centers and to assist in their function and activities

(vi) Maintain liaison with state and other libraries associations and co-operation with international organizations with similar aims

(vii) Coordinate the activities and to assist amongst the different libraries, scientific and research institutions, learned societies, business and industrial organizations, etc.

CONCLUSION

Hence, it may be concluded that public library is considered an integral portion of present society and perform a very crucial role in the community. It should be regarded as a social force which can greatly influence the modern society. It aims at securing for all the citizen of nation; justice, liberty and equality. It is establishing new horizon of social structure. It is to be considered as an instrument of social change. It is difficult to visualize a prosperous country without establishment, enlargement, development and advancement of public libraries. Therefore, it is the duty of government of national, state and local to establish and maintain nation- wide public library system under the clear mandate of laws and regulations and also shall support & give priority to promote research for this purpose.

REFERENCES

1. RAMAN (M). Establishing relationship with wider society: Role of media relation unit in university. University News. 47,32; 2009, p.18-21.
2. RAO (KS). Union budget: A serious concern toward economic growth. Kurukshetra. 58,6; 2010, p .19-23.
3. MUKHERJI (B). Books, libraries and culture. IASLIC Bulletin. 54,1; 2009, p.3-8.
4. SARDANA (JL). Libraries and information studies in retrospect and prospect. 2002. Concept Publishing, New Delhi, p.338-347.

5. KISHAN KUMAR. Library Organization. 2003. Vikas Publishing House, New Delhi, p.201-219.
6. http://www.unesco.org/webworld/libraries/manifesto/libraman.html
7. BOTTOMORE (TB). Sociology: A guide to problems and literature. 1972. George Allen & Unwin, Bombay, p.113-133.
8. NAYAK (J). An investigation into the awareness, knowledge and attitude of students, teachers toward climate change. University News. 48,27; 2010, p.8-12.
9. ABDUL KALAM (APJ). Technology is the foundation for the sustained development of the nation. University News. 48,2; 2010, p.24-28.
10. BHATNAGAR (CP). The crisis in Indian society. 1971. National publishing, Delhi, p.1-17.
11. SENGUPTA (B) and CHAKBORTY (B). Library, Library science and Librarianship. 1981. World Press, Kolkata, p.29-40

14
Preservation And Conservation in Archives Management

Jadhav Vandana S.
Asst. Professor, Vidyadhan Mahavidyalaya, CIDCO, Aurangabad
Dr. Khaparde V.S.
Associate Professor & Head Dept. of LIS,
Dr. Babasaheb Ambedkar Marathwada University, Aurangabad, (MS), India

ABSTRACT

The term, archive has come to used to refer to a wide variety of storage and preservation and conservation functions and systems. Traditional archives are understood as facilities or organizations, which preserved records originally generated by, or for a government organization, institution or corporation for access by public or private community. Historically, these records have been in such types as books, papers, maps, photographs and films, audio visual, tapes, e-forms etc. All these types of records were damaged by various ways like environment, insects water, light but for saving from these damages there were used various preservation methods. For saving and developing, the archival records the ICA (International Council on Archives)is working since 1910.

KEYWORDS: Archives, Preservation, Conservation, Fumigation, ICA (International Council on Archives), Archivum.

1. INTRODUCTION

An archive is the record of any institution, public or private, preserved because of their value. The term is a collective noun derived from the Greek word "archcion" and originally was applied to government records (public archives). While usage varies throughout history and from country to country, in the United States the term archives has been extended to include the records of private as well as public institutions. Less common is its application to the records of families and individuals, which are generally described as "private" or "personal papers", or less aptly, as "historical manuscripts."

An archive is a collection of historical records, as well as the place they are located. Archives contain primary source documents that have accumulated over the course of an individual or organization's lifetime. In general, archives consist of records that have been selected for permanent or long-term preservation on grounds of their enduring cultural, historical, or evidentiary value.

Archival records are normally unpublished and almost always unique, unlike books or magazines for which many identical copies exist. This means that archives are quite distinct from libraries with regard to their functions and organization, although archival collections can often be found within library buildings. A person who works in archives is called an archivist. The study and practice of organizing, preserving, and providing access to information and materials in archives is called archival science.

The term archives is also used to designate (1) an agency of administrative unit responsible for identifying appraising, accessioning, preserving, arranging, describing, and providing reference service on archives material and for approving the destruction of records of transitory value and,

(2) A building or part of a building housing archival materials and providing office space and facilities for both archivists those engaged in the administration of archives and users.

Originally archival and library materials were preserved in the same places. Archives administration shares a common purpose with library and information science: to acquire, preserve, and make information, in the form of documentation available as effectively and as economically as possible.

2. TYPES OF ARCHIVES

2.1 Academic Archives

Archives used in colleges, University and other educational institution. The use it typically exaction a library, may be archivist or a librarian. Now a day special archivist is formed. Some time professor of history an archivist. He preserves academic community. (History of university).

Contain, professor, president, memorial related to school archives and activities and the items. (Speech, chief gust). The academic library archive store T.C. there is close stack. The users of academic archives are often respective student.

2.2. Business Archive

The archives located profits make institution ex. Reliance, WOKHARD this co-operates archive business history or history of their company. The milestones of the company are preserved. Record management is different and history archives are different. These archives are not open to public. This is maintaining for company and it is close access it is concern with their parent company. Is whole and soul is director of company.

2.3. Government Archives

It includes those institution, which is run by local, and government institution it is any one can use it because, it is public archives. History of whole archives as far as government archives is considered France is richest which covers 26 km stack area record for storage of archives.

2.4. Non-profit archives

It include historical society such as hospital and repository within foundation. It is typically establish with private fund, donor, and history of specific person cases often these institution relied on funding from government depending on fund non-profit area. The employee may be professional or volunteers.

2.5. Electronic Archiving

Archives can be of many forms. However when pertaining to specifically databases there are three main form, described by new media artist Bill Viola; matrix, and schizo.

In the branching format one option can potentially lead to numerous other option can potentially lead to numerous other options. Imagine a tree diagram, where multiple branches branch of one branch. The same rule applies here. We start at a single beginning point then are given choices as to what we wish to see next based on topics.

The matrix form is not as linear as the branching form. The matrix structure is like a grid where there is no direct path to follow. An individual has the ability to view any archival information regardless of their previous selection. Thus, it is a non-linear archival structure. The user is only restrained by the amount of content there is to view.

Also referred to as the spaghetti style by Bill Viola, Schizo is a form of archives that is completely random. The user has no control over what they are capable of experiencing. Information is presented to them without any preordained trend. There is no restriction due to topics but in return, the user has no control over the information being presented to them.

2.6. Web Archiving

The process of collecting data from the World Wide Web and preserving it in an archive, such as an archive site, for the web user to see.

Examples of web archives are:

- Side bars

- Blogs
- Calendar
- Tag cloud
- News websites

Some archives deft categorization. There are tribal archives within the Native American nations in North America, and there are archives that exist within the papers of private individuals. Many museums keep archives in order to prove the provenance of their pieces. Any institution or persons wishing to keep their significant of archival science may have an archive. In the 2004 census of archivists taken in the United States, 2.7% of archivists were employed in institutions that defied categorization. This was a separate figure from the 1.3% that identified themselves as self-employed.

The archives of an individual may include letters, papers, photographs, computer files, scrapbooks, financial records or diaries created or collected by the individual - regardless of media or format. The archives of an organization tend to contain other types of records, such as administrative file, business records, memos, official correspondence and meeting minutes.

2.7. Audiovisual Archives

The audiovisual heritage is an important element within the cultural heritage and has achieved prominence in the twentieth century, the first to have been recorded on audiovisual formats. Audiovisuals are not new but have become of increasing importance as art, entertainment and information carriers. In some cases the transmission of sound and visual data has greater value and impact than the printed document where, for example, there is a literacy or language barrier. Audiovisual may also be the only suitable records for the oral or sonic transmission of culture and the arts, news and other current items. The spread and development of modern technologies mean an increase in the role of audiovisual data carriers for communication, information and culture. Today's radio and television rely heavily on archive material and it is estimated that more than 60% o radio and television programmes use archival or stock material for programming.

Audiovisual archives vary in type, purpose and function, and until recently most of them wee single material archives: moving image, sound and still-image archives, the latter frequently housed in more conventional archives of print materials. As the technologies converge so do the archives, to unite effort and conserve resources. Some archives take responsibility for all recorded materials, others take smaller bites and combine on or two of the material. The larger archives cannot always combine materials in one department; the physical techniques required to deal with each material from the point of view of storage, headlining and restoration need different expertise and materials and materials are therefore separated by this parameter alone.

3. PRESERVATION OF ARCHIVES

The main function of any archive is to preserve the heritage and the artifacts that make up that heritage. These are the major concerns of audiovisual archives. Many of the difficulties encountered result from the fragility or the volatile nature of the materials. The carriers are the weak link and the materials have to be transferred to other carriers that are more stable, with a longer life expectancy or more up to date. Audiovisual materials are made of polymers, and all polymers.

Decay! Progress is being made to slow this decay and prolong the life expectancy of the carriers and thus the source material, but preservation measures will simply retard deterioration, not prevent it. The life expectancy of audiovisual material is dependent on chemistry and storage and handling conditions. After 100 years much early film has been lost, especially volatile nitrate. Sound and video recordings are subject to attack from many enemies. No universal panacea has been found and the new technologies of optical disks are as prone to damage as the old. For example, there have been problems with vinegar syndrome producing tape and laser rot affecting optical disks designed to act as storage media for tape and laser rot affecting optical disks designed to act as storage media for tape materials. Archives must copy material from one format to another to save the content, to overcome the obsolescence of equipment and systems, and to provide copies for research and other uses. There are three steps in preservation work:

- Conservation
- Preservation
- Restoration

3.1. Preservation

3.1.1. What is Preservation?

Preservation encompasses the activities, which prolong the usable life of archival records. Preservation activities are designed to minimize the physical and chemical deterioration of records and to prevent the loss of informational content.

Preservation is a branch of library and information science concerned with maintaining or restoring access to artifacts, documents and records through the study, diagnosis, the tenant and prevention of decay and damage.

It should be distinguished from conservation, which refers to the raiment and repair of individual items to slow decay or restore them to a usable state. Conservation is occasionally used interchangeably with preservation, particularly outside the professional literature.

The preservation of library and archival materials in the library is varying impotent aspect of library management which generally find a neglecting aspects and the least attention is paid by the library authorities to this. it is generally acknowledged that in the present day circumstances the main attentions are laid down only the use of library materials but it is preservation aspects has received little attention. The books and other library materials which contain and deal with the developments of or ancestor's civilization and history of human beings are precious. It in facts not preserves but also mirrors of a countries cultural heritage. The ancient and old cultural heritage of nation can be traced out only from reliable source of literature in the form of books and other kinds of non book materials.

"The act of process of preserving, or keeping safe; the state of being preserved, the kept from injury, destruction or decay; security; safety as, a picture in good preservation". (Dhiman.2004).

3.1.2. Why Preservation

The library material may be damaged or defaced due to certain causes such as:

1. Climatic Factors
2. Light
3. Moisture
4. Dust and Dirt
5. Insects
6. Human being, the readers.

That reason the preservation of library material is vary essential to the library (Dhiman.2004).

3.1.3. Types of Preservation

- Intellectual preservation.

- Art preservation.
- Film preservation.
- Historical preservation.
- Photograph record preservation.
- Digital preservation. (Dhimian, A. 2004.)

3.2. Conservation

What is Conservation?

Conservation attempts to preserve records in their original format. Conservators examine records and assess their condition and the materials, which comprise them. Conservators then recommend remedial treatments to arrest deterioration or to improve condition. As they perform the recommended treatments, conservators carefully document the condition of the record as well as the procedures performed and materials used.

3.3. Fumigation

3.3.1. *What is fumigation?*

There are several chemicals which are volatile i.e. they evaporate, if left open, either in normal room temperature or with slight rise in the same. As the vapors of some such volatile chemicals are poisonous to the insects, fungi etc., those can be used for protection against such enemies of the library collections. This method is known as fumigation.

Gaseous poisons used to kill insects etc, are called fumigants. The chemicals that are normally used for this purpose are either liquid or solid in normal condition. In those libraries and archives centers where the problems of fungi and insects attack are moderate to high, or where there are enough possibility of such problems, fumigation will prove to be an extremely effective measure.

3.3.2. *Need of fumigation*

In the areas where rainfall is quite high, cases of fungi attack, to full or part of the library collection and archival collection, is not very rare. The first sign of fungi attack indicate that the internal environment in the library or archival center is not suitable to conservation- atmosphere is moist, i.e., the relative humidity is high, and arrangement of light and air circulation is not adequate. These environments should be rectified immediately by taking various necessary measures, but for collection, which is already effected, application of fumigation is essential to get rid of fungi and insects.

3.3.3. *Types of fumigation*

There are two types of fumigation:

1. Ordinary fumigation
2. Vacuum fumigation

3.3.4. *Types of chemicals used in fumigation*

1. Ethylene oxide (1 part) and Carbon dioxide (9 parts) mixture
2. Thymol
3. Formaldehyde
4. Para dichlorobenzene
5. Carbon tetrachloride and Ethylene dichloride (mixture of 1:3) or Carbon tetrachloride (8) with Carbon disulphide (20)
6. Methyl bromide
7. Carbon disulphide
8. Hydrocyanic acid gas.

4. THE TREATMENT NEEDED BY DAMAGED BOOKS AND ARCHIVES

The repair and restoration of damaged rare and valuable books, archives and extra important documents, maps, prints and broadsides, should be done by professional bookbinders and conservators, because they only have the training and experience, scientific apparatus, tools and equipment necessary for that sophisticated work.

The following are suggestions for making treatment of damaged documents and Archives:

4.1. Soiled and stained book and archives

Collections of books and paper archives that are defiled only by erasable dirt can be cleaned easily on the premises. It is a time consuming job but well worth the effort. The survey report should identify the items that need that attention and recommend that the work be done in-house.

The removal of grime involves washing, and the use of solvents and bleaches to remove the embedded soil. That is work for professionals, if the book or archives are of sufficient importance to warrant the cost, and that should be recommended after obtaining cost estimates.

The removal of stains books and archives requires the skill and experience of professionals who, can identify the stains and reduce them by washing, by the use of solvents, or by bleaching as the circumstances dictate. That is not inexpensive, but it should be recommended if the stains are obliterating the text. Because it is so easy to expunge important information by the treatments, bleaching and the use of solvents for stain removal must never be attempted by any one who has not been trained in those conservation procedures.

4.2. Worn and torn books and archives

The overall condition of any category of books and archives collections are minor wear and tear, it is often possible to repair them in house. The first consideration in the decision making in regard to heavily damaged books and archives the general collections is whether the books or archives available in reprint, or on microform, and at what cost. It will usually be the case that replacement cost, when replacement of general collection book and archives are available, is less than the bookbinders estimates for restoration.

Damaged books and archives in the special collections and rare books and archives are another matter completely. They are seldom replaceable in their original edition, and microform copies would be a most unsatisfactory substitute. Restoration by professional book restorers should be the recommendation here. The bookbinders should be asked to provide cost estimates for each item. Those estimates should describe the damage how the damage would be corrected, and the probable cost. The priorities for treatment will have to be made by the librarian and archivist.

Because of the number of moderately to heavily damaged books and archives in special collections almost always far exceeds the availability of finds to pay for their treatment, repair and restoration will have to programmed over a period o f years. In many libraries and archives unbound documents are very often not in good quality, acid free folders and boxes. When that is the case the report should recommend a high priority in-house program to refill the documents in acid free folders, and repackage the folders in archival quality storage boxes that have been labeled so as to lay flat on the shelves.

4.3. Acid damage

The pages in most of the books printed after the mid-19th century will be acid to some extent, sometimes to the point of embitterment. Those printed on ground wood pulp paper will often be brittle even if they are now only a few years old. All acid contaminated books are doomed to self-destruct if the acid in them is not neutralized.

The treatment alternatives for acid contaminated books

that could be recommended are

(a) Replacement with reprints on good paper, if they are available - which is unlikely,

(b) Copy on microfilm or microfiche- the currently favored method,

(c) Spray deacidification of individual items selected because of their particular importance to the institution- costly but a quite satisfactory solution, if the paper has not already become brittle, and

(d) Mass deacidification. Mass deacidification, is the ideal solution for all but the already embrittled books and archives in libraries.

Unfortunately mass deacidification will not be available in most countries in the foreseeable future. In the United States it is expected to become available from commercial sources, or from regional coöperative mass deacidification facilities, in a few years.

Acid contamination of unbound records is equally serious even though the paper on which they were created is sometimes of better quality- even very high quality. When acid contaminated single sheets are discovered and the damage is discoloration only, they can often be spray deacidified in-house even if only modest treatment facilities are available. When the damage includes discoloration and embrittlement, they can be spray deacidified and encapsulated in-house. Encapsulation is a simple, easily learned, inexpensive method for enclosing brittle paper between sheets of thin, transparent, polyester film that can be done on any flat surface using only a knife and scissors for tools.

4.4. Mould damage

Important books with heavy fungus damage are discovered they require priority attention. The report should recommended, if replacement copies or copies on microfilm are not available, that the damage books be sent at once to a bookbinder/ restorer for disassembly, sterilization, stain reduction, page reinforcement, and rebinding as necessary.

4.5. Insect Damage

Books and boxes of documents containing insect and/ or traces of insect, or in which the paper has been damaged by insects, must be fumigated as soon as possible. That can be done easily with vacuum fumigation equipment that is frequently available in preservation workshops, sometimes in large libraries and archives, and often in industrial establishment such as food processing businesses. If the traces of insects are wide spared, the whole area should be repeatedly treated by commercial exterminators until there is assurance that that problem is under control.

4.6. Rodent Damage

The possibility of disease, evidence of rodents in the building should be a matter of major concern. The report should recommend that exterminators be hired at once at once to destroy the pests. Together with that, there should be recommendations for increased emphasis on housekeeping, and the strict observance of regulations in regard to the consumption of food and beverages by the staff and patrons. When leather book covers, and sometimes even the text blocks, have been chewed by rats or squirrels, restoration by professionals is required if the book, is important as an object. Otherwise it can be replaced, or microfilmed to preserve the intellectual content.

4.7. Water damage

Books and documents that have been wet in the past

are usually stained. Slight staining can safely be ignored if there is no evidence of mould and the paper is dry. Heavy staining, that is offensive, and sometimes even obliterates the text, has to be removed by professional bookbinders or paper archives conservators. That should be recommended, unless the damaged item is one that can be replaced or microfilmed.

Often the covers and text blocks of books that have once been wet are twisted and distorted, making the book unusable. If the book is important, and it cannot be replaced, it can be restored to first class condition by bookbinding restorers. A recommendation to do so should include a statement that the price will be high, but the results will be most satisfactory.

4.8. Photochemical damage

Damage by natural and fluorescent light and the ultraviolet radiation that is always associated with such lighting, to boxed records is improbable because that dangerous energy cannot reach the enclosed materials. Documents that have been displayed under, or otherwise exposed to, natural light or fluorescent artificial light for any length of time have undoubtedly been damaged often to the point where, in addition to the loss of strength, the paper has been discolored, and the ink faded. When the discoloration and /or fading has made the text difficult, or impossible, to read, professional conservators can often recover the printed or written information by infra-violet photography, or by chemical means.

The dangerous lighting by blocking or screening the windows through which the sunlight is coming and by putting ultra-violet filtering sleeves on any fluorescent tubes used for lighting the spaces in question. If that is not done the light will soon begin to destroy the cloth, paper, or leather material covering the back of the book first to the spine will fall off thus exposing the book block itself to further damage.

5. PRESERVATION PROGRAMS AT THE NATIONAL ARCHIVES

Preservation Programs at the National Archives consist of two major organizational units committed to the physical well being of Federal records in the custody of the National Archives and Records Administration.

6. INTERNATIONAL COUNCIL ON ARCHIVES (ICA)

As in several other sectors of intellectual scientific and professional activities, the need for international exchange and cooperation has been felt within the archival field for more than half a century. However, before the end of World War II the efforts had to be interrupted on relatively limited achievements prior to the creation of permanent co operational structures. In 1910, there was the First World Congress of Librarians and Archivists, Brussels, Belgium.

Between the two wars, a group of archive experts met under the aegis of International Institute for Intellectual Co-operation, which prepared the first volume of an International Guide to Archives, devoted to Europe.

7. MEMBERS OF INTERNATIONAL COUNCIL ON ARCHIVES

In January 1974, the council had 560 members of all vive categories from ninety nine countries. The following countries are represented by category A and/or B members.

1. Africa: (A Category) Algeria, Cameroon, Congo, Dahomey, Egypt, Gabon, Gambia, Ghana, Guinea, Ivory Coast, Kenya, Lesotho, Libya. **Africa: (B Category)** Malagasy Republic, Mauritania, Morocco, Niger, Nigera, Rhodesia, Senegall, Sierra Leone, Sudan, Tanzania, Uganda, Upper Volta, Zaire, Zambia.

2. America: (A Category) Argentian, Bahamas. **America: (B Category)** Barbados, Brazil, Canada, Colombia, Cuba, El Salvador, Guyana, Haiti, Jamica, Mexico, Netherland Antilles, Panama, Puerto Rico, Unit States, Venezuela.

3. Asia: (A Category) Bangladesh, Republic of China, Hong Kong, India, Indonesia, Iraq, Israel, Japan, Jordan, Khmer Republic. **Asia (B Category)** Kuwait, Lebanon, Malaysia, Nepal, Pakistan, Papua and New Guinea. Philippines. Singapore, Sri Lanka, Syria, Thailand, United Arab Emirates. Vietnam, Yemen Republic.

4. Europe (A Category) Australia, Belgium, Bulgaria, Byelorussia, Czechoslovakia, Denmark, Finland, France, Germany, Germany FR, Greece, Holy See, Hungary, Iceland, Ireland, Italy, Luxembourg, Netherlands, Norway, Poland, Portugal, Romania, Spain. Sweden, Switzerland, Ukraine, UUSR. United Kingdom, Yugoslavia. **Europe (B Category)** Oceania, Australia, Fiji, New Zealand.

8. THE INTERNATIONAL ROUND TABLE CONFERENCE ON ARCHIVES

In 1954, President Charles Braibant of ICA decided to convene each year in which an International Congress was not being held the leaders of the profession at an annual Round Table Conference in order to study problems of general interest concerning archival policies, methods, and techniques.

Sr. No.	*Place of Conference*	*Year*
1	Paris	1954
2	Namur	1955
3	Zegreb	1957
4	Wiesbaden	1958
5	Lisbon	1959
6	Warsaw	1961

7	Madrid	1962
8	Budapest	1963
9	London	1965
10	Copenhagen	1967
11	Bucharest	1969
12	Jerusalem	1970
13	Bad Godesberg	1971
14	Luxembourg	1973
15	Ottawa	1974

9. TECHNICAL ASSISTANCE ACTIVITIES AND COMMITTEE FOR DEVELOPMENT OF ARCHIVES

Since 1966, the highest priority among the council's activities has been given to technical assistance to developing countries. These activities are carried out in close cooperation with UNIESCO. Beginning in1970, the technical assistance activities of the council are planned and supervised by the Committee for the Development of Archives.

9.1. Archivum

Archivum, the review of the council, is a yearly periodical dedicated to all the professional aspects of archive and records management and to the problems of access to archives and research in archive repositories. Articles are written in five languages: English, French, German, Italian, and Spanish. Until 1960 Archivum published a current international archival bibliography, but this activity had to be interrupted due to lack of funds.

9.2. General Objects of the International Council on Archives

1. To hold periodically an international congress on archives;
2. To establish, maintain and strengthen relations

between archivists of all countries and between all institutions, professional bodies and other organizations, whether public or private, where ever located, which are concerned with the custody, organization or administration of archives;

3. To promote all measures for the preservation, protection and defense against all manner of hazards of the archival heritage of mankind, and to further the progress of all aspects of the administration and techniques of the preservation of archives by facilitating exchange of ideas and information on problems relating to archives;
4. To facilitate the more frequent use of archive repositories and the effective and impartial study of archival documents by making their contents more widely known and by encouraging greater ease of access to archive repositories;
5. To promote, organize and co-ordinate, on an international scale, activities in the field of archive administration;
6. To co-operate, with other organizations concerned with documentation that ensures the preservation of human experience, and the use of that documentation for the benefit of humankind.

10. CONCLUSION

An archive is a collection of historical records, it contain primary source documents that have accumulated over the course of an individual or organization's lifetime. In general, archives consist of records that have been selected for permanent or long-term preservation on grounds of their enduring cultural, historical or evidentiary value.

There were various types of archives like, Academic archives, business archives, government archives, non-profit archives, electronic archives, web archives, audiovisual archives, these all were damaged by worn and torn, acid, mould, insect, rodent, water, photo-chemicals, light, ultraviolet sun rays etc. For the protection of archives, the various preservation methods were used and for already damaged archives, there were used conservation and fumigation method for their unique value. By seeing the cultural, historical, scientific, evidentiary value of archives ICA (International Council on Archives) working since 1910 for the development of archives. In 1974, the council had 560 members from 99 countries. The ICA (International Council on Archives) taking the conferences for archival development. The ICA (International Council on Archives) started the journal on archives named as 'Archivum'.

11. REFERENCES

- Antonio. B. (2004). The conservation and preservation of film and magnetic materials (2): Magnetic Materials. *Library Reviews*. 53 (7). 372-378.
- Bathnagar. A. (2006). Digitization in academic libraries. *Information Studies*. 72 (1) 35-54.
- Beagrie, N. and Jones, M. (2001). Preservation Management of Digital Materials: A handbook, London.
- Bessot, B. (2001) Libraries of printeg legal deposit: The presentation of the regional daily press. *Bulletin des Bibliotheques defrance*. 46 (3).96-97.
- Carroll, B. & Hodge, G. (1999). "Digital electronic archiving :The state of the art, the state of practice". (Online). Available: *http://www.icsti.org/Dig Archiving Report 1999.pdf.*
- Chilling Worth, M. (2004). Heavy demand bring online WW2 Photo archive to a grinding helt. *Information World Review* (199).
- Darlington, J. (2003). Domesday redax: the resources of BBC Domesday project videodics. *Records Management Bulletin* (117). 19-24.
- Das. J. (2003), Digital Libraries: Theory and Practices. *https://drtc.Isibang.ac.in.*
- Dhiman, A. and Dhiman, Y. (2004) Library Management. Ess Ess

Publication, New Delhi. 337-385.

- Faundeen, J. (2003). "US Land Remote Sensing Archive." Presented at the ERPANET/CODATA International Archive Workshop on the Selection, Appraisal and Rotation of digital Scientific Data healed in Lisbon, Portugal, 15-17.
- Feeney, M. (1999). Towards a national strategy for archiving digital materials. *Alexandria* 12(2). 107-20.
- Khouagio, B. (2002). The Management & Archiving of Institutional Web site. *Archives*. 34(2)17-49.
- May, S. (2004). The biblioteque Orientade: History conservation & arrangement. *International preservation news*. (33) 16-19.
- Niess, U. (2006). Digitization of archival collection, recommendation of the fedeal conference of Local Archives at the congress of municipalities. Der Archival multiang splatt for deatches archiv weason 59 (4). 323-329.
- Research Library Group. (2002). "Open Archival Information System (OAIS) Resources."Oct2002(Online).Available:*http://www.rlg.org/longterm/oais.html*
- Roosa, M. (2000), Library of congress plans for digital future. *International preservation news*. 22 (23). 32.
- Stephens, C (2005). Digital preservation : A global information management problem. *Information management Journal*. 34 (3) 68-71.
- Timmy Leyssens. (2003). Preservation metadata; metadata for digital archives using the OAIS information system. (*Bibliotheek – en Archiefgids*). 79 (4) 15-18.

15

Knowledge Audit: An Overview

Dr. Mukhyadal B. G.
Asst. Prof., Dr. Babasaheb Ambedkar, College of Arts & Commerce, Nagsenvana, Aurangabad
Dr. (Mrs) Vaishnav A. A.
Prof. & Head, Dept. of LIS, Dr. Babasaheb Ambedkar, Marathwada University Aurangabad
Dr. Sonwane S. S.
Assistant Professor, Dept. of LIS, Dr. Babasaheb Ambedkar, Marathwada University Aurangabad

ABSTRACT

The paper deals with the definition of the Knowledge Audits concepts, Evaluation of the concepts, Types of knowledge, views, Aims & objectives, Purpose, Needs, benefits, components, models, and methods were used for Knowledge Audit.

Keywords: Information, Knowledge, Knowledge Audit, Knowledge Audit Model,

DEFINITIONAL ANALYSIS

Audit

Audit means to go through the process of examining and verifying a organization's financial records and supporting documents. (Ward, 2009); an examination of systems, programming and datacenter procedures in order to determine the efficiency of computer operations, a systematic process of objectively obtaining and evaluating evidence regarding assertions about economic actions and events to ascertain the degree of correspondence between those assertions and established criteria and communicating the results to interested users, is a Latin word meaning "he hears", in its modern sense, an audit is process whereby the accounts of business entities, including charities, trusts and professional firms, are subjected to security in such details as will enable the auditors to form an opinion as to their accuracy, truth and fairness. This opinion is embodied in an audit report. Before conducting the audit, the auditor should examine the relevant books, statements and records. He should call for explanation on different aspects, ask for such information as he deems fit. He should then apply his judgment in the light of all these available material. After going through all records, he will be able to certify that the cost is correct, true and fair (Answer, 2010).

Information

Information is the meaning that a human assigns to data by means of conventions used in their presentation, data that has given shape. It may be considered as processed data, data plus the meaning, which has to be a result of human action. (Seetharama, 1999); facts and data organized to characterize a particular situation (Wiig, 1999); Processed data, (Bollinger and Smith 2001); Organized data (Bhatt, 2001; Perez et al., 2002); an expression of knowledge (Stonier, 1990).

Knowledge

Knowledge is a sum total of information conserved by civilization, perception of the agreement or disagreement of two ideas (Clark, 2004); totality of the ideas conserved by the humans. In this sense, Knowledge= Universe of Ideas

(Ranganathan, 1990); fluid mix of framed experience, values, contextual information, and expert insight that provides a framework for evaluating and incorporating new experiences and information. It originates and is applied in the minds of knower. In organizations, it often becomes embedded not only in documents or repositories, but also in organizational routines, processes, practices, and norms (Davenport and Prusak, 1998; 1998a; 2000; Quintas, 2002).

Knowledge Audit

Knowledge audit is a systematic and scientific examination and evaluation of the organization. The knowledge audit investigates and analyses the current knowledge environment. (Hylton, 2009, 2010; Choy, Lee, and Cheung, 2004); a systematic process through which an organization can understand its knowledge and information needs, what it knows, the information flow and gaps (Anand and Anand, 2007); the all important first major phase or step of a knowledge management initiative, and is used to provide a sound investigation into the company or organization's knowledge 'health', a fact-finding, analysis, interpretation, and reporting activity, which includes a study of the organization's information and knowledge policies, its knowledge structure and knowledge flow, (Paramasivan, 2003; Admin, 2006).

EVOLUTION OF CONCEPT

Knowledge

Knowledge is a sum total of information conserved by civilization. Knowledge is the perception of the agreement or disagreement of two ideas, (Clark, 2004).

Knowledge is a fluid mix of framed experience, values, contextual information, and expert insight that provides a framework for evaluating and incorporating new experiences and information. It originates and is applied in the minds of knower. In organizations, it often becomes embedded not only in documents or repositories, but also in organizational routines, processes, practices, and norms (Davenport and Prusak 1998).

Types of Knowledge

Knowledge is classified by different experts in different ways there are five categories of knowledge viz.

1. Practical knowledge, which is useful in an individual's work, decisions, and actions.
2. Intellectual knowledge, which satisfies intellectual curiosity
3. Small-talk and pastime knowledge, which satisfies non-intellectual curiosity or the desire for light entertainment
4. Spiritual knowledge, which relates to religion and mystical experiences
5. Unwanted knowledge, which is outside one's interests and is usually accidentally acquire (Machlup, 1990).

Knowledge can also be classified as:

- Tacit Knowledge
- Explicit Knowledge
- Cultural Knowledge

Tacit Knowledge

Tacit knowledge is the knowledge that a person posses and that it is described as knowledge embedded in the individual's experience and it has a personal quality, which makes it hard to formalize and communicate (Nonaka and Takeuchi, 1995); subconsciously understood and applied, difficult to articulate, developed from direct experience and action, and usually shared through highly interactive conversation, story-telling and shared experience (Shehabat, Mahdi and Khoualdi , 2008); personal knowledge embedded in individual experiences and is shared and exchanged through direct, eye-to-eye contact. Clearly, tacit knowledge can be communicated in a most direct and effective way (Nonaka and Takeuchi, 1995; Boisot, 1999); knowledge that is hard to encode and communicate. It is ephemeral and transitory and cannot be resolved into information or itemized in the manner characteristic of information (Polanyi, 1962; Polanyi, 1967); more difficult to define, and "is deeply rooted in action, commitment, and involvement in a specific context" (Nonaka, 1994).

Explicit Knowledge

Explicit knowledge is the output of tasks and activities that can be documented as reports, databases, procedures, etc., in contrast, can be more precisely and formally articulate. Therefore, although more abstract, it can be more easily codified, documented, transferred or shared. Explicit knowledge is playing an increasingly large role in organizations, and it is considered by some to be the most important factor of production in the knowledge economy (Shehabat, Mahdi and Khoualdi, 2008; Platts and Yeung, 2000); formal knowledge that can be packaged as information and can be founding the documents of an organization: reports, article, manuals, patents, pictures, images, video, sound, software etc. (Nonaka and Takeuchi, 1994, 1995); can be articulated in formal language including grammatical statements, mathematical expression, specifications, manuals, and so forth (Nonaka and Takeuchi, 1995).

Cultural Knowledge

It is the knowledge which includes assumptions, and beliefs that are used to understand, describe, and explain the reality, as well as conventions, values and significance to new information. These shared beliefs, norms, and values from the frame work in which organizational members construct reality, recognize the new information, and evaluate alternative interpretations and actions (Banka, 2001).

VIEWS ON KNOWLEDGE AUDIT

Knowledge audit is an accepted management technique, many different types of audits currently exist in the commercial world, e.g. financial audits, communication audits, technical audits, employment audits, and also more recently, information audits or knowledge audits. The major purpose of an information audit or knowledge audit is the identification of users' knowledge needs as well as how well these needs are met by the information services department (Botha, 2000; Boon, 1990); a knowledge audit is a planning document, which provide a structural overview of a designated section of an organization's knowledge as well as details of the qualitative and quantitative characteristics of the individual chunks of knowledge within that designated section (Debenham and Clark, 1994).

The knowledge audit may identify the following (Wiig, 1993):

- Information glut or lack of information
- Lack of awareness of information elsewhere in the organization
- Inability to keep side by side of relevant information
- Significant "reinventing the wheel"
- Common use of out-of-date information and
- Not knowing where to go for expertise in a specific area.

A knowledge audit assesses potential stores of knowledge. It is the first part of any knowledge management strategy. By discovering what knowledge is possessed, it is then possible to find the most effective method of storage and dissemination. It can then be used as the basis for evaluating the extent to which change needs to be introduced to the organization.

AIMS AND OBJECTIVES OF KNOWLEDGE AUDIT

The aims and objectives of knowledge audit are:

1. Knowledge audit helps an organization to clearly identify what knowledge is needed to support overall organizational goals and individual and team activities;
2. To give high-level view of the extent, nature, and structure of the knowledge in a specific section;
3. To provide a statement of the qualitative characteristics of the chunks of the knowledge within a particular knowledge repository;
4. To provide scientific estimates for the quantitative characteristics of the chunks of knowledge with in a particular knowledge repository.
5. To provide meaningful hard data input to the strategic plan for knowledge processing
6. To identify the relevant knowledge repositories with in the organization (Paramasivan, 2003; Debenham and Clark 1994).

PURPOSE OF KNOWLEDGE AUDIT

The main purpose of the knowledge audit is to help the audited unit to determine what it knows, who knows what, what it does not know, what it needs to know, and how it should go about improving the management of its existing knowledge. The knowledge audit also assesses the efficiency and effectiveness of corporate, departmental and process-driven knowledge lifecycles. (Hylton, 2009).

NEED OF KNOWLEDGE AUDIT

A knowledge Audit is a rigorous examination of an organization's knowledge and information user. It is intended to make visible the knowledge and information assets that drive its core activities. Organizations conduct knowledge audits for a number of reasons, such as to:

1. Identify what and where key knowledge assets can be found
2. Identify knowledge gap (what they should know but don't)
3. Use them as evidence for developing a corporate taxonomy
4. Identify high priority documents (in terms of demand and value) for migrating into a portal
5. Use them to set knowledge management priorities and needs in a knowledge management strategy exercise.
6. Map the knowledge flow and current bottlenecks within those flows
7. Develop an information and knowledge map of the organization
8. Review the use of external knowledge resources and how it may be used more effectively
9. Review the use of internal knowledge resources, how valuable they are, and how they may be improved (DiMattia and Blumenthal, 2000).

BENEFITS OF KNOWLEDGE AUDIT

The main benefit of knowledge audit is the development of a much better understanding of this prize asset and how it can be used to stimulate creativity and innovation. Specifically knowledge audit will be to identify how the organization can:

1. make better use of its intellectual assets
2. make better use of external knowledge
3. avoid inefficiencies and duplication of knowledge
4. avoid knowledge overload
5. save real time and money through efficiencies (Anand and Anand, 2007).

The benefits of knowledge audit can be categorized as:

- Validity Benefits
- Diagnostic Benefits
- Feedback benefit
- Information benefits
- Training benefits

Validity benefits : one of the results of a properly performed knowledge audit is valid and accurate knowledge on the status of knowledge as a corporate resource. The quality of planning and management should therefore improve, as accurate, relevant and valid knowledge is readily available.

Diagnostic benefits : The researchers have determined that the diagnostic benefit is one that is characteristics of the majority of audits. The diagnostic element of an audit allows for strong points and weak points (or "gaps") to be identified. This knowledge can be used to build on the strong points and weak points and to eliminate the weak ones.

Feedback benefit : knowledge audit is an important element in the process of feedback. The knowledge audit is used to determine whether specific knowledge inputs deliver the expected/ desired knowledge outcomes. The knowledge audit is therefore an instrument of evaluation and provides knowledge that can be used to plan and implement corrective actions.

Information benefits : a communication audit focuses attention on the process of communication in an organization and the improvement there of in the same manner, the knowledge audit can help to focus staff members' attention on the value and benefits of the use of knowledge as a corporate resource.

Training benefits : The knowledge audit provide the

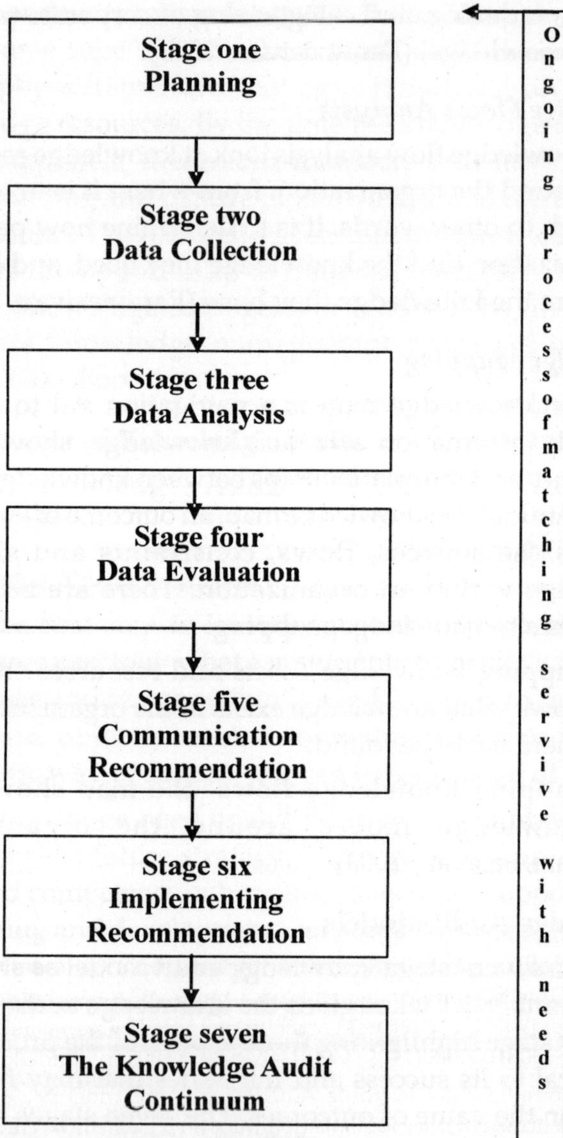

Fig. 1. The Seven Stage Modal of Knowledge Audit

5. Communicating recommendation
6. Implementing recommendation

7. The knowledge audit as a continuum

The model is not a highly structured and controlled process that operates in a tightly defined manner. Rather it is a structured framework that is flexible and can 'bend' to meet the varying conditions and constraints of an organization. In other words, the components can be 'tailored' to suit to the objectives of the organization and the resources available (Susan, 2000).

METHODS OF KNOWLEDGE AUDIT

There are a variety of methods that can be used but as a general rule most knowledge audits involve: Identifying knowledge needs by using questionnaires, interviews and focus groups and the development of a knowledge inventory mainly focusing on the types of knowledge available (Liebowitz, 2000).

CONCLUSION

The Knowledge Audit identify of an organization's structure, how it was functioning, its Goals, objectives, flows, identification of knowledge needs, and identify the gaps and duplications in the organizations.

REFERENCES

- Admin (2006). KMTips: Knowledge Audit. *http://www.kmtalk.net/ article.php? Story=2006012301144652 andquery=knowledge%2BA udit.* Accessed on 23rd July, 2011.
- Anand, V. and Anand, S. (2007). Information and Knowledge Management: Role of Knowledge Audits, Benchmarks, Maturity Measures in Knowledge Management. *In*:5th International CALIBER-2007. Panjab University, Chandigarh, 8-10 Feb-2007, 273-282.
- Answer (2010). Audit. *http://www.answer.com/topic/audit.* Accessed on 28th June, 2011.
- Banka, Bihari Chand, (2001). Knowledge Management :Tools and Techniques for Librarians. *Journal of Library and Information Science, 26(2),* 175-186.
- Bhatt, G. (2001). KM in organizations: Examining the interaction

between Technologies, Techniques, and People. *Journal of Knowledge Management, 5(1)*, 68-75.

- Boisot, M. H. (1999). Knowledge assets: Securing competitive advantage in the information economy. Oxford: Oxford University Press
- Bollinger, A. and Smith, R. (2001).Meaning organizational knowledge as a strategic asset. *Journal of Knowledge Management, 5(1)*, 8-18.
- Boon, J. A. (1990). Information Management: an educational perspective. *South Africa Journal of Library and Information Science, 58(4)*, 319-327.
- Botha, H. (2000). *The information audit: principles and guidelines. Unpublished Master's dissertation. Pretoria*: University of Pretoria. Pretoria,
- Choy, S. Y., Lee, W. B., and Cheung, C. F. (2004). A systematic approach for knowledge audit analysis: Integration of knowledge inventory, mapping and knowledge flow analysis. *Journal of Universal Computer Science, 10(6)*, 674-682.
- Clark, Donald (2004). Knowledge. *http://www.nwlink.com/~donclark/Knowledge/knowledge.html*. Accessed on 1st Mar. 2011.
- Debenham, J. and Clark (1994). The Knowledge Audit. *Robotics and computer Integrated Manufacturing Journal*, 11(3).
- Devenport, T. and Prusak, L. (1998). *Working knowledge: how organizations manage what they know*. Boston: Harvard Business School Press
- Devenport, T. and Prusak, L. (1998a). *Working knowledge*. Boston: Harvard Business School Press (MA)
- Devenport, T. and Prusak, L. (2000). *Working knowledge: how organizations manage what they know*. Boston: Harvard Business School Press
- DiMattia, S. and Blumenstein, L. (2000). In search of the information audit: essential tool or cumbersome process? *Library Journal, 125(4)*, 48-50.
- Hylton, A. (2009). A Knowledge Audit must be people-centred and people focused. *http://www.knowledgeboard.com*. Accessed on 22nd June, 2011.
- Hylton, A. (2010). Knowledge Auditing. *http://communityknowledge.co.uk/KMIntro/part_e.html*. Accessed on 22nd June. 2011.
- Liebowitz, J.(2000). The Knowledge Audit. *Knowledge and Process*

Management, 7 (1), 3-10.

- Machlup, F. (1990). *Knowledge: Its creation, distribution and economic significance.* Princeton: Princeton University Press
- Nonaka, I. (1994). A dynamic theory of organizational knowledge creation. *Organization Science, 5(1),* 14-37.
- Nonaka, I. and Takeuchi, H. (1995). *The knowledge-creating company: How Japanese companies create the dynamics of innovation.* New York: Oxford University Press
- Paramasivan, T. (2003). Knowledge Audit. *http://icai.org/resource_file/11294p498-506.pdf.* Accessed on 1st July, 2011.
- Perez, M. et al., (2002). Knowledge tasks and teleworking: a taxonomy model of feasibility adoption. *Journal of Knowledge Management, 6(3),* 272-284.
- Platts, M. J. and Yeung, M. B. (2000). Managing learning and Tacit Knowledge. *Strategic Change, 9(6),* 347-356.
- Quintas, P. (2002). Managing knowledge in a new country. In P. Quintas and T. Ray (Ed.), *Managing knowledge: An essential reader.* London: Sage, 1-14.
- Ranganathan, S. R. (1990). *Prolegomena to Library Classification* (3rd ed.). Bangalore: Sarada Ranganathan Endowment for Library Science
- Seetharama, S. (1999). Information Management: Tools and Techniques. *In:* National Workshop on Information Management including ISO 9000 QMS, held at Documentation Research and Training Centre, Banglore on 6-8 January 1999. Papar No. BA.
- Sharma, R. and Chowdhury, N. (2007). On The Use of a Diagnostic Tool for Knowledge Audits. *Journal of Knowledge Management Practice, 8(4),* 1-7.
- Shehabat, I., Mahdi, S. and Khoualdi, K. (2008).E-Learning as a Knowledge Management Approach for Intellectual Capital Utilization.*Turkish Online Journal of Distance Education, 9(1),* 205-216.
- Stonier, T. (1990). Information and the internal structure of the universe: An exploration into information physics. London: Springer- Verlag
- Ward, Susan (2009). Auditing. *http://www.sbinfocanada.about.com/cs/taxinfo/g/audit.htm.* Accessed on 27th June, 2011.
- Wigg, K. M. (1999). Introducing knowledge management into the enterprise. *Information Research, 8(1)*
- Wiig, K. (1993) *Knowledge Management Foundation.* Boston: Schema Press.

16
Collection Development in Modern Digital Era

Dr. Dharamraj K. Veer
In-Charge University Librarian
Dr.Babasaheb Ambedkar Mararthwada University, Aurangabad

ABSTRACT

Each library is facing a problem of budget. Prices of books, journals are increasing day by day on one hand, while library budget are decreasing on the other. In the technological development, library can acquire digital resources in economic way. Present paper attempts to emphasizes on collection development policy, internet based collection and challenges in building digital collection.

Keywords: Library Budget, Collection Development, *books, journals, collection development policy, digital collection.*

INTRODUCTION

Libraries are about many things. But, Collections have always been at the heart of Libraries, be they digital, traditional brick and mortar, or hybrid between the two. Moreover, collections will retain that role in the future as well. Any academic library that aims to satisfy the information needs of academics & researchers must take great care with the development & management of its collection. It is generally considered that both the quantity & quality of a library's collection depend almost entirely upon the library's acquisition program , including its acquisition policy , its acquisition procedures & of most importance , its selection methods. Collection development is a term that is used by the library community to refer to "the selection and acquisition of material for an expanding collection and decisions on the material to be included in that collection". Guidelines from the IFLA (International Federation of Library Associations and Institutions) Acquisition and Collection Development Section say that the primary function of collection development policies is to provide guidance on selecting and deselecting resources from a collection. Typically, collection development decisions apply at different stages of an institution's workflow, including the selection, acquisition, processing, housing, weeding, retention, preservation, relegation and discarding of library materials. Much of the focus in the library world has been on the development and implementation of written collection development policies and guidelines, although the practical value of these has sometimes been questioned.

The new concept of a digital collection is evolving incorporating adaptations of many old features and standards, and creation of many brand new ones. This conceptual and pragmatic evolution is far from over. The concepts and processes of collection development and collection management are undergoing a transformation as well. This is due to the effect of great many and diverse digital resources and tools that can be used in collection development and that are generally and easily available through the Internet. New processes and tools for collection development has emerged, used for development and management of both, traditional and digital collections. In addition, the process of collection management became more closely connected than ever with means, ways, and policies for access, adding an additional dimension.

COLLECTION DEVELOPMENT IN ICT ENVIROUMENT

The electronic revolution affects the traditional role of the academic and research library as an institution that collects and stories information and makes it available to its users would be obvious and is indisputable. In order to cope the multidimensional information needs of the modern users, libraries should rethink about the forms and types of information resources. In this IT era, low cost of e-resources, their easy availability, 24x7 accesses, up-to-date information, e-resources are becoming a vital component of library collection & hence gaining importance in the collection development policy. With the digitization of books, documents, journals and other forms of material, modifications of policies would take place. Overall the policy set for published material could be modified accordingly; the entire philosophy of Collection needs to be changed as simply duplicating the collection practices evolved for print materials in the new information (network) environment.(Seetharama and Ambuja, 2000).

As builds of collections, librarians now have a larger and more complex set of resources from which to select. These resources range from analogue versions of books, journals, encyclopedias and sound, to digital versions of these in a variety of formats such as CDROM, DVD, digital video tape, to online digital e-journals, e-books and online databases. Digitization would also have an effect on the preservation and archiving as resources would also be available in digital format.

INTERNET BASED COLLECTION DEVELOPMENT:

i) e-books

Online Dictionary of Library & Information Science defines e-books as –"A digital version of a traditional print book designed to be read on a personal computer or on e-book reader." There are two major categories of e-books i.e.

i) Off-line (CD-ROM)

ii) On-line

There are number of e-books in multidisciplinary subject available free-of-cost on internet.

ii) e-journals

In order to provide latest information to the researchers & scholars, the concept of e-journals had been raised firstly in 1945. E-journal may be defined as –"One which is available electronically, to be used with the help of computer & other communication technologies." With the development of communication technology, the usage & popularity of e-journal has been increased Today e-journal is becoming the main source of scholarly information & its use has been increased.

Golnessa, G. M. & Talawar, V. G. (2008) conducted a study at Indian Institute of Science entitled "The use of scholarly Electronic Journals at the Indian Institute of Science: A Case Study in India", with the purpose to investigate the use of scholarly electronic journals at the Indian Institute of Science. The results of the study showed a growing interest in electronic journals among the users at IISc. The electronic journals were mostly used for research needs & PDF format was the most preferred format. The fact is that users have free access to electronic journals at all hours from their own computers seems to be the most appealing feature.

iii) E-databases

E-databases are also one of the important digital resources. A study about knowledge & use of digital library resources by engineering faculty members affiliated to Acharya, Nagarjuna University, A. P. India shows the usage pattern of digital resources by faculty members.

iv) E-consortia

E-consortia provide seamless access to thousands of e-journals, databases & thus playing important role in digital collection development. Some of the major consortia projects in India are – UGC-INFONET, INDEST-AICTE Consortium, FORSA, HELNET etc providing access to seamless digital information.

CHALLENGES IN BULIDING DIGITAL COLLECTION

The major challenges in building digital collection are:

- Technical Architecture
- Copy right Management
- Preservation

Technical Architecture

Libraries will need to enhance and upgrade current technical architectures to accommodate digital materials. The architecture will include components such as:

- High-Speed local networks and fast connections to the Internet;
- Relational databases that support a variety of digital formats;
- Full text search engines to index and provide access to resources;
- A variety of servers, such as Web servers and FTP servers; and
- Electronic document management functions that will aid in the overall management of digital resources.

Copyright Management

Copyright has been called the "single most vexing barrier to digital library development". The current paper-based concept of copyright breaks down in the digital environment because the control of copies is lost. Digital objects are less fixed, easily copied, and remotely accessible by multiple users simultaneously. The problem for libraries is that, unlike private businesses or publishers that own their information, libraries are, for the most part, simply caretakers of information they don't own the copyright of the material they hold. It is unlikely that libraries will ever be able to freely digitize and provide access to the copyrighted materials in their collections. Instead, they 25 will have to develop mechanisms for managing copyright, mechanisms that allow them to provide information without violating copyright, called rights management.

Preservation

In the preservation of digital materials, the real issue is technical obsolescence. Technical obsolescence in the digital age is like the deterioration of paper in the paper age. Libraries in the pre-digital era had to worry about climate control and the de-acidification of books, but the preservation of digital information will mean constantly coming up with new technical solutions. When considering digital materials, there are three types of preservation are:

The Preservation of the storage medium

Tapes, hard drives, and floppy discs have a very short life span when considered in terms of obsolescence. The data on them can be refreshed; keeping the bits valid, but refreshing is only effective as long as the media are still current. The media used to store digital materials become obsolete in anywhere from two to five years before they are replaced by better technology. Over the long term, materials stored on older media could be lost because their will no longer have the hardware or software to read them. Thus, libraries will have to keep moving digital information from storage medium to storage medium.

The Preservation of access to content

This form of preservation involves preserving access to the content of documents, regardless of their format. While files can be moved from on physical storage medium to another, what happens when the formats (e.g., PDF, Adobe Acrobat) containing the information become obsolete? This is a problem perhaps bigger than that of obsolete storage technologies. One solution is to do data migration that is, translate data from one format to another preserving the ability of users to retrieve and display the information content. However, there are difficulties here too-data migration is costly, there are as yet no standards for data migration, and distortion or information loss is inevitably introduced every time data is migrated from format to format.

The preservation of fixed-media materials through digital technology

This slant on the issue involves the use of digital technology as a replacement for current preservation media, such as microforms. Again, there are, as yet, no common standards for the use of digital media as a preservation medium and it is unclear whether digital media are as yet up to the task of long-term preservation. Digital preservation standards will be required to consistently store and share materials preserved digitally.

CONCLUSION

Considering, the importance of digital resources in the age of information technology. It is necessary to provide necessary infrastructure to all libraries for acquiring the required digital resources. It is also concentrate on awareness of digital resources and open source digital resources available on various websites.

REFERENCES

1. Arms, W.Y. (1995). Key concepts in the architecture of the digital library. D-lib Magazine, July.
2. Galyani,Moghaddam,Golnessa & Talwar,V.G.(2008).The Use of Scholarly Electronic Journals at the Indian Institute of Science : A Case Study in India . *Interlending & Documentry Supply* ,36(1).pp.15-29.Retrieved from : *www.eprints.rclis.org/archive*. Accessed on 25 October 2009
3. Lellavathi,N & Doraswamy,M.(n.d.).Knowledge & Use of Digital Resources by Engineering Faculty Members Affiliated to Acharya Nagarjuna University,A.P.India.Retrievedfrom: *www.ulib.org/conference/genpub/Leelavathi.doc*. Accessed on 25 October 2008.
4. Shreeves, E. (1997). Is here a future for cooperative collection development in the digital age? *Library Trends*, vol. 4 , No.3, pp.373-390.
5. Seetharama, S and Ambuja, R. Collection Development in Electronic Era: DRTC Annual Seminar on Electronic Sources of Information, March 2000

UNIT 5

LIS EDUCATION, LIBRARIES & LIBRARY PROFESSION

term finance that are essential to keep pace with the requirements of developments on technological fronts.

Keywords : Information technology, Libraries, Internet, Electronic library, Costs

1. INTRODUCTION

These days, Internet, electronic resources, and automation have become as important as printed documents. These offer very fast and easy search, access and downloads. The consortia based approach has brought down their cost for and very wide coverage which was unthinkable in case of printed resources. These hardly need any space. However, it requires information technology (IT) infrastructure involving large expenditure. The available resources in any institutes are limited. Institutes have limitless opportunities to invest in IT and content services but have finite budgets. Competition for institutional resources is intense. Thus, the choices are crucial. It is important that the limited resources are invested wisely. (Rosenblatt, 1999)

While the demands of IT are becoming more intense and resources are limited, and to maintain infrastructure of IT requires a long-term investment. However, funding agencies generally support the initial cost and budget accordingly. Most libraries in the developing world have invested in the IT in the first half of this decade with the one time grant. It was generally not realized that the hardware, software and networking would require upgradation and maintenance. It is important that the librarians and institutional administration and grant agencies realize a need and plan for the same. This article discusses with these aspects. It will help to foresee priorities and ensure more appropriate budgets for maintenance, up gradation for the IT infrastructure created or to be created.

One-time funding for IT is evident at the institutional level, it is also apparent at the library level. Librarians must develop strategies for long-term funding, to keep pace with technological developments. Even if hardware and software seldom 'wear out', their usefulness becomes limited because of the need for increased capabilities to meet the demands of users for new applications and expanded resources. The author

2. INITIAL VERSUS RECURRING COSTS

The initial costs for IT implementation are usually well planned, especially if special funding is required. A major source of 'start-up' money is supplied by grants and fundraising efforts. Most of libraries have learned that in order to maintain the essential balance between technology and books, they need to seek alternative sources of income. Only through such fiscal dexterity libraries are able to deliver the latest technologies to users while maintaining the breadth and diversity of their collections.

While it is clear that libraries are getting funds from alternative sources for initiating technology, it is less clear how funding for the continuing costs like AMC for maintenance, up gradation are being planned and secured. However, significant questions arise for many of these libraries: How will they maintain their Internet services and upgrade their hardware and software once the grants are exhaust?

From grants, for technology initiatives libraries have benefited greatly. However, it is vital that librarians recognize the fast developments nature of technology and the need for strategies for and financial sources of long term funding. They or their parent institutions cannot rely on 'windfalls' or stopgap measures to ensure regular supply of funds to maintain the systems.

In the early days of technological development, systems lasted for several years and upgrades to hardware and software were less frequent, telecommunications requirements were limited, and the Internet was just a dream.

At that time, one-time funding was sufficient and the need for continuing funds was less critical. But with the fast development it has become essential to have budgets that reflect the reality. Academic institutions are only now trying to develop methods to deal with the situation. They're struggling to find the more effective ways of incorporating technological needs into institute budget and planning processes. Before developing strategies to support the ongoing funding needs, it is essential to look at the elements of technology and the costs associated with them.

3. ELEMENTS OF RECURRING COSTS

3.1. Hardware

Hardware, including computers, printer and other peripherals, used to last for a few years and expenditures could be planned in an orderly manner much as other major equipment purchases. Recently, however, it has become apparent that product cycles have accelerated due to fast technological developments. As McCollum points out "... the constant evolution of IT guarantees that spending will continue to rise; no matter how nice the computers and network wires are today, in a year they'll be outdated."

It is essential to develop priorities and determine replacement cycles. Obviously, no one buys all new computers in a one go the moment a new model arrives. People use varying age equipment, but it loses its effectiveness and may impair performance as capability diminishes as time span increases. To develop a buying strategy it is essential to ask some basic questions.

3.1.1. How important is it for users to purchase the latest machine?

This question is of utmost importance because if users' do not have the latest equipment then they will not be able to run the latest software, connect to the networks, or work with graphics. Speed and memory limitations will prevent them down from taking advantage of the latest developments. On the other hand, it is very expensive to keep obtaining the latest devices or software when there is an upgrade with minimal improvements.

3.1.2. *Can the hardware support the software?*

It is an obvious, but often overlooked question! Does the computer have sufficient memory, chip speed and storage to run without any degradation of performance when the user load increases? If it does not, then one may have to reconsider what impact a new machine will have on the total costs.

3.1.3. *Can computers connect to network and handle graphics and other content available on Internet? Must they?*

In the networked environment, it is a key question as the speed and memory capabilities are essential to the effective use of the Web with its intensive graphic content. So much information is now available over the Internet that it is becoming essential for libraries to be connected with appropriate machine.

3.1.4. *How is productivity being affected by aging machine?*

Computers still operate and perform the original operations for which they were designed long after their optimum efficiency has been reached. It is important to take into consideration how old equipment is affecting the user, and whether significant improvements in software and speed are being sacrificed as the hardware cannot handle the upgradations.

3.1.5. *Is library able to deliver needed services and products on available machine?*

It is, of course, an essential question. Hardware decisions should be based on needs of the applications as they relate to specific services and functions of the institution. If a specific application or upgrade to an existing program is necessary then the software and hardware of required configuration should be purchased. If not, then it may be wise to delay the equipment purchase.

3.1.6. How often should hardware be replaced even if it still functions?

This question is related to some of the previous questions regarding the necessity for the latest features, more speed or additional memory. In addition, it is important to consider maintenance costs. Old machine can become very expensive in terms of high maintenance costs and troubleshooting.

3.1.7. Should hardware be replaced in regular cycles? If so, what should the length of time be?

It is an important question, as it is best if one can avoid crises and eliminate 'crashes' and other hardware problems. Regular replacement cycles can help to predict expenditures and to establish corresponding budgets in a consistent manner.

3.1.8. Should latest, most powerful, model be purchased regardless of application or should one be purchased based on requirements even if slightly older?

While it might seem best to purchase the most powerful hardware so it will last longer, it is highly debatable. The latest equipment is often on the 'cutting edge', and the 'bugs' may not have been removed of the system. Experts differ on whether it is most cost effective to purchase the latest model or the model prior to that. If the latest is chosen, it may be necessary to do some "troubleshooting." There is usually an optimum time to buy a machine when it is new enough to handle the software and networking demands, but not so new that it has not been carefully tested.

Items pertaining to the hardware purchasing strategy include:

- Develop a detailed list of the equipments with model numbers, manufacturing dates, and capabilities;
- study market and keep up-to-date on current developments;
- decide on an optimum replacement cycle;
- determine a replacement schedule based on age, function, and software requirements as well as the optimum replacement cycle;
- schedule a regular program of annual purchases to eliminate crises;
- rotate equipment through various functions to lengthen its lifespan; and
- develop plans for surplus used equipment to recover some costs or eliminate expensive and time-consuming disposal procedures.

3.2. Software

Software development is one of major factors driving the fast pace of technology. Enhancements to software resulting in new versions and updates require more memory and faster computers. As software applications grow ever larger and World-Wide Web pages more elaborate, administrators cannot question whether to replace aging computers, only how often their institutions can afford upgrades.

Expert opinion varies on how often software should be upgraded. Some believe one should always upgrade to the latest version while others feel that as long as the software is performing adequately it is not necessary to upgrade. Each position has budgetary and performance implications. Constant upgrading requires hardware enhancements to accommodate the increased memory requirements and faster processing time. It also has an impact that new versions of applications software often require training of staff and also requires time to be familiar with the package. On the other hand, old software is familiar and users may be fast and productive using it. However, it may be slow or cumbersome in execution. It may only operate on older hardware, which can become a problem.

As James ' writes in an article on upgrading application software, the best approach may be to not automatically either upgrade or retain old software, but to analyze the needs, uses, and hardware requirements of the new software version.

The following list of questions would be helpful in determining whether and when to purchase new software.

3.2.1. What enhancements does the new software version provide?

Software upgrades come out regularly and it is important to decide whether it is necessary to implement each new version. Software memory requirements can become very demanding on existing hardware. A review of the enhancements will determine applicability to a particular application and determine advisability of acquiring the new version.

3.2.2. What are hardware requirements?

Any decision to upgrade the software is a careful examination of the corresponding hardware requirements. Most upgrades require additional memory and faster processing speeds. Does computer have sufficient memory, chip speed and storage to be able to run without any degradation of performance when user load increases? If it does not, then it may be necessary to reconsider acquiring the upgrade.

3.2.3. Will the vendor still support the older version?

This question may seem obvious, but vendor support is a major consideration in determining the viability of the older software version. While it may be possible to postpone minor upgrades and vendor support may not be critical, major upgrades may be essential.

3.2.4. What are the costs associated with remaining with older version in terms of vendor support or local assistance?

There are hidden costs related to running old software that may not be readily apparent. As the software ages, it may become costly in terms of its interfacing with other applications or network connections. It may require more time and effort to get it to operate efficiently and therefore be more costly than it would be to upgrade completely.

3.2.5. Will older version still interface with other software applications? Conversely, will newer version require different versions of other applications software?

A new software version may have implications for other software applications running on the hardware. A careful review of the interconnections to determine the impact of the upgrade is essential in predicting the full cost of the proposed implementation.

3.2.6. What impact will the new version have on staff? Training requirements? Support issues?

Depending on extent of upgrade there will be associated costs in terms of staff training and support. Estimating these related costs prior to purchase will eliminate any 'surprises' in the future. What are costs connected to switching to new version including installation, related hardware needs and training requirements? In determining actual costs of an upgrade it is important to take into consideration all related costs that may not be readily apparent such as installation, training and support in addition to hardware and networking costs that are more obvious. For instance, can installation of new software take place automatically over the organization's local area network, can it be done *in situ* at user's desk, or must the machine be taken to some central computer department (in that case the user may be without a PC for several hours or even days).

Action items in determining software requirements include:

- Develop a list of software detailing requirements and specifications in connection with the hardware inventory;
- establish criteria to be used to determine whether to upgrade software or not;
- attempt to integrate upgrading of software with the purchase of new hardware to better utilize resources;
- determine impact of software upgrade on related applications and peripherals; and
- ascertain how the upgrade will actually be handled and any training requirements and support issues.

3.3. Infrastructure and Network Access

Networking is essential for the development of the modern electronic and automated library. Access to the Internet with its variety of resources and requirements for graphics, images and video are requires better, faster equipment along with robust network connections. Additional workstations require more electrical outlets and telecom ports. This often requires expenditures for facilities upgrades. With judicious planning, these expenditures need not occur as often as upgrades of hardware and software. However, it is to be expected that there will be some annual expenditures related to new outlets or telecommunications hook-ups. In addition to these costs, there are network access fees that are a recurring charge and must be budgeted accordingly.

Libraries are beginning to realize the expense related to network access. While major facilities upgrades, including additional electrical outlets and telecom connections, may occur infrequently, annual adjustments may be required. A campus network usually provides access to Internet and is budgeted centrally. However, concerns regarding the funding capability at the institutional level exist. As Clifford Lynch explains Large organizations, both higher education and corporate, will be increasingly unable to afford (and in some cases even obtain, at any price) the capacity they need to connect to their backbone Internet service providers.

Whatever library's size or affiliation, it is essential to budget for costs associated with network access.

Again, a checklist of relevant questions is helpful.

3.3.1. *Will new hardware purchases require additional electrical and telecommunications outlets?*

When making hardware purchases, it is always important to determine facilities requirements. New hardware may require different physical configurations, new printers, or additional peripherals. Investigating these needs, estimating feasibility, and predicting costs prior to purchase will eliminate frustration and hidden costs later.

3.3.2. *Will new hardware and software interface with the existing network connections?*

It is, of course, a primary consideration, and it is important to determine whether new software will interface with the networking software. In the case of very new releases, it is important to find out if sufficient testing has been done to eliminate "bugs."

3.3.3 Will the telecommunications configurations and current network providers be able to handle increased capabilities?

Related to the above questions, contacting network providers to be sure they can accommodate the new hardware and software system before purchase will reduce the possibility of surprises.

3.3.4. What will be the initial costs for connecting new hardware and software to the network?

Ascertaining the true initial costs of connecting hardware and software to the network has to take into account factors such as installation and set-up costs, additional facilities work (electrical and telecommunications outlets), and network fees.

3.3.5. What will be the ongoing costs related to the telecommunications connections?

While most people are aware of ongoing maintenance charges, it is important to remember that there are ongoing telecommunications charges associated with network access. If additional connections are required, then the continuing fees need to be calculated.

Action items to prepare for infrastructure and network access include:

- Be familiar with available network connections and capabilities of network providers;
- develop plans for implementation of new hardware and software detailing electrical and telecommunications implications;
- estimate and budget for additional outlets and telecommunications connections;
- estimate annual costs for telecommunications connections; and

- review telecommunications options and network providers to determine best choice in terms of performance and cost.

3.4. Support

Systems personnel, training, and maintenance have to be included in this category. As the electronic and automated aspects of the library continues to grow and expand the elements necessary to support this effort increase. The entire library staff is involved in all aspects of electronic and automated library, but staff dedicated to maintaining the hardware and software as well as managing the intricacies of the network is essential to the smooth operation of the system. As more of libraries growing electronic and automated, it is necessary to have more personnel committed to hardware, software, and network support. It is essential to plan for this consequence. It may be possible to outsource some of this support either to institutional computing facilities, such as campus computing, or purchase support from vendors or local suppliers. However, it is likely that some support on-site in the library will be required. As the electronic components increase, more of this support is necessary.

Training is essential, and librarians must plan on providing on going support for staff and users in learning and using new software and hardware. Funds for this should be incorporated into the budget. Of course, maintenance has to be considered in the hardware and software negotiations. Either this support has to be performed locally or vendor-supplied. Either way, it is an important factor that must be included in the planning and budgeting for technology. This paper will not go into details on these support elements. Suffice it to say that they must be included in the budget as ongoing expenses.

4. BUDGETING FOR TECHNOLOGY

From the preceding discussion, it is clear that technology-related issues cut across all sectors of the budget: personnel, equipment, facilities, and operating expenses. There are also both one-time expenditures and recurring costs. From discussions in the literature it is also obvious that funding agencies as well as libraries themselves have not addressed the financial implications of technology in their budgeting. An article in Educom Review states that these one-time budgeting allocations are not adequate to meet out requirements of technology. These stopgap approaches do not reduce costs or increase productivity. It is time to consider how to restructure budget to support the reengineering of libraries around the available technology. Institute needs to abandon current short-term, unit-cost-based funding approaches and develop in their place new approaches that encourage longer-term investments in course and program development.

Academic libraries are struggling with the need to integrate technology into their operations without sacrificing other services: ". . . most libraries have long since learned that in order to maintain the essential balance between technology and books, they need to search alternative sources of income. Only through such fiscal dexterity are libraries able to deliver the latest IT to users while maintaining the breadth and diversity of their collections". In addition to finding new sources of funding, libraries are analyzing their costs and services ". . . given effectively static funding, the only way that institute IT organizations can offer either increased levels of services or new services is to eliminate some current services or to reduce the unit costs of those services provided currently. Measurement of the cost and the quality of these services is a necessary first step".

Essential to budgeting for technology is careful planning and analysis of costs. When implementing new technology one must consider the continuing costs and develop plans for upgrades, maintenance, and support. Once a realistic budget has been established, it is essential to devise funding strategies, both one-time and long-term, to generate the needed revenue and to meet out various purchasing requirements.

5. TECHNOLOGY, FUNDING STRATEGIES AND OPTION

5.1. Revenue Generation

5.1.1. User Fees

In some respects this is a controversial option for libraries, which always prefer not to institute user fees. However, academic institutions, especially private ones, are charging fees to generate financial resources for recurring technology expenses. They also are passing on to the students some costs, such as those for printing charges, especially for full-text documents.

5.1.2. Fundraising

Typically, it is easier to receive financial grant and private donations for innovative projects than for ongoing maintenance or recurring costs. However, the integration of these elements into grant proposals and funding requests for new initiatives may meet with success and ensure the successful continuation of project. Academic libraries have realised the need to secure additional funds to support technology. "In the early 1990s, following the boom-boom 1980s, library funding mirrored the country's economic slowdown. Property values began to slide, jobs were lost, and library budgets were cut, and in some cases decimated, as a result. Thus, libraries turned to their own revenue generating devices, starting and expanding Friends' groups, launching foundations, and becoming more determined in

18

Changing Role of Librarian in Digital Environment

Dr. Adhe G. D
Associate Professor & Head ,
Dr. Babasaheb Ambedkar, College of Arts & Commerce Nagsenvana, Aurangabad

Mukhyadal B. G.
Asst. Prof., Dr. Babasaheb Ambedkar College of Arts & Commerce Nagsenvana, Aurangabad

ABSTRACT

The role of librarian has changed in the digital library environment, therefore pertinent on the part of the librarian to acquire new skills required for developing and managing the digital libraries. The library and information professionals are required to acquire such knowledge and skills as the library is one of the highly IT influenced service profession. The empowerment of library and information professionals with IT skills is aimed at providing services that are expected of from the clientele in the new environment.

Key Words : Digital Environment, Role of Librarian, Traditional Library, Digital Library, Virtual Library, Electronic Library, Automated Library, Digital preservation.

1. INTRODUCTION

Digital libraries have a short history. While discussing about digital libraries, under various names. Digital libraries are collections of digital content and services selected by a curator for use by a particular user community. Digital libraries offer direct access to the content of a wide variety of intellectual works, including text, audio, video, and data; and may offer a variety of services supporting search, access, and collaboration. In the last decade digital libraries have rapidly become ubiquitous because they offer convenience, expanded access, and search capabilities not present in traditional libraries. This has greatly altered how library users find and access information, and has put pressure on traditional libraries to take on new roles. However, information professionals have raised compelling concerns regarding the sizeable gaps in the holdings of digital libraries, about the preservation of existing holdings, and about sustainable economic models.

2. DEFINITIONS OF DIGITAL LIBRARY

What is a digital library? There is much confusion surrounding this phrase, stemming from three factors. First, the library community has used several different phrases over the years to denote this concept-electronic library, virtual library, library without walls-and it never was quite clear what each of these different phrases meant. "Digital library" is simply the most current and most widely accepted term and is now used almost exclusively in the literature or everywhere.

The concept of a digital library can be defined in a variety of ways. The expressions Virtual Library, Digital Library and Hybrid Library are often used interchangeably, some definitions regarding a digital library are: Digital Libraries acting as knowledge depositories can be considered as complex information systems, development and use of which require solution of numerous scientific, technological, methodological, economic, legal and other issues. (Kalinichenko, et al, 2002).

A digital library is a collection of information that is both in digital (electronic) form and is organized. Information may take many forms, such as images, video, audio, text, formatted documents and interactive software (Hunter, and Mardis, 2001).

2.1. Traditional Library

Libraries are where the access points such as, library catalogues as well as library collections are print based and their management is by and large manual.

2.2. Automated Library

A library where access points and house keeping operations are computerized is called an automated library. The graphic records are still print-on-paper publication.

2.3. Electronic Library – Digital Library

The access point as well as the graphic records are in electronic/digital form when these electronic/digital libraries are connected via various networks, particularly the INTERNET, this is called virtual library.

Digital library is not only digitization of physical resources, but also thoughtful organization of electronic collection for better access. Such organization provides coherence to a massive amount of shared knowledge base. While the method of access provides convenient information retrieval for a wide range of global user. Essentially a digital library deals with organization and access of a large information repository. In all probability, digital libraries are likely to augment traditional libraries, such as an on-line card catalogue augments, rather than strictly replacing, a book collection. The reason for this could be than the digital medium tends to be better for searching and the physical medium better for reading. Lets us know about digital library and the skills required to build up digital collection

3. ADVANTAGES OF DIGITAL LIBRARY

The advantages of digital libraries are given below;

- Preserve the valuable documents, rare and special collections of libraries, archives and museums.
- Provide faster access to the holding of libraries world wide through automated catalogues.
- Help to locate both physical and digitized versions of scholarly articles and books through single interface.
- Search optimization, simultaneous searches of the Internet make possible, preparing commercial databases and library collections.
- Offering online learning environment.
- Making short the chain from author to user.
- Save preparation/ conservation cost, space and money.
- Digital technology affords multiple, simultaneous user from a single original which are not possible for materials stored in any other forms

4. DIGITAL LIBRARY SERVICES

Digital Library Services provides a wide array of services to assist members of the library with organizing collections of materials or making them more widely available. The following services offered by the Digital Libraries.

- Catalogue Databases,
- Current Awareness Bulletins,
- Externally Purchased Databases,
- CD-ROM Databases,
- Remote Information Services,

- Internally Published Newsletters, Reports & Journals,
- Internet Information Sources Mirroring & Cataloguing,
- E-mail,
- Bulletin Board Service,
- Netnews system,
- Audio and Video Communication,
- Electronic Table of Contents,
- Electronic Document Delivery Service,
- Electronic Theses and Dissertations,
- Reference Service,
- Electronic Publishing,
- Discussion groups and forums,
- Central storage facilities for Hosting digital collections and indexes,
- Tools for loading, storing, searching, and displaying digital objects,
- Special Collections service.

5. DIGITAL LIBRARY PROCESSES

5.1. Content selection

The content selection for the Dl is depends on the utility, value and rarity of collection. It may be Internal or external, free or commercial, owned or licensed, print or electronic formats. The content may includes Staff publications, e-mail archive, news, reports, policies and plan documents, drawings, software, press releases, presentations, courseware, lectures, best practices, etc. for education and corporate purpose.

5.2. Content acquisition

Digital Library acquired contents already in digital form as well as to be converted and they may be loaded in central or distributed sites. The format (PDF, TIFF, postscript, html, xml) of the digital content may selected as those supported subsequent presentations today & tomorrow and It should not needs special access mechanism.

5.3. Content organization

The concept of content management has been around in intellectual organization and physical organization. Intellectual organization consist object description, categorization, indexing control and automatic content extraction. Physical organization includes databases, indexes, storage, content granularity (full text tagging or hierarchical browsing support), search and retrieval. Digital object identity fire also paying important role in content organization. The content organization needs special attention in DL because it is the base of the DL services and products.

5.4. Content access and delivery

Digital library is changing landscape for access and delivery of digital contents globally. This allows various type search such as Structured search (meta-data driven), Object search (full-text, multi-media object search), Search at finer granularity (tables, figures, paragraphs, section headings), Global search and resource type search (e.g. bibliographic databases, e-journals, reports, experts). The searching features includes Relevance ranking, Search refinement, search history, search set combination, Personalization, customization. It also facilitates structured presentation (display), Hierarchical browsing (subject schemes/ topic directory). Access and delivery area of Digital library are developing new innovative technologies and processes in these areas that will capitalize upon the digitized status of DL content, and allow quicker, easier and cheaper access to content, which in turn will be a powerful justification for your digitization effort. Access and delivery process are aided by conversion to digital mass storage.

5.5. Access management

Access management consist various operations such as access control, content security, object identification, ownership establishment, License metering, user Id and password management, Proxy/IP authentication management, etc. All the above operations have been controlled by the various software's and techniques that facilitate to DL has access control over the owned and licensed contents.

5.6. Usage and monitory

DL have integrated usage and monitory system that gives answers of such question like what digital sources are being used, how much and by whom. Those answers may help you to evaluate system performance and information services.

5.7. Networking and interoperation

Networking enhances digital information services and resource sharing. Metadata and Open access initiative allows federated access to different collection within and across DL. Interoperation allows to DL users to find out desired information from different system across the word.

5.8. Preservation

Digital preservation involves quite different methods, skills, and outcomes and can complement traditional preservation services, while simultaneously providing unique and dynamic new uses of information. Digital Library ensures perpetuity and long-term access through time and changing technologies.

6. TYPES OF RESOURCES

The resources provided by the digital libraries can be classified into in-house resources and external resources. In-house resources are those resources that are stored in the web server locally and made accessible through the network. E-books, course notes, and application notes etc. are examples of the in-house resources.

The external resources are those materials that are not stored in the web server. External resources include online journals, online databases, online e-books etc. External resources are provided by different publishers - ASME, ACM, IEEE, Oxford University Press Journal (OUP) and many more are there. The publisher provides access to their full text materials by two methods:

(i) Username and password

(ii) Internet Protocol (IP) address based Access Control Method

7. CHANGING ROLE OF LIBRARIAN IN DIGITAL ENVIRONMENT

The ready availability of information on the Internet, and its widespread use, really presents Librarians with an opportunity, not a threat. Technology Survey users realize they need help, which Librarians can provide. Librarians now face difficulties and complicity challenges due to new trends in information access. In the present technological/ Internet era the professionals have to change themselves as the information profession is being changed. Now information specialists have to work as information resources in which various professional groups are expected to map strategies that lead to produce, manage, maintain and service the information. Information professional has to work as:

7.1. Librarian

In addition to being library manager, they also act as collection development, technical processors and so on, taking care of information quality.

7.2. Information Manager

To meet information need of the user they should know how to manage and deliver appropriate information services.

7.3. Information adviser/instructor

Ensure that user/staff know how to access relevant sources of information (literacy).

7.4. System & Networking

For delivery of information to their users in an appropriate manner develop and design appropriate systems.

8. SKILLS, KNOWLEDGE, COMPETENCIES ARE REQUIRED FOR LIBRARIAN

The basic goal of library and information profession has always been to provide access to information to those who need it. The activities realizing this goal have evolved and transformed over the years. This includes - Available technology, and need of an evolving information society. Information activities have been guided by the developments in the field of storages, presentation and archiving of knowledge, collection development and organization of knowledge, information explosion and computers in information retrieval. Librarian and information professional involved in information gathering, storage, retrieval and dissemination on one hand and on the other hand the computer specialists who supports the library and informational professionals in this endeavor. For successful implementation of Digital Library, it is essential that LIS professionals are well trained and possess requisite knowledge and skills in this respect.

8.1. Knowledge & Skills

Librarians need to know understand

- Financial resources (Budget) Human resources (Skills for manpower training)
- Knowledge resources (books, journals, i.e. resources, Internet)
- Technological facilities and resources (computer, online catalogues, websites, LANs file servers etc.)

8.2. Competencies that required possessing in LIS professional

- Provide quality service.
- Be resourceful
- Acceptance of change.
- Knowledge of user interaction with knowledge resources.
- Be adoptive, flexible and resistant.
- Posses excellent communication skills, constantly update personal knowledge base by keeping in touch with the latest development
- Create awareness among the users, make them accept the changes
- Be an information management strategist, etc.

8.3. Technical Knowledge required

- World processing, Graphics, Spread sheet & Presentations.
- Operating systems - Windows, UNIX, LINUX.
- Database Management Systems including the skills in Bibliographic Database Management Systems.

- Information Retrieval software for online, CD-ROM and Internet.
- Library software packages, acquaintances with Digital Library Tools.
- General purpose programming, Networking
- Web page Development and Content Management

8.4. Capacity to used/download free Software /resource

The Librarian should have capacity to used/ download free software. (e.g. DSpace, NewGenlib, Koha, GSDLS etc)

9. CONCLUSION

The day has arrived when it is most important to learn to access, analyze apply and evaluate such information. As traditional custodians of information, librarians need to be aware of the implications of these changes and develop technological and managerial skills, which will enable them to make effective use of information and to meet their organizations goals and objectives.

10. REFERENCES

- Arms, Williams Y. (2000). Digital Libraries, Cambridge, MA: MIT Press.
- Hunter, B., and Mardis, M. (2001). K-12 Education considerations for a National SMETE Digital Library. Virginia: Piedmont Research Institute.
- Klinichenko, and Leonid A., et. al. (2002). Digital libraries: advanced methods and technologies, digital collections. <*http://www.dlib.org/dlib/ january03/ kalinichenko/01kalinichenko.html*>. Accessed on 24 August, 2011
- Kanjilal, Uma (2004). Education and training for digital libraries: Model for web enhanced continuing education programme. *In*: International Conferences on Digital Libraries. New Delhi, 629-635.
- Marchionin, Gary and Maurer, Hermann (1995). The role of Digital Library in teaching and learning. Communication of the ACM, 38(4), 124-133
- McMillan, Gail (1999). Digital Libraries support distributed

education. *http://www.ala.org/content/navigationmenu/ACRL/ Events and conference/ macmillan99.pdf.* Accessed on 21st August 2011

- Nyamboga, Constantine and et. Al. (2004). Required skills of Information technologies for Library & Information professionals: A case of University Libraries in Kenya-Africa. *In* International Conferences on Digital Libraries. New Delhi, p. 629-635.
- Rajkumar, P. V. (1996). The Internet : a global cluster of Computing Networks its presence and Impact. In Advance in Information Technology Impact on Library, Banglore, p. 1- 6.
- Wiederhold, G. (1995). Digital Libraries: Value and Productivity. *Communication of the ACM, 38(4)*,23-29.
- Wilensky, Robert (1995). U C Berkley's Digital Library Project. *Communication of the ACM, 38*(4)7-13

19
Medical Libraries & Librarianship in India

Dr. (Mrs.) Shaista Parvin Muqueem
Assistant Librarian, Dr. Babasaheb Ambedkar Marathwada University, Aurangabad Maharashtra, INDIA.

MEDICAL LIBRARIES, INDIA, FIVE YEAR PLANS, RESEARCH LIBRARIES

Introduction

With the unprecedented advancements in the world of medical science in the last five decades, the study of medicine has become very challenging and complex. New discoveries in almost all the fields related to medicine have made medical education an extremely specialized field that now forces students and resource-people to keep themselves updated in their knowledge of what is happening at present I their field. In making this large corpus of knowledge accessible to the user, medical libraries play the most significant role in the medical society. The main objective of these libraries is to assist the students, researchers and practitioners in not only upgrading their knowledge but also in providing information about new innovations, views, theories and the latest treatment for better patient care. No educational or research program can culminate into fruitful and valid results unless backed by an efficient support system, i.e. the library. (Library Herald, 2007)

MEDICAL LIBRARIES IN INDIA

Medical Library has played an important role in the great advances of medical knowledge. It is the link between the past and the present. The history of the medical library is closely related to the history of medicine. In fact, the particular attitude towards medicine at any given time affected the state of the medical library. India has a long history of keeping under systematic control the medical writings. The Sanskrit manuscripts on Ayurvedic medicine, mostly research works of Susruts, Charaka and the commentaries on these by their successors, found their existence in University of "Takshila", "Nalanda" and "Vikramshila". The time was the 2nd century B.C. Libraries attached to these was sources to classical medical education, research and practice. The treaty of Charaka on "Kaya Chikitsa" or medicine is known as the most standard work on Indian medicine. Around 1000 B.C. Dhanwantari, the King of Varanasi, flourished. His famous disciple, Susruts, is regarded as the first surgeon of the world who used performs plastic surgery in an age when no anesthesia had been discovered. His famous treatise "Asthang Hriydaya" related both to surgery and medicine. One thousand three hundred instruments of Susruta find mention in the "Surgical Instruments of the Hindus". Hippocrat, the founder of the modern medicine came 200 years later than Susruta. For about 700 years during the Muslim rule, no researches were done in Ayurveda. By then surgery and traditional medicine had risen to the highest pitch in Europe and America. During the medieval period, the Mughal rulers, nobles and courtiers had their own personal medical libraries. (Dixit, 1995)

With the rise of European medieval period, the Mughal

rulers, nobles and courtiers had settlements in the seventeenth and eighteenth centuries; libraries became a part of social and educational institutions, however, the origin of modern medical libraries in India can be traced to the establishment of the British rule in the country. Some members of the medical professions, mostly Europeans of the Armed Forces Medical Services, felt that it would be helpful to record their experiences and views in medical and allied sciences with a view to communication with, and be some benefit to ,

Their colleagues scattered all over India. The efforts taken in this direction resulted in the formation of the, Medical and Physical Society of Calcutta in March 1823. The Transactions of the Medical and Physical Society of India, which brought out its first issue in March 1823 was the first professional medical periodical published in India.

The credit for first suggesting cooperative effort among medical men in India for their professional advancement by forming subscription libraries should probably go to John Peter Wade (Chitale and Bhatt, 1974, pp. 406-414) an Assistant Surgeon of the Bengal Medical Services, a pioneer in clinical observations and author of three works on diseases of India. (Neelameghan, 1963)

By the end of the nineteenth century, the three provincial capitals of India viz., Bombay, Calcutta and Madras, and many of the towns had their medical colleges. The first medical library attached to the Institute of Anatomy, Madras Medical College, came into being in 1830. After a gap of five years, Madras Medical College had also established its own library for the use of students and faculty members. In the same year, i.e., 1835 Calcutta Medical College opened its library. Later on, the medical libraries at Goa Medical College and Grant Medical College were established in the years 1842 and 1845 respectively. Besides medical colleges, health, medical and allied institutions had also started taking initiative in establishing their own libraries. For example, T.N.F.S. Laboratory, Forensic House Kamarajaisalan had opened the library in 1850, Institute of Mental Health in 1867 and Indian Veterinary Research Institute in 1890.

In the beginning of the twentieth century, the concept of medical libraries changed totally. In 1901, the Government of India declared open the Imperial Library (now the National Library) to all. From 1900 onwards, India witnessed a strong movement for the establishment of medical libraries in different parts of the country. Officials of provincial governments, rulers of Princely states, eminent citizens and librarians played an active role in the library movement. With the result that a number of medical libraries were established by the several medical colleges, research institutions, medical, health and allied institutions of India. Some of the prominent medical libraries that came into existence during the period 1901-1944 are; Central Research Institute Library (1905), Library of Kasturba Hospital (1906), Mary Calvert Holdswarth Memorial Memorial Hospital Library(1906), Library of Pasteur Institute of India (1907), Library of National Institute of Communicable Diseases (1909), E.T.C.M. Hospital Library, (1910), Indian Council of Medical Research Library (1911), Library of College of Physicians and Surgeons of Bombay, (1913), Library of Lady Hardinge Medical College and Hospital (1916), R.G. Kar Medical College Library (1916), King Edward VIH Memorial Pasteur Institute and Medical Research Library (1917), Library of National Institute of Nutrition (1918), Library of Topiwala National Medical College (1921), king George Medical College Library (1922), Andhra Medical College Library (1923), Mysore Medical college Library (1923), Calcutta Tropical Medicine School Library (1923), Shilpauk Medical College Library (1924), Glancy Medical College Library (1925), National Medical Library (1926), Library of All India

Institute of Hygiene and Public Health (1932), Dayanand of R.G.Kar Medcial College (1939), Library of Christian Medical College and Hospital (1942), Library of Amritsar Medical College (1943), Library of S.C.B. Medical College (1944), Sri Ram Chandra Bhanja Medical College Library (1944) (Dixit, 1995).

FIVE YEAR PLANS & MEDICAL LIBRARIES

It has been observed that since 1951, when the First Five Year Plan was launched a great momentum has taken place in the establishment of medical libraries. Several medical libraries were either established or developed by institutions: research/academic/ medical, notably the libraries of Post-Graduate Institutions of Chandigarh, Pondicherry, New Delhi and Varanasi; the libraries of research institutes under the Indian council of Medical Research, such as National Institute of Nutrition, National Institute of Virology, National Institute of Occupational Health, National Institute of Diarrhoeat Disease and Cholera; IRR and the libraries under Council for Scientific and Industrial Research (CSIR)-such as National Engineering Research Institute Library, Central Food Technological Research Institute Library, the Library of the Cancer Research Institute etc. Several other institutes, such as, National Institute of Health and Family Welfare, National Institute of Mental health and Neurosciences, National Tuberculosis Institute, National Institute of Communicable Diseases, National Institute of Immunology and in the field of traditional systems such as National Institute of Ayurveda, National Institute of Homoeopathy etc. have started improving their libraries and documentation centers.

Apart from the above, National Botanical Research Institute and Vallabh Bahi patel Chest Institute opened their libraries in 1953. The Maulana Azad Medical College Library and the Library of Institute of Nuclear Medicine and Allied

Science came into existence in 1958 and 1961 respectively. A documentation center in the field of toxicology was established at the Indian Toxicology Research Institute in 1965.Later on in 1971, the University College of Medical Sciences opened its library. A well-planned documentation center in the field of immunology had been established at the Institute of Immunology in 1981.

The information concerning the establishment of 240 medical colleges, medical, health and allied institution (allopathic system) and their libraries is given in during the planning period 1961-1965, the maximum numbers of academic/research/medical institutions were established and simultaneously the maximum number of medical libraries opened. Thus, it could be inferred that after the introduction of national plans well-planned medical libraries came into existence. There are more than 744 medical libraries different systems such as allopathic, dental, nursing, pharmacy, homoeopathy, unani, ayurveda, yoga and naturopathy, etc. in existence. Theses libraries are providing the various information services to over 10-15 million health workers of different categories spread over about 14,000 institutions (colleges/schools, research institution, hospitals/dispensaries, Department of Health/Medical/ Family Welfare Services, etc.) in both modern as well as indigenous systems of health care (Dixit, 1995).

These days information technology is the most widely talked about concept. Information technology is the science of gathering, storing, manipulation, processing and communication. Most medical libraries around the world provide information through modern technologies, such as E-mail, CD-ROM, CD-Net, On-Line service, etc.

INTERNATIONAL

W.H.O. : Regional Office for South East Asia Library: This Library is primarily meant to provide reference services to WHO staff in the regional office and to the member countries of the region, provided the request is received from the national focal point. The library has four independent CD-ROM drives and a CD-NET tower consisting of.28 drives. It has different databases viz. AIDSLINE, POPLINE and MEDLINE . Besides it also has Encyclopedias on CD-ROM. It also provides information services through INTERNET.

National

National Medical Library : It is one of the largest medical libraries in the South Asia region. It functions as a focal point for collecting, processing and supplying all biomedical information, generated within the country and abroad. It has a total collection of 3, 10,000 volumes and receives 2,100 periodicals annually. It has a separate audiovisual section with the 240 A.V. cassettes and uses the LIBSYS software package for library automation. It has two normal CD-ROM drives and six databases viz. MEDLINE, HEALTHSTAR, CANCERLIT, EMBASE and AIDS-CD. It has 2 Pentium computers. Searching of information through CD-ROM is being done by users as well as library staff it also gives the print out facility without any charge.

B.B. Dikshit Library AIMS : The library was established is 1956 and supports teaching, research programmers of the Institute, besides patient case. It has a total collection of 1, 35,000 volumes and receives about 500 periodicals. The library is equipped with all the modern information technologies such as CD-ROM drive, CD-Net, E-mail, multimedia, etc. It has different databases like MEDLINE, POPLINE, CANCERLIT, PSYCLIT, LISA and many one-time-databases.

Central Science Library of Jamia Hamdard University: It was formerly known as Institute of History of Medicine and Medical Research and was established in 1961.

It was changes into Jamia Hamdard University in 1989. The Central Science Library has a total collection of 1, 50,000 volumes of medical science documents and receives abhout 250 periodicals. It has a Pentium computer and 4 CD-ROM drives of Hitachi. It has some databases viz. MEDLINE, TOXLINE and IPA. It also provides free of cost print-out facility to users. Besides this library has a good collection of 2500 microforms and 4,650 manuscripts,. There is provision to acquire the INTERNET connection and to develop the local area network (LAN) for its affiliated departments of Pharmacy and Nursing.

Indian council of Medical Research: The ICMR was established in 1911. Over the years, it has built up a collection of research reports published by the council and it has a total collection of 30.000 volumes and receives 150 periodicals. Although this library is of national status but it does not have any modern technology, the searches are done through the NIC and the National Medical Library.

Research Libraries

These are eight institutions, which are engaged in active health science research.

National Institute of Immunology : It was established in 1982. The library has total collection of 6,500 books, 4,000 back volumes of periodicals and subscribes to 128 periodicals. It has two CD-ROM drives and different database like MEDLTINE, LIFE SCIENCES and DERWENTO. It uses CD/ISIS software package for in house activities and has a personal computer. Library does not give the printout facility but it provides downloading facility on floppies. Besides, it has three photocopiers, microfilm reader and printer, and has 375 microforms.

Centre for Biochemical Technology : It was established in 1967 by CSIR and engaged in research work in the field of biochemical technology. It has a total collection of 1,500 volumes and receives 46 current periodicals. It has only one MEDLINE database and provides free of cost print-out facility to researchers.

Institute of Nuclear Medicine and Allied Science : The library of the institute is known as Technical Information and Documentation services and was established in 1962 by Defense Research and Development organization (DRDO). It has a total collection of about 30,000 volumes and receives 69 periodicals. The library has a PC 286 computer. It also has a normal CD-ROM drive of Hitachi and three databases namely MEDLINE, CANCERLIT and BIOETHICLINE. It gives free of cost print-out facility to scientists and forwards their MEDLARS search requests to NML and NIC.

Defense Institute of Psychological Research : It is also a specialized research institute of DRDO. It caters to the needs of Scientists of Psychology; It has a total collection of 7,200 books, 10,000 back-files of journals and receives 64 current periodicals. It has only one personal computer for in house activates. It does not have any CD-ROM drive for CD-Net listed in the questionnaire.

Defense Institute of Physiology and Allied Sciences: It was established in 1962 and the total collection of the library is approximately 10,000 volumes, and subscribes to 75 subscribed journals. The, library does not have CD-ROM drive and CD-Net facility listed in the questionnaire.

National Institute of Communicable Diseases : It was established in 1963 and has a total collection of 29,000 volumes, with subscription to 236 journals (including those received as gifts and in exchange). It has one PC 486 computer and the connection through NIC for MEDLARS search. The library has a photocopier but no micrographic facilities.

Institute of Human Behavior and Allied Sciences : It was established in 1995 and attached to Mental Diseases Hospital. It has a total collection of 3,000 volumes and receives 65 journals. It has one PC 386 computer and the online connection of MEDLARS though NIC. Meddlers search is being done by library staff only and it provides free of cost printout facility.

Institute of Pathology, ICMR : It was established in 1965 by ICMR to cater to the needs of researchers in pathology. It has a total collection of 4,000 books 5,000 back - volumes of journals and subscribed to 45 journals. The library does not have any of the modern information technology gadgets. (Kumar & Vishwakarma, 2002).

CONCLUSION

The medical library is own of the several major resources and academic medical center. That together makes possible the flow of information through quality health education & research. Health Science education and research have considerably changed in their concept and character due to advances in bio-medical science. These changes demand support from Libraries to collect, sort and recall the vied variety of information.

The CD-ROM is a better alternative for providing medical information in a developing country such as India. It is cheaper than the Online- search and also a one- time investment. The proper in -house training should be imparted to the professionals. The Medical library Association of India has taken a lead in conduction training programmers on modern technologies for librarians.

REFERENCES

1. Dixit, R.P. (1995) - Information Management *in* Indian Medical Libraries, New Delhi, New Concepts.
2. Dixit. R.P. and Sharma A.K. (1998) – Medical Libraries *in* jain M.K., Fifty Years Library and Information Services in India., Delhi, Shirpa Publication.
3. Kumar R.P. and Vishwakarma M.K. (2002)- Medical Information through CD-ROM in The Health Science Libraries *in* Sardana J.L.

ed., Libraries and Information and prospect Essays in Honour D,.R.Kalia, New Delhi; Concept Publishing co.

4. *Library Herald*. vol. 45, no.3 September 2003.
5. Neelmeghan, A (1963) - Development of medical societies and medical periodicals in India 1780-1920, IASLIC Special Publication, no.3, Calcutta, IASLIC.

UNIT 6

Statistical Research Methods in LIS

20

Impact of Personal Background on Publication of Faculties of Languages in Marathwada Region: A Case Study

Mr. Sanjay S. Waghmare

Asst. Prof., Dagdojirao Deshmukh Arts, Commerce & Science College, Waluj, Aurangabad, Maharashtra, India

Dr. Shashank S. Sonwane

Assistant Professor, Dept. of Library and Information Science
Dr. Babasaheb Ambedkar Marathwada University
Aurangabad, Maharashtra State, India

ABSTRACT

Publication Patterns needed to analysis of research performance of faculty members in their profession. Publication patterns to identify the role faculty members in promotion of language studies in department and to increase the publication of languages education. The present paper attempts to analysis the publication patterns of the faculty members of languages.

Keywords: Publication Patterns; Publication Outlets; Publication Density; Publication Concentration; Babasaheb Ambedkar Marathwada University.

1. INTRODUCTION

The word publication means the act of publishing, and it also means any writing of which copies are published, and any website. Among publications are books, and periodicals, the latter including magazines, scholarly journals, and newspapers.

The distribution of copies or phonorecords of a work to the public by sale or other transfer of ownership, or by rental, lease, or lending. The offering to distribute copies or phonorecords to a group of persons for purposes of further distribution, public performance, or public display, constitutes publication.

To publish is to make content publicly known. The term is most frequency applied to the distribution of text or images on paper, or to the placing of content on a website.

2. NEED OF PUBLICATION

Publication is needed to increment there knowledge. Common man can not understand the foreign language. Therefore, faculties of languages write in their regional languages. So it can easily understand the common man. Therefore publication is needed.

3. DEFINITIONAL ANALYSIS

3.1. Publication Patterns

Publication patterns mean the information resources for effective and efficient use, it is necessary that characteristics of in information sources are studied. Studied has broadly in two ways publication pattern of journal and information generator of the authors. The term publication reflects on total publication outlets, journal publication outlets etc.

3.2. Languages

The origin of language is a topic that has attracted considerable speculation throughout human history. The use of language is one of the most conspicuous and diagnostic traits that distinguish Homo sapiens from other species. Unlike writing, spoken language leaves no concrete evidence of its nature or even its existence. Hence linguists have to resort to indirect methods in trying to decipher the origins of language.

A language is a dynamic set of visual, auditory, or tactile symbols of communication and the elements used to manipulate them. Linguistics -someone expert in the study of languages and its personal relationship.

3.3. Marathwada Region

Aurangabad division popularly known as Marathwada was basically founded as a military camp and a seat of Subhedari Deccan. Later on it was developed as a big trading town and a lending cultural center of Deccan. Aurangabad is an ancient city with great historical tradition. It was a part of Nizam's territory. After the police action in 1948, Aurangabad came under the Jurisdiction of the overmanned if India and the recognition of states in 1956. The Marathwada became a part of bilingual state of Bombay. Marathwada can well be describing on the home of art, religion and literature. The caves of Ajanta and Ellora which lie in this region attract scholars, artist, students and visitors from distant part of the world.

3.4. Personal Background

Personal background means the historical information

regarding a family. It includes the Surname, historical events, various personalities in the family etc. In the study the family background is consider as place of residence of a family, Type of family, how many members are there in the family, educated members in the family, working members in the family, who governs the family etc.

4. OBJECTIVES OF THE STUDY

- To survey the factors which motivate them to write etc.
- To analyze domain wise productivity.

5. SCOPE AND LIMITATION OF THE STUDY

Present study is limited to the languages departments in the Dr. Babasaheb Ambedkar Marathwada University, Aurangabad.

The study consists of 7 departments in Languages of Dr. Babasaheb Ambedkar Marathwada University, Aurangabad. In the 7 departments having 33 faculty members are working at present.

6. POPULATION SAMPLE AND PUBLICAIONS

Dr. Babasaheb Ambedkar Marathwada University in all 33 teaching department out of 33 teaching departments, 7 departments are languages viz. English, Foreign Languages, Hindi, Marathi, Pali and Buddhism, Sanskrit, and Urdu. In these languages departments total 33 faculty members are working in the designation of Professors, Readers and Lectures. Means the population sample is 33 faculty members. The subject wise distribution of faculty members covered and study is given in following table.

Table 1. Number of Faculty Members and Publications

Sr. No.	Departments	Total Faculty Members	Public-ations	Respondent Response	%age
1	English	08	34	08	100%
2	Foreign Languages	04	21	01	25%
3	Hindi	07	109	07	100%
4	Marathi	08	13	08	100%
5	Pali and Buddhism	02	01	02	100%
6	Sanskrit	01	37	01	100%
7	Urdu	03	00	03	100%
	Total	**33**	**215**	**30**	**100%**

7. SURVEY METHOD

Present study was done with the help of survey method. Survey research is distinguished by its reliance upon the selection of person from large and small population and the making of observation. So that inference can be applied to present population. A population is a group of person, objects institution or other units that passes at least on common characteristics.

Encyclopedia of library and information science defined this method as "the survey research methods enable investigation to conduct complete enumeration of population survey. It is save time and money without scarifying accuracy or information adequacy.

8. DATA COLLECTION METHOD

The researcher has collected Curriculum Vitae (CV) of individual faculties regarding their publication & education information. But Curriculum Vitae (CV), Annuals Reports of BAMU, as well as by using structured Questionnaire separately designed foe the faculties. The data collected from the respondents through the CV as well as questionnaire was tabulated and analyzed.

8.1. Questionnaire Design

Questionnaire is often using in survey as primary data collection tools. Questionnaire is a device for securing answer to questions by using a form which the respondent fills in him. It is a fairly reliable tool for gathering data from large, diverse, varied and scattered social group.

9. DATA ANALYSIS AND INTERPRETATIONS

Information was collected from the faculties in the form of curriculum viate (CV), annual report of BAMU, as well as by using structured questionnaire separately designed for the Faculties. The data collected from the respondents through the CV as well as Questionnaire was tabulated and analyzed.

An attempt was made to analyze the data which was collected from the faculty members of Dr. BAMU, Aurangabad structured questionnaire was used to collect the data; the questions which were responded by the faculty members are analyzed one by one and are presented under following heading, viz.

9.1. Age and Publication

The data which was collected from faculty members of Dr. Babasaheb Ambedkar Marathwada University was analysis according to age group is shown in table no.2

Table 2. Age and Publication

Age Group	*No. of Faculty Members Respondent*	*Publications*	*Percentage*
1950-1959	15	165	76.72%
1960-1969	04	27	12.59%
1970-1979	09	18	08.37%
1980-1989	02	05	02.32
Total	**30**	**215**	**100%**

It is observed from the table no. 4.16 that out of total publications, 165 (76.72%) publication were published by 1950-1959 years age group; 27 (12.59%) publications were from the 1960-1969 age groups; 18 (08.37%) publications were published by the 1970-1979 years age group and 05 (02.32%) publication were from the 1980-1989 years age group.

9.2. Place of residence and publication

The data collected from the faculty members of Dr. Babasaheb Ambedkar Marathwada University was categorized onto two group's i.e.;

i) Urban Area

ii) Rural Area

Table 3. Place of residence and publication

Place of Residence	*No. of Faculty Members Respondents*	*Publications*	*Percentage*
Urban	21	153	71.16%
Rural	09	62	28.84%
Total	**30**	**215**	**100%**

It can be observed from the table no.3 that is, out of the total publication 215, 153 (71.16%) publications were of the faculty members from urban area and 62 (28.84%) were of the faculty members from rural area.

9.3. Types of family and publication

The data collected from faculty members of BAMU was analyzed according to joint and nuclear family, this is shown in table no. 4.

Table 4. Types of family and publication

Types of Family	*Total No. of Faculty Members Respondent*	*Publications*	*Percentage (%)*
Nuclear Family	15	100	46.51%
Joint Family	15	115	53.49%
Total	**30**	**215**	**100%**

It can be observed from table no.4 that is, out of the total 215 publications, 100 (46.51%) publications were of the faculty members from nuclear family and 115 (53.49%) were of the faculty members from joint family.

9.4. Number of educated member in family and publication

The data collected from the faculty members of Dr. Babasaheb Ambedkar Marathwada University was analyzed and presented table no. 5.

Table 5. Number of educated member in family and publication

Educated Members	*No. of Faculty members Respondent*	*Publications*	*Percentage*
One	1	13	06.05%
Two	2	12	05.58%
Three	5	27	12.56%
Four	7	65	30.23%
More than four	15	987	45.58%
Total	**30**	**215**	**100%**

It can observed from the table no.5 that out of the total 215 publications, the highest percentage i.e. 45.58% publications is in the more than four educated members in a family and minimum percentage i.e. 06.05% and 05.58% publications is in the one and two educated members in a family.

9.5. Members working in family and publication

The data collected from the faculty members of Dr. Babasaheb Ambedkar Marathwada University was analyzed as per the number of members working in the family.

Table 6. Members working in family and publication

Working Members	*No. of Faculty Members Respondent*	*Publications*	*Percentage*
One	08	68	31.63%
Two	12	46	21.39%
Three	05	59	27.44%
Four	05	42	19.54%
More than four	00	00	00.00%
Total	**30**	**215**	**100%**

It is observed from table no. 6 that, the highest percentage i.e. 31.63% in that families of the faculty members where on member are working; where as two members are working in 12 faculties that is 21.39%. Three members are working in the 5 faculty members and four members are working in the 5 faculty members that is (27.44%) and (19.54%). No any family members working in the more than four.

9.6. Governs of family and publication

The data collected from the faculty members of Dr. Babasaheb Ambedkar Marathwada University was analyzed and present table no. 7 .

It can observe from the table no.7 that is, out of 30 faculty members 24 (92.09%) faculties are governed by self; 1 (0.46%) faculties are governed by spouse; 4 (2.32%) faculties are governed by father and 1 (5.13%) families are governed by Mother.

Table 7. Governs of family and publication

Governs of Family	*No. of Faculty Members Respondent*	*Publications*	*Percentage*
Father	04	05	02.32%
Mother	01	11	5.13%
Brother	00	00	00.00%
Sister	00	00	00.00%
Spouse	01	01	0.46%
Your Self	24	198	92.09%
Total	**30**	**215**	**100%**

9.7. Marital status

An attempt was made to find out the publication of faculty members before and after marriage.

Table 8. Material status and publications

Marital Status	*No. of Faculty Members Respondent*	*Publications*	*Percentage*
Married	28	202	93.95%
Unmarried	02	13	06.05%
Total	**30**	**215**	**100%**

It is observing from table no. 8 that out of 30 faculty members, the maximum 28 married faculty members publication i.e. 202 (93.95%) and 2 unmarried faculty members publication i.e. 13 (06.05%).

9.8. Education of spouse and publication

The data was collected from the faculty members of BAMU was analyzed and presented in table no. .

It can observe from table no. 9 that is, out of 215 publications 102 (47.44%) were from the faculties whose spouse education is post-graduate (P.G.), 65 (30.28%) were from the faculties whose spouse education is S.S.S., 9 (04.19%) were from the faculties whose spouse education is Non-

Educated and 15 (06.97%) were from the faculties whose spouse is Under-graduate, 13(06.05%) were from the faculties whose spouse is any other and 11(05.12%) were from the faculties whose spouse is Doctorate.

Table 9. Education of spouse and publication

Education of Spouse	*No. of Faculty Members Respondent*	*Publications*	*Percentage*
Doctorate (Ph.D.)	01	11	05.12%
Post Graduate	18	102	47.44%
Under-Graduate	02	15	06.97%
S.S.S.	06	65	30.23%
Non-Educated	01	09	04.19%
Any Other	02	13	06.05%
Total	**30**	**215**	**100%**

9.9. Working of spouse and Publication

An attempt was made to find out the impact of working spouses as well as non working spouses on the publication of faculty members, which is shown in the table no.10

Table 10. Working of spouse and publication

Status of Souse	*Total No. of Faculty Members Respondent*	*Publications*	*Percentage*
Employed	13	88	40.94%
Unemployed	17	127	59.06%
Total	**30**	**215**	**100%**

The table no. 10 revels that out of total 30 faculty members 13 (40.94%) faculties spouses are employed and 17 (59.06%) faculties spouse are unemployed.

9.10. Number of children and publication

The data collected form the faculty members of BAMU are presented in the table no. 11

Table 11. Number of children and publication

Number	No. of Children Male	Female	Total	Res-ponse	Public-ation	Percentage
1	05	06	11	11	77	35.81%
2	12	06	18	09	70	32.58%
3	06	06	12	04	32	14.88%
4	03	05	08	02	13	06.05%
5	01	04	05	01	09	04.17%
No Children	00	00	00	01	01	00.46%
Not Response	00	00	00	02	13	06.05%
Total	**27**	**27**	**54**	**30**	**215**	**100%**

The table no. 11 revels that, out of the total 30 faculty members 2 (2.39%) faculties have not responded to the researcher. It can be observed that, the faculties have single children the publication is 77 and percentage is 35.81%; when faculties members have two childrens the publication is 70 and percentage is 32.58% and when faculty members have three childrens the publication is 32 and percentage is 14.88%. While, faculties have four childrens the publications is 13 and percentage is 06.059% and faculties have more than four childrens the publications is 9 and percentage is 04.17% respectively.

Only one faculty member has no child that is publication is 1 and percentage is 00.46%.

9.11. Parent Education and Publication

Parents include mother and father. The education of parents is considered fewer than two scientists viz.

i. Father

ii. Mother

9.11.1. Father Education and Publication

The data collected from the faculties of BAMU was analyzed and presented in the table no. 12

Table 12. Father Education and publication

Father education	*No. of Faculty Members Respondent*	*Publication*	*Percentage*
Post Graduate	07	37	17.21%
Under-Graduate	06	53	24.62%
S.S.S.	10	70	32.59%
Non-Educated	07	55	25.58%
Any Other	00	00	00.00%
Total	**30**	**215**	**100%**

It can be observed from the table no.12 that Non-Educated, S.S.C. which is considered as low education but the publication percentage of this group is higher i.e. 55 (25.58%); 70 (32.59%). While, Under-Graduate and Post-Graduate faculty members publication is 53 (24.62%) and 37 (17.21%) respectively.

9.11.2. Mother education and publication

The data collected from the faculties of BAMU was analyzed and presented in the table no. 13

Table 13. Mother education and publication

Mother Education	*No. of Faculty Members Respondent*	*Publication*	*Percentage*
Post Graduate	01	00	00.00%
Under-Graduate	01	01	00.46%
S.S.S.	15	142	66.05%
Non-Educated	12	72	33.49%
Any Other	01	00	00.00%
Total	**30**	**215**	**100%**

The table no. 13 that is, S.S.C., Non-Educated which is considered as low education, but the publication percentage of this group is higher i.e. 142 (66.05%); 72 (33.49%); only one that Under-Graduate facilities publication percentage is 0.46%. While one faculties mothers education is Post-Graduate but he has not any publication.

However, one faculty member literate to her mother, but he has no publication.

9.12. Teaching experience

An Attempt was made to see the impact of teaching experience on publication of faculty members.

9.12.1. P.G. level experience and productivity

An attempt was made to see the impact of teaching experience on publication of faculty members. A question was asked regarding the teaching experience at PG and UG level. The data was collected from the faculties and as been analyzed and presented in the tale no. 14.

Table 14. P.G. level experience and publication

Experience on Years	*Responded Faculties*	*Publication*	*Percentage*
1 to 5	10	29	13.49%
6 to 10	08	29	13.49%
11 to 15	03	65	30.23%
16 to 20	05	57	26.51%
21 to 25	02	14	06.51%
26 to 30	02	21	09.77%
Total	**30**	**215**	**100%**

It is observed from table no.14 out of 215 faculties the highest publication of 11 to 15 years experience group i.e. 30.23% after that 16 to 20 years experience group i.e. 26.51% publication and 21 to 25, 26 to 30, years experience group i.e.6.51%, 9.77%. While, 1 to 5 and 6 to 10 years experience group that are same 29(13.49%) respectively.

9.12.2. U.G. level experience and publication

An attempt was made to find out the impact of UG level teaching experience on publication of faculty members. The data was collected from the faculties of BAMU was analyzed and presented in the tale no. 15.

Table 15. U.G. level experience and publication

Experience on Years	*Responded Faculties*	*Publication*	*Percentage*
1 to 5	09	48	22.32%
6 to 10	07	27	12.56%
11 to 15	05	39	18.14%
16 to 20	05	78	36.28%
21 to 25	02	11	05.12%
26 to 30	01	12	05.58%
Total	**30**	**215**	**100%**

Out of total 30 respondent that is, 26 to 30, 21 to 25, 16 to 20 , 11 to 15, 6 to 10 and 1 to 5 years experience of faculty members publication that is 22.32%, 12.56%., 18.14%, 36.28%, 5.12% and 05.58% respectively.

9.12.3. Research experience for guiding PH. D. students and publication

The data collected from the faculties of BAMU was analyzed is presented in the table no.16

Table 16. Research experience for guiding and publication

Research Experience For Guiding	*Responded Faculties*	*Publication*	*Percentage*
Ph. D. Awarded	12	128	59.53%
Ph.D. Research in Progress	11	68	31.63%
Not Awarded	7	19	08.84%
Total	30	215	100%

The table no.16 indicate that the research experience for guiding is Ph. D. awarded 128 i.e.59.53% publication, Ph. D. research in Progress is 68 and 31.63% publications and not awarded Ph. D. is 19 and their faculty members publication is 08.84%.

9.13. Motivating factors

Motivation is essential in every ones life. An attempt was made to see which factor motivate to faculty member to write. The data collected form the social scientists of BAMU was analyzed and presented in the table no.17

Table 17. Motivated factors

Motivating Factors	*No. of Faculty Members Respondent*	*Percentage*
Providing Weight age for Promotion	01	03.33%
Monetary Benefits	00	00.00%
Certificated of Merits	01	03.33%
Medals	00	00.00%
Cash Incentives	00	00.00%
Publicity	00	00.00%
Family Members	01	03.33%
Friends	06	20.01%
Any Other Factors	21	70.00%
Total	**30**	**100%**

It can be observed from the table no. 17 that is, 06 (20.01%) faculty members were motivated by Friends. While, Providing Weightage for Promotion, Certificated of Merits, Family Members; i.e. 1 (03.33%) respectively, and 21 (70.00%) faculty members motivated by any others factors.

9.14. Factors helping to write

The data collected form the faculty members of BAMU was analyzed and presented in the table no. 18

Table 18. Factor help to write more

Factors	*No. of Faculty Members Respondent*	*Percentage*
Well Situation of Working	13	43.33%
Funding Agency	04	13.34%
Current Information Material	07	23.33%
Guidance from family	02	6.67%
Moral Support of Souse	04	13.33%
Total	**30**	**100%**

It can be observed from Table No.18 that is, well situations of working and living conditions helps to 13 (43.33%) faculty members to write more. Funding agency, Current information material, Guidance from family and moral support of spouse, 17 (56.67%) faculty members write.

9.15. Encouragement by friend circle

An attempt was made to find out the impact of encouragement by friend circle on publication of faculty members. The data was collected from the faculties of BAMU was analyzed and presented in the tale no. 19

Table 19. Encouraging factors

Factors	*Total No. of Faculty Members Respondent*	*Publications*	*Percentage*
Encourage	30	334	100.00%
Discourage	00	00	00.00
Total	**30**	**334**	**100%**

It can observe from the table no.19 that is, out of 30 faculty members 30 (100%) faculty members were encouragement by the friend circle.

It indicated that family environment motivate the faculty members to write.

10. CONCLUSION AND IMPLICATIONS

It is observed that (Table No. 4.16) out of total publications, 165 (76.72%) publication were published by 1950-1959 years age group; 27 (12.59%) publications were from the 1960-1969 age groups; 18 (08.37%) publications were published by the 1970-1979 years age group and 05 (02.32%) publication were from the 1980-1989 years age group.

It is indicate the (Table No.4.17) that is, out of the total publication 215, 153 (71.16%) publications were of the faculty members from urban area and 62 (28.84%) were of the faculty members from rural area.

It can be observed (Table No.4.18) that is, out of the total 215 publications, 100 (46.51%) publications were of the faculty members from nuclear family and 115 (53.49%) were of the faculty members from joint family.

It is indicate that (Table No.4.21) that is, out of 30 faculty members 24 (92.09%) faculties are governed by self; 1 (0.46%) faculties are governed by spouse; 4 (2.32%) faculties are governed by father and 1 (5.13%) families are governed by Mother.

It is observed (Table No.4.22) that out of 30 faculty members, the maximum 28 married faculty members publication i.e. 202 (93.95%) and 2 unmarried faculty members publication i.e. 13 (06.05%).

Out of 215 faculties the highest publication of 11 to 15 years experience group i.e. '30.23% after that 16 to 20 years experience group i.e. 26.51% publication and 21 to 25, 26 to 30, years experience group i.e.6.51%, 9.77%. (Table No.4.28) While, 1 to 5 and 6 to 10 years experience group that are same 29 (13.49%) respectively.

The (Table No.4.30) indicate that the research experience for guiding is Ph. D. awarded 128 i.e.59.53% publications, Ph. D. research in Progress is 68 and 31.63% publications and not awarded Ph. D. is 19 and their faculty members publication is 08.84%.

The 06 (20.01%) faculty members were motivated by Friends. (Table No. 4.31) While, Providing Weightage for Promotion, Certificated of Merits, Family Members; i.e. 1 (03.33%) respectively, and 21 (70.00%) faculty members motivated by any others factors.

It can be observed (Table No. 4.32) that is, well situations of working and living conditions helps to 13 (43.33%) faculty members to write more. Funding agency, Current information material, Guidance from family and moral support of spouse, 17 (56.67%) faculty members write. It is indicate (Table No.4.33) that is, out of 30 faculty members 30 (100%) faculty members were encouragement by the friend circle.

It can be concluded that **Family environment i.e. urban residences, nuclear family, educated members in the family, lesser number of children, spouse & friends circle motivate the scientists to write.**

IMPLICATIONS OF RESULTS

Based on the results of the study following are the implications.

1. Incentives should be given foe the faculties foe undertaking highest number of projects.
2. Heads of the Department should motivate the faculties to write their articles in journals.
3. Research is a continuous process; the scientist should publish their research work on regular basis.

REFERENCES

Cole, F. G. and Eagles, N. B. (1917). The history of comparative anatomy. Part I. A statistical analysis of the literature. Science Progress, 11, 578 - 596.

Concise Oxford dictionary of Current English edited by H W Fowler and F G Fowler.-9th ed. - Calcutta: Oxford University Press. (1974)

Das, S K (1986). *An introduction to research.* Culcutta: MukherjeePvt. Ltd.

Kasyap, M M (1969). *Planning of survey Library Herald,* 2 (1&2), 195-199.

Kumar, PSG (2004).*Research methods and statistical techniques.* Delhi: B R Publishing Corporation.

Ona, Vocerience and Andre, Trumpiene (1994). Bibliometrics, Scientometrics and Informetrics: their relationship and interactions. *ILA Bulletin,* 39(4)175-179.

Panda, B. D. (1997). *Research methodology for library science (With statistical methods and bibliometrics).* New Delhi: Anmol Publication

Pritchard, A. (1969). Statistical bibliography or bibliometrics. *Journal of Documentation,* 24 (4), 348–349.

Ravichandrarao, I.K. and Neelameghan, (1992).From Librametry to informetrics: An overview and Ranganathan's contributions. *Libri,* 43 (3), 242 - 257.

Soman, Anu P. (2002). Growth of knowledge in humanities.A Bibliometrics study. *In* Devrajan G (Ed) *Research in Library and Information science* New Delhi: Ess Ess Publications, 87-104.

21

Citation Metrix of Commerce and Management Teachers

Dr. Jagdish N. Kulkarni

Assistant Librarian, Swami Ramanand Teerath Marathwada University, Nanded (MS), India

Prof. (Dr.) R D Biradar

Director, School of Commerce and Management Sciences

Mr. Shyam M. Sarsare

Project Fellow, Swami Ramanand Teerth Marathwada University, Nanded, (MS), India

ABSTRACT

Present paper analyzes the publications and prepares ranking of the most productive teachers in Commerce and Management from Maharashtra. Bibliometric indicators such as number of papers, authorship pattern, degree of collaboration (Quantitative indicators), number of citations, impact factor (Qualitative indicators) and h-index, g-index and p-index (composite indicators) have applied for preparing a rank list.)

Key Words : Commerce, Management, Research Papers (Papers), Bibliometric indicators, Citation, etc.

1. INTRODUCTION

Commerce and management education is an essential aspect for the growth and development of trade, commerce, industry and agriculture. To cope-up with modern trends in industry, commerce and management teachers have to update their knowledge through extensive reading and doing research. The best teacher is known from his class room teaching but his recognition to the rest of world comes from his research publications.

Rank list of teachers has been prepared with the help of analysis of their research publications. Analysis of research publication is based on certain indicators such as quantitative indicators (number of papers), qualitative indicators (citations, average citations, collaboration, and degree of collaboration) and composite indicators (h-index, g-index, p-index etc.). In the previous studies it was found that the ranking based on composite indicator gives much better results than other indicators as it combines both quantity and quality aspects (Gupta, 2011). Having this in mind, this study is conducted to know the research contribution of teachers. The analysis of citation of such publications helps in analyzing the quality of research publication.

Citation is one of the tools of measurement of research publications. Citation metrix is a quantitative, qualitative and composite study of research publications based on citation. Science citation index (SCI), Social science citation index (SSCI), Web of science, SCOPUS are some of the databases which keeps track of publications and their citations. There is no special citation index for commerce and management publications. However Google scholar lists publications of all subjects along with their citations.

2. SCOPE & LIMITATIONS

The scope of the study is wider covering commerce and management teachers, but due to limitation of time, the study has confined to teachers in commerce and management from Maharashtra only.

3. OBJECTIVES OF THE STUDY

Following are the objectives of the study.

i) To know the publication contribution of the commerce & management teachers.

ii) To trace authorship pattern of paper publication.

iii) To calculate degree of collaboration

iv) To find out citations received to their publication.

v) To know & compare h-index, g-index and p-index.

vi) To prepare rank list of teachers based on different indicators

4. DATA COLLECTION

List of commerce and management teachers in Maharashtra were prepared with the help of oral and written communication with the different institutions and persons. A questionnaire was distributed amongst the teachers and data was collected. A search engine Google Scholar, was used for further information.

5. METHODOLOGY

Questionnaire and Survey method is used. Though the data was collected for 311 teachers, only 43 teachers who were having at least one paper shown in Google Scholar was considered for analysis. Further, the data was analyzed for the teachers who were having at least one citation shown in Google Scholar. The data from Google Scholar was collected in the month of March and April, 2011.

6. ANALYSIS

The collected data analyzed on following parameters,

6.1. General analysis

There were 43 teachers of commerce and management with at least one publication contribution shown in Google Scholar. The collected data was analyzed on different parameters viz. Gender, Designation and Ranking list based on number of publication of teachers.

6.1.1. Gender-wise Distribution

Figure 6.1.1 shows the gender wise distribution of commerce & management teachers according their paper contribution.

Fig. 6.1.1. Gender-wise distribution of Teacher (Authors) and their Paper Contributions

Figure 6.1.1 clearly demonstrate that the 5 (11.63 percent) female teachers contribute 7 (9.59 percent) papers where as, 38 (88.37 percent) Male teachers contribute 66 (90.41 percent) papers which depicts that the contribution of male teachers was more than the female teachers. The average paper per male teachers was 1.74 whereas for female teachers was 1.40. Overall average paper per author was 1.70.

6.1.2. Designation-wise distribution

The designations were grouped under three categories viz. "A" (Professor & Head, Director, Principal), "B" (Reader, Associate Professor, Vice-Principal) and "C" (Assistant Professor, Senior Lecturer, Lecturer, Teacher). The Table 6.1.2 shows designation-wise distribution of teachers along with contributions of their paper.

Table 6.1.2. Designation-wise Distribution of Teachers & their Paper Contribution

Sr. No.	*Designation Group*	*Number of Teachers (Authors)*	*Number of Paper Contribution*	*Average (Paper/ Authors)*
1	A	16 (37.21%)	34 (46.57%)	2.1
2	B	11 (25.58%)	11 (15.07%)	1
3	C	16 (37.21%)	28 (38.36%)	1.8
	Total	**43 (100%)**	**73 (100%)**	**1.7**

The Table 6.1.2 reveals that near about same number of teachers are in all three groups however, the productivity was varied in nature. The "A" grouped teachers have maximum 34 (46.57 percent) papers followed by 28 (38.36 percent) papers of "C" group teachers. The average paper per group of designation (among data available groups) is highest 2.1 for "A" group followed by 1.8 for "C" group. There was very low contribution of "B" group teachers compare to "A" & "C" group teachers.

6.2 Authorship Analysis

Authorship analysis has done on following parameters,

6.2.1. Authorship Pattern

Authorship pattern means number of authors per paper. Details of Authorship pattern has shown in table 6.2.1

Table 6.2.1. Authorship Pattern

Sr. No.	*Authorship*	*Number of Papers Contributed*	*Cumulative (Papers Contributed)*
1	Single Author	53 (72.60%)	53 (72.60%)
2	Two Authors	12 (16.44%)	65 (89.04%)
3	Three Authors	6 (8.22%)	71 (97.26%)
4	More than Three Authors	2 (2.74%)	73 (100%)
	Total Papers	**73 (100%)**	

The table 6.2.1 explains that the highest 53 (72.60 percent) papers were contributed by single authors (teachers) followed by 12 (16.44 percent) and 6 (8.22 percent) papers written by two & three authors respectively. More than three author's papers were 2 (2.74 percent). It depicts that majority papers were contributed by single author. It shows that there is trend of individual research and publications in commerce and management.

6.2.2. *Degree of Collaboration*

The degree of collaboration of papers may be counted based on the formula by Subramanyam (1983).

$C = Nm / Nm + Ns$

$C = 20 / 20 + 53$

$C = 20 / 73$

$C = 0.2739$

Where, C = Degree of Collaboration in a discipline, Nm = Number of Multi Authored citation, Ns= Number of Single authored citation.

Here, the degree of Collaboration in paper is found 0.2739

When value of C decreases it means the level of collaboration is decreasing. As degree of collaboration is less than 0.5, it means that the trend of research in commerce and management is solo than collaborative research.

6.3. Analysis based on quantitative indicators

The quantitative indicators are papers shown in the questioners by respective teachers and number of papers shown in Google scholar on their name.

6.3.1. Rank list of teachers based on papers shown in the questioners:

Table 6.3.1. Shows rank list of teachers based on papers shown in the questioners.

Sr. No.	*Name of the teachers*	*No. of Papers as filled in questionnaire*	*Rank*
1	Bhatia B.	100	1
2	HM Jha Bidyarthi	95	2
3	Sarwade WK	38	3
4	Shitole GY	32	4
5	Wawge RS	25	5
6	Tapkir MM	25	5
7	Biradar RD	21	6
8	Lokhande MA	21	6
9	Karangutkar SR	20	7
10	Wagh VW	19	8
11	Joshi JV	18	9
12	More VS	17	10
13	Luhar AS	16	11
14	Sadar SB	15	12
15	Thombre KA	14	13
16	Bhola SS	13	14
17	Jagdale PR	13	14
18	Bokad PV	12	15
19	Sondge MN	11	16
20	Ingle MR	11	16
21	Sable RM	10	17
22	Waghmare PD	10	17

23	Sawant BS	9	18
24	Jugale YV	8	19
25	Mahajan SS	8	19
26	Ujagare DV	8	19
27	Deolankar VS	7	20
28	Bhavsar AC	7	20
29	Laturkar VN	7	20
30	Pimplapure V	7	20
31	Dandekar VS	5	21
32	Raut SN	5	21
33	Mane SV	5	21
34	Patil VS	4	22
35	Rayate BB	3	23
36	Murtadak JB	3	23
37	Jadhav SS	2	24
38	Chacharkar DY	1	25
39	Sinha Ritu	1	25
40	Patil DY	1	25
41	Barbole AN	NM	26
42	Kawday DS	NM	26
43	Dande MA	NM	26

NM= Not mentioned

The table 6.3.1 reveals that Prof. B. Bhatia ranked first with 100 papers. HM Jha Bidyarthi (95) and (38) Sarwade W K ranked second and third respectively. Three authors have not filled up the column of number of papers.

6.3.2. Rank list teachers based on papers shown in Google Scholar

Table 6.3.2 shows rank list of commerce & management teachers who were having at least one paper on Google Scholar.

Table 6.3.2. Rank list teachers based on papers shown in Google Scholar

Sr. No.	*Name of the teachers*	*Papers shown in Google Scholar*	*Rank*
1	Wawge RS	6	1
2	Biradar RD	5	2
3	Bhatia B.	3	3
4	Wagh VW	3	3
5	Deolankar VS	3	3
6	HM Jha Bidyarthi	3	3
7	Shitole GY	3	3
8	Jagdale PR	3	3
9	Luhar AS	3	3
10	Joshi JV	2	4
11	Bhola SS	2	4
12	Jugale YV	2	4
13	Mahajan SS	2	4
14	Thombre KA	2	4
15	Sawant BS	2	4
16	Sinha Ritu	2	4
17	Sarwade WK	1	5
18	More VS	1	5
19	Dandekar VS	1	5
20	Rayate BB	1	5
21	Lokhande MA	1	5
22	Sable RM	1	5
23	Sondge MN	1	5
24	Barbole AN	1	5
25	Patil VS	1	5
26	Bhavsar AC	1	5
27	Murtadak JB	1	5
28	Ujagare DV	1	5
29	Laturkar VN	1	5
30	Raut SN	1	5

31	Karangutkar SR	1	5
32	Kawday DS	1	5
33	Bokad PV	1	5
34	Dande MA	1	5
35	Ingle MR	1	5
36	Waghmare PD	1	5
37	Pimplapure V	1	5
38	Chacharkar DY	1	5
39	Jadhav SS	1	5
40	Mane SV	1	5
41	Sadar SB	1	5
42	Tapkir MM	1	5
43	Patil DY	1	5

The above table 6.3.2 illustrates that, Wawge R S, Lecturer from Department of Business Administration & Research, SSGMCE, Shegaon ranked first with 6 publications followed by Biradar R D, Professor & Director, from the School of Commerce & Management Sciences, SRTM University, Nanded with 5 publications. There were seven teachers with 3 publications and another seven teachers with 2 publications. Rests of twenty seven teachers were with single publication. It represents that very less number of publications of the teachers were appeared in Google Scholars.

6.4. Analysis based on qualitative indicators

There are qualitative indicators like citations and impact factor

6.4.1. Rank list of teachers based on citations:

The primary function of citation is to provide a connection between two documents, one which cites and the other which is cited. Citation counting is a technique that determines how many citations a given document, author, journal, etc. has received. Table 6.4.1 gives rank list of teachers based on citations received to their publications.

Table 6.4.1. Rank list of teachers based on citations

Sr. No.	*Name of Teachers*	*Citations shown in Google Scholar*	*Rank*
1	Bhatia B	14	1
2	Sarwade WK	8	2
3	Biradar RD	5	3
4	More VS	4	4
5	Joshi JV	3	5
6	Bhola SS	3	5
7	Wagh VW	2	6
8	Deolankar VS	2	6
9	Dandekar VS	2	6
10	Jugale YV	2	6
11	Mahajan SS	2	6
12	Rayate BB	2	6
13	Lokhande MA	1	7
14	Sable RM	1	7

The table 6.4.1 shows that the rank list of authors based on citations analysis. Dr. Bhatia B, Professor, from K. J. Somaiya Institute of Management Studies & Research, Vidyavihar, Mumbai is ranked first with 14 citations. Dr. Sarwade WK, Assistant Professor, from Department of Commerce, Dr. BAM University, Aurangabad ranked second with 8 citations followed by Dr. Biradar RD, Professor & Director, from School of Commerce & Management Sciences, SRTM University, Nanded and More VS, Director, Mahatma Gandhi Vidya Mandir's Institute of Management & Research, Nashik with 5 and 4 citations respectively. There are two authors having 3 citations, six authors are with 2 citations and two authors with 1 citation.

6.4.2. *Rank list of teachers based on impact factor*

Impact factor is a ratio. In essence this ratio is a measure that an item in asset of citable items receives on an average the citations during a particular period, usually a year after the publication of citable items. Here the overall period has been considered. Table 6.4.2 shows rank list of teachers based on impact factor (Thomson, 2011; Kademani, 2007; Tiwari, 2006).

Table 6.4.2. Rank list of teachers based on impact factor

Sr. No.	*Name of the Teachers*	*Impact Factor = C/P*	*Rank*
1	Sarwade WK	8	1
2	Bhatia B	4.666667	2
3	More VS	4	3
4	Dandekar VS	2	4
5	Rayate BB	2	4
6	Joshi JV	1.5	5
7	Bhola SS	1.5	5
8	Biradar RD	1	6
9	Jugale YV	1	6
10	Mahajan SS	1	6
11	Lokhande MA	1	6
12	Sable RM	1	6
13	Wagh VW	0.666667	7
14	Deolankar VS	0.666667	7

Table 6.4.2 reveals that W.K. Sarwade ranked first with impact factor 8 where as B. Bahtia and V S More ranked second and third with impact factor 4.66 and 4 respectively.

6.5. Analysis based on Composite indicators:

There are various Composite indicators such as h-index, g-index, p-index etc.

6.5.1. *h – index*

The h – index is an index that attempts to measure both the productivity and impact of the published work of scientist or scholars. The h – index is based on the set of the scientists most cited papers and the number of citations that they have received in other peoples publications. The h – index of teachers is shown in the table 6.3.2 (Kulkarni, 2011).

Table 6.5.1. h – index

Sr. No.	*Name of the teachers*	*h-index*	*Rank*
1	Bhatia B.	2	1
2	Biradar RD	2	1
3	Sarwade WK	1	2
4	Lokhande MA	1	2
5	Joshi JV	1	2
6	Wagh VW	1	2
7	Deolankar VS	1	2
8	Dandekar VS	1	2
9	Jugale YV	1	2
10	Mahajan SS	1	2
11	Bhola SS	1	2
12	Sable RM	1	2
13	Rayate BB	1	2
14	More VS	1	2

The above table 6.5.2 depict the rank list of teachers based on h – index. Dr. Bhatia B, Professor, from K. J. Somaiya Institute of Management Studies & Research, Vidyavihar, Mumbai and Dr. Biradar RD, Professor & Director, from School of Commerce & Management Sciences, SRTM University, Nanded have maximum 2 h – index and ranked first. Rest of 12 authors has 1 h – index with second rank.

6.5.2. *g-index*

g-index given a set of articles ranked in decreasing order of the number of citations that they received, the g-index is the (unique) largest number such that the top g articles received on average at least g citations (Kulkarni, 2011).

Table 6.5.2. g – index

Sr. No	*Name of the teachers*	*g-index*	*Rank*
1	Bhatia B.	3	1
3	Biradar RD	2	2
2	Sarwade WK	1	3
4	More VS	1	3
5	Bhola SS	1	3
6	Joshi JV	1	3
7	Dandekar VS	1	3
8	Rayate BB	1	3
9	Mahajan SS	1	3
10	Jugale YV	1	3
11	Wagh VW	1	3
12	Deolankar VS	1	3
13	Lokhande MA	1	3
14	Sable RM	1	3

Table 6.5.2 depicts rank list of teachers by g-index. In the present case the g-index gave same results as the h-index.

6.5.3. p-index

Gangan Pratap of NISCAIR suggested p-index which is used for ranking of institutions as well as the authors. It can be calculated by $(C^2/P)^{1/3}$. where P stands for papers and C for citations.

Table 6.5.3. g – index

Sr. No	*Name of the teachers*	*P-index*	*Rank*
1	Bhatia B.	4.03	1
2	Sarwade WK	4	2
3	More VS	2.52	3
4	Biradar RD	1.71	4
5	Bhola SS	1.65	5

6	Joshi JV	1.65	6
7	Dandekar VS	1.59	7
8	Rayate BB	1.59	7
9	Mahajan SS	1.26	8
10	Jugale YV	1.26	8
11	Wagh VW	1.1	9
12	Deolankar VS	1.1	9
13	Lokhande MA	1	10
14	Sable RM	1	10

Table 6.5.3 reveals that Bhatia B ranked first with 4.03 as his p-index followed by Sarwade W K with 4 and More V S with 2.52 as their p-index.

6.5.4. Average of composite indicators

For having single rank list based composite indicators average value of h-index, g- index and p-index was calculated and rank list was prepared accordingly.

Table 6.5.4. Rank list of teachers based on average value of composite indicators

Sr. No	*Name of the Teachers*	*h-index*	*g-index*	*p-index*	*Average*	*Rank*
1	Bhatia B.	2	3	4.03	3.01	1
2	Sarwade WK	1	1	4	2	2
3	Biradar RD	2	2	1.71	1.9	3
4	More VS	1	1	2.52	1.51	4
5	Bhola SS	1	1	1.65	1.22	5
6	Joshi JV	1	1	1.65	1.22	5
7	Dandekar VS	1	1	1.59	1.2	6
8	Rayate BB	1	1	1.59	1.2	6
9	Mahajan SS	1	1	1.26	1.09	7
10	Jugale YV	1	1	1.26	1.09	7
11	Wagh VW	1	1	1.1	1.03	8
12	Deolankar VS	1	1	1.1	1.03	8
13	Lokhande MA	1	1	1	1	9
14	Sable RM	1	1	1	1	9

The Table 6.5.4 notifies that Bhatia ranked first with 3.01 followed by W K Sarwade (2) and R D Biradar (1.9) respectively.

6.6. Conclusions

The average paper per male teachers was 1.74 whereas for female teachers was 1.40. Overall average paper per author was 1.70.

Out of 311 Commerce and Management teachers only 43 teachers' papers were shown in the Google scholar. It means 13.82% could find place on scholarly platform. In that too only 14 (4.5%) teachers had at least one citation to their paper.

Professors and equivalent position teachers have maximum 34 (46.57 percent) papers followed by 28 (38.36 %) papers by Assistant professors and equivalent position. Associate professor and equivalent position had little contribution.

The highest 53 (72.60%) papers were contributed by single authors (teachers) followed by 12 (16.44%) and 6 (8.22%) papers written by three authors. The degree of Collaboration in paper is found 0.2739. It shows that there is trend of individual research and publications in commerce and management.

By quantitative indicators analysis Prof. B. Bhatia, HM Jha Bidyarthi, W K, Sarwade, R S Wawge, R D Biradar, V S More found most productive teachers. Where as in qualitative indicators few teachers disappeared as there were no citations to there publications.

The analysis by composite indicators shows that Dr. B Bhatia, Professor, from K. J. Somaiya Institute of Management Studies & Research, Vidyavihar, Mumbai is ranked first followed by Dr. W K Sarwade, Assistant Professor, from Department of Commerce, Dr. BAM University, Aurangabad ranked second and Dr. R D Biradar, Professor & Director, from School of Commerce & Management Sciences, SRTM University, Nanded ranked third. Dr.V S More, Director, Mahatma Gandhi Vidya Mandir's Institute of Management & Research, Nashik also was in good position in the overall ranking.

(**Acknowledgement:** We are grateful to Professor Dr. S. B. Nimse, Hon'ble V.C. for his constant encouragement in this research project.)

(This paper is an outcome of UGC sanctioned MRP 2009-11 on "Research and Publication Contribution of Teachers in Commerce & Management: A Bibliometric Study".)

REFERENCES

- Adhe, G. D. (2008). *Productivity Patterns of Scientists in Marathawada: A Bibliometric Study.* Unpublished Doctoral Thesis, Dr. Babasaheb Ambedkar Marathawada University, Aurangabad.
- Biradar, R D, Kulkarni, J N and Sarsare, S M, (2010) Doctoral Research in Commerce - A Bibliometric Analysis, *Journal of Commerce & Management Thought,* I(2), Pp. 140-154.
- Gupta, B M (2011) Ranking of Indian institutions in agriculture & allied sciences for their research output during 1999-2008 Annals of Library & information Studies, 58(3), pp.63-70
- Harzng website (2010). http://www.hazng.com/pophelp/metrcs.htm accessed on 28 August 2010.
- Kademani, B.S. et al. (2007). Scientometric profile and publication productivity of the radiochemistry division at Bhabha atomic research centre. *SRELS Journal of Information Management,* 44(2), 99-124.
- Keshava and et al., (2009), h-index: A Review of Literature, *Pearl,* 3(2), Pp. 39-44.
- Kulkarni, J N (2011) *Mapping CALIBER, NACLIN and IASLIC proceedings; A Scientometric study,* Unpublished Doctoral Thesis, Dr. Babasaheb Ambedkar Marathwada University, Aurangabad.
- Kumar B. & Dabas, D.S. (2008). Google scholar: An Internet search service for academic content. *University News,* 46(08), 13-17.

- Martell, Charles (2009). A Citation analysis of College & Research Libraries comparing Yahoo, Google, Google Scholar, and ISI web of knowledge with implications for promotion and tenure, *College and Research Libraries*, 70(5), 460-472.
- Pratap, Gangan (2010) Research assessment using bibliometrics indicators (unpublished NISCAIR training notes)
- Pratap, Gangan (2010) Thermo dynamical approach to bibliometrics sequences (unpublished NISCAIR training notes)
- Subramanyam, K (1983), Bibliometric Studies of Research Collaboration: A Review, *Journal of Information Science*, 6(1), Pp. 33-38.
- Thomson Reuters, (2011) *http://thomsonreuters.com/content/press_room/science/448197* accessed on March, 2011.
- Tiwari, A. (2006). *Bibliometrics Informetrics, and Scientometrics: Opening new vistas of information science*. Jaipur: RBSA publishers.

UNIT 7

INFORMATION LITERACY

22

Information Literacy: An Overview

Jadhav Vandana S.

Asst. Professor, Vidyadhan Mahavidyalay, CIDCO, Aurangabad

Dr. Khaparde Vaishali S.

Associate Professor & Head, Dept. of Dept.of Lib & I Sc, Dr. Babasaheb Ambedkar Marathwada University, Aurangabad (MS), India.

Shelke Santosh M.

Librarian, Shri Bhagawan Homoeopathic Medical College, N-6, CIDCO, Aurangabad

ABSTRACT

Information Literacy (IL) has become a crucial issue today for development and progress. Even at the individual level to become an independent learner it is essential to achieve a high level of IL programs are under way across the globe. IL is the vital process in modern changing world. Information Technology (IT) is taking a new shape day by day. People should enable to interpret and make informed choice as user of information sources. IL makes the people capable to recognize when information is needed and how to locate, evaluate, and effectively of the needed information. IL is increasing important in the present context of the information explosion and concomitant uncertainties about its authenticity, validity, and reliability. For student, regardless of their discipline, IL skills enable them to master content and give them to confidence to proceed with investigation be self reliant and have a sense of being in control of their learning.

Keywords: Information Literacy, Information Technology. Visual literacy, Media literacy, Computer literacy, Digital literacy, Network literacy, Library literacy

INTRODUCTION

In 1974, Paul Zarkowski, president of the Information Industry Association, introduced the concept of "Information Literacy" in a proposal submitted to the National Commission on Libraries and information science (NCLIS). The proposal recommended that a national program be established to achive universal information literacy within the next decade. According to Zurkowski, "People trained in the application of information resources to their work can be called information literates. They have learned techniques and skills for utilizing the wide rang of information tools as well as primary source in modeling information solution to their problems".

DEFINITION

According to American Library Association's President Committee on Information Literacy, "To be Information Literate Person must be able to recognize when information is need and have the ability to locate, evaluate, and use effectively the needed information."

"Information Literacy knows when and why you need information, where to find it, and how to evaluate, use and communicate it in an ethical manner". (Chartered Institute of Library and Information Professionals.)

"The ability to recognize a need for information, find, evaluate and use that information in whatever format (print index, online database, Internet)."

www.dced.fov.be.ca/irp/it 1112/apf.html

OBJECTIVES OF INFORMATION LITERACY

Basic objectives of IL are as follow;

- To teach the students, user and people how to find information;
- How to prepared it for lifelong learning;
- To enable the learner to master the contents and extend their investigation;
- To become self directed a person or the people;
- To assume ability of greater control over their own learning or situation or problems by the people.

IMPORTANCE OF INFORMATION LITERACY

Importance of IL can be summed up by Boundy as "Information Literacy is a prerequisite for participative citizenship, social inclusion, the creation of new knowledge, personal empowerment and learning for life". We see that importance of IL as follows;

- IL is important to understand the difficult questions of ownership of information and copyright;
- Students should learn to respect author's rights;
- To be an independent lifelong learner it is essential to achieve a high level of IL;
- IL is to help close the gap between the information poor the information rich;
- IL is required to have a critical thinking approach, that would lead to economic and cultural progress of nation;
- A sheer abundance of information in electronic format has made IL increasingly important.

NEED FOR INFORMATION LITERACY

- The significant changes in the information environment;

- Information available through libraries by any sources free from geographical boundaries;
- Authenticity, validity and reliability and needs valid consideration of Information;
- It is worth special mention, abundance of information will not create informed citizenry;
- Skill for handling electronic sources of information in new digital environment.

TYPES OF INFORMATION LITERACY

1. Visual literacy

When we look at visual information such as photographs, illustrations, or computer graphics, we rely on our previous perceptions of the world to make sense of the visual image. Braden and Hortin define the visual literacy as "to understand and use images, including to think, learn and express own self in terms of images"

It is divided into three contracts;

1.1 Visual Learning

2.2 Visual Thinking

3.3 Visual communication.

2. Media literacy

Representative of the media literacy movement met at the national leadership conference on Media Literacy and agreed to define Media Literacy as an ability of a citizen to "access, analyze and produce information for specific outcomes"

Those who advocate media literacy recognize the influence television, motion picture, radio, recorded music, news-papers and magazines have on us daily.

3. Computer literacy

Computer Literacy is generally thought of familiarity

with the personnel computer and the ability to create and manipulate documents and data via word processing, spreadsheets, databases and other software tools. Computer literacy is seen as an integral part of education and not as separate entity.

The Computer Science and Telecommunication Board of National Council are defining computer Literacy as fluency with Information Technology (FIT ness) in the higher education arena.

4. Digital literacy

Digital Literacy considers the broad range of resources that are importance of looking at each of these resources with a critical eye. Emphasis is placed on the format of the information presented and a special consideration that each type of resources presents.

5. Network literacy

It closely related to computer literacy it's called "Network Literacy" a term that is still evolving. To locate, access, and use information in a networked environment such as the WWW, users must be network literate that called network literacy.

6. Library literacy

To educate the users about the Library facilities and services, how to access information, to evaluate it this education is provided by the library to the users that means Library Literacy.

CHALLENGES IN INFORMATION LITERACY

So many challenges are facing by Information Literacy like as follow;

Political Hurdles

The basic challenges are created by government,

bureaucrats and politicians of the country. They don't encourage any Programme that may lead to information literacy.

Inadequacy of Technological Infrastructure and IT

As digital Literacy and network literacy are also encapsulated in information literacy on of the big challenges to IL is the lack of technological infrastructure. In India there are numerous institutions with poor technological infrastructure.

Traditional System of Education

So many developing countries that still follow a traditional-education system that is based on memorizing instructor's notes do not encourage student's initiative and critical thinking.

Low Literacy Rate

In developing countries the literacy rate are vary low. According to 2001 census fingers, in India the literacy rate was 65.38%.

Lack of Finance & Human Resources

The staff in the libraries and teachers in schools and collages are often inadequate in the developing countries funds for even some basic activities like printing a library manual for students awareness is often inadequate by that information literacy programmes can not carried by the institutions.

Lack of Libraries

Lack of libraries especially school libraries, which are the basis of information literacy, are a big challenge for develop information literacy programmes. In many developing countries lack of school libraries is a common phenomenon.

ROLE OF INDIAN GOVERNMENT IN INFORMATION LITERACY

To see the importance of IL and low rate of I L Indian government concluded the IL Programmes are as follows;

Sr. No.	*IL Programmes*	*Launched Date/Year*
1	Sarva Shiksha Abhiyan (SSA)	2001-2010
2	District Primary Education Programme (DPEP)	1994
3	National Literacy Mission	1988
4	TARA Akshar	2005-06
5	Computer-based Functional Literacy (CBFL)	-
6	Portal of Government of India	-

This programmes were taken by India for develop Information Literacy skills in learners, to become independent leaders to make the common people a part of IT revolution, to help librarian to develop, assess and improve their information literacy programmes.

CONCLUSION

The definition, objectives, needs, types and importance of Information Literacy concluded that, Information Literacy is a key component in the information age and democracy and information a strategic resource that cannot be fully exploited without information literate citizenry. About the challenges of information literacy, it is not possible for any individual library to overcome these challenges single-handedly. For overcome from these challenges Indian Government conducted some programmes like; SSA, DPEP, PEP, National Library Mission, TARA Akshar, CBFL, Portal of Government of India.

REFERENCES

American Library Association, (1989). President Committee on Information Literacy. (Final Report) Retrieve on Aug -2010 from *http://*

www.ala.org/ala/acrl/asrl standards/informationliteracycompetacy.htm

American Library Association, (2003). Introduction to Information Literacy. Retrieved on Aug-2010 from *http://www.ala.org/ala/acrl/acrissues/acrlnfolit/ infolitoverview /intotoinfolit/introinfolit. html*

Dennis, N. (2001). Using inquiry methods to foster information literacy partnerships. *Reference Service Review*, 29,122-132.

Farmer, L S.J. (2003). Facilitating faculty incorporation of information literacy skills into the curriculum through the use of online instruction. *Reference Service Review*, 31,307-312.

Gedam, P.G. and Agashe, A. T. (2009). Information Literacy Competencies and Programmes in India.

Kavulya, J. M. (2003). Challenges facing information literacy efforts in Kenya: a case study of selected university libraries in Kenya. *Library Management*, 24,216-222.

Rajaram, S. (2006). Information Literacy Gap: Challenges in bridging the divide. *International convention CALIBER, 4,* (pp-193-198).

Vishala, B. K. and Bhandli, M. K. (2006). Information Literacy teaching in higher education environment. *International Convention CALIBER,* 4, (pp-201-208).

23

Information Literacy the Role of Library in UNISWA

Thiyam Satyabati Devi
Assistant Librarian Cataloguing Head,
University of Swaziland, Swaziland.

ABSTRACT

The Library has a leadership role in the development of information literate, the effective embedding of information literacy programmes within the mainstream of the learning process requires close co-operation between all stakeholders. There is still much to be done to promote integrated information literacy in higher education. Teamwork between teachers and libraries is well developed in some countries but many are only just beginning to realize what libraries can do for them. The Faculty of humanities in UNISWA has a separate department for Academic communication skill which aims at upgrading the academic communication skills of students. This paper will give an overview of the role played by the library in teaching information literacy.

Keywords: UNISWA, Information literacy, Vision, Mission statement, ACS, Library.

0. INTRODUCTION

The University of Swaziland (UNISWA) has been for a long time the only university in Swaziland comprising of three campuses situated in Mbabane, Luyengo and Kwaluseni. It was established in 1982 by an Act of Parliament with a mandate to teach, conduct research and carry out community service. The three campuses offer Master's degrees, Bachelor's degrees, Diplomas and Certificate programmed with English as medium of instruction. To cater mainly for employed learners, the institution offers a limited number of programmed through distance education. It is the centre of academic and intellectual excellence. It has the responsibility of preserving and transmitting the nation's cultural heritage while at the same time contributing to the generation of new knowledge through research. The university provides programmed and courses that are relevant to the human resources needs of the country that are in line with regional and global trends. The university has embarked on a programmed to all the first year students to ensure a smooth introduction of information literacy.

1. VISION AND MISSION OF THE UNIVERSITY

The vision of the University is Leadership through Excellence in Education.

The mission of the University of Swaziland is to achieve Excellence in teaching and learning, research and training, community service, provision of opportunities for consultancy, professional leadership and enterprise development in the contemporary context. The mission shall be achieved through:

- Providing education opportunities at undergraduate and postgraduate levels;
- Establishing new academic programmed designed to meet the emerging needs of society;

- Conducting a regular review of the academic programmed to make them demand-driven to stakeholders;
- Creating continuing education opportunities for the inculcation of life-long learning;
- Generating, disseminating and preserving knowledge through research, stakeholders' participation and development of an institutional repository;
- Teaching that encourages participation of students in entrepreneurship endeavors;
- Accounting to stakeholders that fosters efficient utilization of resources;
- Coordinating and monitoring performance among all employees and periodic evaluation and review of activities; and
- Providing an excellent working and learning environment for staff and students.

2. MISSION AND OBJECTIVES OF THE UNISWA LIBRARY

2.1. Mission

The Mission of UNISWA Library is to provide efficient service and access to quality academic information resources to support the instructional, Learning, Research and Administrative functions of the University. In this regard, the library provides both print and electronic resources.

2.2. Objectives

- To computerize library operations and services to optimize information access through local, regional and internet connectivity.
- To develop library infrastructure in the three campuses in order to provide equitable services.

- To develop a responsive collection that is sufficiently comprehensive and representative of the universe of knowledge and ideas to keep pace with the changing need of users.
- To select and acquire relevant and current documents, irrespective of format, to support the teaching learning and research needs of the users.
- To reduce the time lag between the ordering of resources and their accessibility.
- To create and maintain up-to date and user-friendly information retrieval tools to facilitate access to information sources.
- To develop and maintain efficient and effective services to meet user needs.
- To equip users with necessary skills which will enable them to fully exploit and utilize effectively the full range of information resources.
- To foster library research skills for life-long independent learning.
- To collaborate and cooperate with other information centres in order to provide access to a wide range of information sources.
- To develop a responsive management system to ensure efficient and effective delivery of library and information services.
- To promote library staff development through education and training.
- To build and maintain a stable team of competent, motivated and dedicated library personnel.
- To install and maintain reliable library environment monitoring systems to promote document preservation.
- To contribute in the development of libraries in schools

by equipping student teachers with the necessary skills for establishing schools libraries.

3. INFORMATION LITERACY:

Information literacy is a set of abilities requiring individuals to recognize when information is needed and have the ability to locate, evaluate, and use effectively the needed information. It is a prerequisite for lifelong learning. Information literate graduates of the University of Swaziland will be able to:

- Recognise the need for information .
- Determine the extent of information needed .
- Access information efficiently.
- Critically evaluate information and its sources.
- Classify, store, manipulate and redraft information collected or generated.
- Incorporate selected information into their knowledge base.
- Use information effectively to learn, create new knowledge, solve problems and make decisions.
- Understand economic, legal, social and cultural issues in the use of information.
- Access and use information ethically and legally.
- Use information and knowledge for participative citizenship and social responsibility.
- Experience information literacy as part of independent learning and lifelong learning.

4. WHO TEACHES INFORMATION LITERACY?

The groups that coordinate and conduct the activities that constitute the Information literacy program are the professional staffs of the library.

- Designs, coordinates, teaches and assesses information

literacy programs for the first-year entrants.

- Provide special training to post graduates and Law students.
- Provides opportunity for all students to achieve the competencies outlined by the program.
- Coordinates with the staff to identify the information literacy needs of each discipline.
- Offer students a variety of ways to achieve the competencies in information literacy.
- Coordinates orientations, trainings, workshops & seminars for the staff. .
- Attends visitors, scholars and others who visited the library.

5. WHO PROVIDES DIRECTION FOR THIS PROGRAM?

The department of Academic Communication Skill and the library together provide the direction for information literacy in the University of Swaziland. They aim at upgrading the academic communication skills of students by offering English for Academic purposes, as a means of enabling students to acquire the requisite English proficiency to cope with the demands of University studies. The programmed includes the teaching of study skills, listening, writing and reading for academic purposes, remedial grammar and the writing of research papers and project reports. The main objectives are to:

- Provide instruction in English for Academic Purposes to all students of the University.
- Inculcate productive, receptive and study skills which are appropriate and adequate for students' learning activities in their various disciplines.
- Provide individualized attention to students through Computer assisted language learning (CALL) programmed offered through the self access centre.

- Carry out research in Academic communication skills and related fields.
- Teaching library skill to the entire 1st year entrant.

6. ROLE OF LIBRARY IN INFORMATION LITERACY

- The development of information literacy skills and knowledge throughout the University community is an essential element of the Library's mission.
- The responsibility for supporting the development of information literacy knowledge and skills is a partnership between the Library and academic and other University staff.
- The Library has particular expertise to support staff and students in the development of their own information literacy.
- Information literacy is an essential priority for the Library, and Library staff.
- Develops, promotes and delivers information literacy training and support to the academic and student communities.
- Works with academic staff to integrate information literacy objectives into course curriculum and unit outlines and content
- Works with a team to evaluate the quality and effectiveness of the information literacy programmes of the University.

7. INFORMATION LITERACY THE NEED

Information literacy forms the basis for lifelong learning. It is common to all disciplines to all learning environments and to all level of education and it is required because of proliferating information access and resources. Individuals are faced with diverse, abundant information choices in their studies, in the workplace, and in their lives.

Increasingly, information comes unfiltered. This raises questions about authenticity, validity, and reliability. In addition, information is available through multiple media, including graphical, aural, and textual. These pose special challenges in evaluating, understanding and using information in an ethical and legal manner. The uncertain quality and expanding quantity of information also pose large challenges for society. Sheer abundance of information and technology will not in itself create more informed citizens without a complementary understanding and capacity to use information effectively. To address the information literacy needs and awareness we offer the following:

- New faculty orientation to introduce the library's information literacy program.
- Workshops for all faculties to introduce new library materials and services.
- Consultations with other teaching faculty to develop models of collaborative instruction where information literacy skills can be built into the curriculum.
- Promote currently existing library services and expertise to facilitate the research process.
- Participate as facilitators outlining integration of information literacy skills in course material.

8. CURRENT EXPERIENCE

Information literacy is not just about learning facts but about learning to learn, a skill that lasts a lifetime. It is not simply library instruction; rather, it is preparing students to learn from a variety of resources. It comes through a mixture of lectures, hands-on assignments, written research projects using technical skills, and critical thinking abilities in the use of print, electronic, and oral information resources. A solid understanding of information needs and uses results from a broad, continuing, and repetitive program throughout. Further, it requires sustained cooperation among all on campus if it is to become a part of the learning process across the curriculum. Because research indicates that the professor plays a large role in determining how students find and use information, any information literacy effort must actively involve faculty. The development of information literacy skills is a collaborative effort of the librarian and the academic staff of the library. The module learning outcomes within many programmes cover aspects of the above in different ways and often implicitly. Librarians are deeply involved in training students in the use of the resources available, how to find and evaluate information and also cover issues of ethics, particularly relating to copyright, referencing and plagiarism. A student who has developed the essential information literacy skills is able to:

- Determine the nature and extent of the information needed.
- Use library to acquire needed information effectively and efficiently.
- Evaluate information and its sources critically.
- Incorporate selected information into one's knowledge base.
- Use information effectively to accomplish a specific purpose.
- Understand the economic, legal, and social issues surrounding the use of information, and access and use information ethically and legally.
- Classify, store, manipulate and redraft information collected or generated.
- Recognize information literacy as a prerequisite for lifelong learning.

9. CONCLUSION

When the students have not grasped the value of Information literacy it is a significant concern so the library should aims to enhance student learning and encourage a critical, analytical and evaluative approach to information resources by promoting information literacy as a graduate attribute. Similarly educationalist knowledge and teaching processes play an important role in assisting the students to develop these responsibilities and skills. Changes are essential to improve the Information literacy skills and understanding of the students. Then only we will find students more capable independent learners, able to use a varied range of resources in assignments with less dependence on recommended texts, and with a good understanding of the importance of referencing and of avoiding plagiarism.

10. REFERENCES

1. Bundy, A, ed. 2004, Australian and New Zealand Information Literacy Framework: principles, standards and practice, Australian and New Zealand Institute for Information Literacy, retrieved from *http://www.anziil.org/resources.*
2. *Hollister Christophe.* Bringing information literacy to career services Reference Services Review 2005 **Vol.** 33 **No.** 1 104-111pp retrieved from *http://oberon.emeraldinsight.com.*
3. *Kaisa Sinikara, Leena Järveläinen* Information literacy development in Finland retrieved from *http://juno.emeraldinsight.com*
4. Nagarajan N. Progress of Women's Literacy in India: Challenges for 21st Century Second Asia Regional Literacy Forum-Innovation and Professionalization in Adult Literacy: A Focus on Diversity, New Delhi, India, February 9-13, 1998.retrieve from *http://www.literacyonline.org/products/ili/webdocs/nagara.html*
5. Nayda, Robyn and Rankin, Elaine. Information literacy skill development and life long learning: exploring nursing students' and academics' understanding [online]. Australian Journal of advances nursing Vol. 26, No. 2 Dec, 2008.
6. University of Swaziland website: http://www.uniswa.sz.

24

Information Literacy in Dr. Babasaheb Ambedkar Marathwada University (BAMU), Aurangabad

Dr. Golwal Madansing D.
Librarian, Nya. Tatyasaheb Athalye Arts,
Yed.S.R. Sapre Commerce & Vid.D.
Pitre Science CollegeDeorukh - 415804 Ratnagiri.

Dr. A. A. Vaishnav
Retd. Professor & Head, Department of Library & Information Science Dr. Babasaheb Ambedkar Marathwada University,Aurangabad - 431003

Dr. S. S. Sonwane
Assistant Professor, Department of Library & Information Science Dr. Babasaheb Ambedkar Marathwada University,Aurangabad - 431003

ABSTRACT

In 21st century, Information Literacy [IL] has become a crucial issue for the political, economic, social & cultural development in all countries. IL is global phenomenon today. The objective of the present paper is to highlight the concept of Literacy, Information Literacy, E-Information Literacy and to specify objectives, hypothesis, limitations, methodology, analysis and findings of the study.

Keywords: Literacy, Information Literacy, E-Information Literacy, BAMU

1. INTRODUCTION

The greatest challenge for society in the 21st century is to keep pace with the knowledge and technological expertise necessary for finding, applying and evaluating information. It is acknowledged that we live in an information-rich society where the amount of information in the world is presently doubling every three years. Therefore it is necessity of 21st century to include information literacy (IL) in education.

The information society calls for all people to become information literate which means that they should not only be able to recognize when information is needed but also be able to identify, locate, evaluate and use effectively information needed for decision making or fulfilling different goals. IL is increasingly important in the present context of the information explosion and related uncertainties about its authenticity, validity, and reliability.

In 21st century, IL has become a crucial issue for the political, economic, social & cultural development in all countries. IL is global phenomenon today. It is information gap that divides the nations & the citizens of a nation into rich & poor. It is information literacy that helps in closing this gap.

2. DEFINITIONAL ANALYSIS

1. Information : Information is data that has given shape. It may be considered as processed data. Thus, information is data plus the meaning, which has to be a result of human action (Seetharama, 1999).

2. Literacy : Literacy involves the ability to use

language in its written form: a literate person is able to read, write and understand his or her native language and expresses a simple thought in writing (*Bawden, 2001*).

3. Information Literacy : Information Literacy is an understanding and set of abilities requiring individuals to recognize when information is needed, have the ability to locate, evaluate, use effectively the needed information and create information within cultural and social context (ACRL,2004; ALA, 1989).

4. E-Information Literacy : Electronic information literacy refers to literacy activities (such as reading, writing, and research) that are delivered, supported, accessed, or assessed through computers or other electronic means rather than paper (Martin & Rader, 2003).

5. BAMU : Marathwada University established in August 1958 was renamed in 1994 as Dr. Babasaheb Ambedkar Marathwada University (BAMU) is located at Aurangabad. The jurisdiction of BAMU is Aurangabad, Jalna, Beed & Osmanbad districts.

3. E-INFORMATION LITERACY

The term "information literacy" was first introduced in 1974 by Zurkowski, in a submission to the US National Commission on Libraries and Information Science, to identify people trained in the application of information resources to their work (Joint, 2005; Singh, 2008; Faust, 2001).

The idea of information literacy, which emerged with the advent of information technologies in the early 1970s, has grown, taken shape and strengthened to become recognized as the critical literacy for the 21st century. He recognized that 'information literates' would be better able to exploit information resources (Bruce, 2002).

E-Literacy and Information Literacy are different but mutually compatible concepts with validity within specific contexts. Most librarians work within hybrid library environments & may feel that e-Literacy is a single medium concept and as a practical tool for promoting the use of their mixed medium information service it is less useful than IL (Joint, 2005).

Electronic information literacy refers to literacy activities (such as reading, writing, and research) that are delivered, supported, accessed, or assessed through computers or other electronic means rather than paper ; is awareness, skills, understandings and reflective-evaluative approaches that are necessary for an individual to operate comfortably in an information rich and IT-supported environment (Martin and Radar, 2003); ability to search retrieves, organize, employ, and evaluate information derived from electronic information resources (Fortier, 1998).

4. AIMS & OBJECTIVES

To study the extent of Information Literacy in PG & Research Students of the Science Departments in BAMU, with special emphasis on the E-Information Literacy.

5. HYPOTHESIS

Awareness of use of Internet is prominent amongst the PG & Research Students in Dr. Babasaheb Ambedkar Marathwada University, Aurangabad.

6. SCOPE & LIMITATION

The present study is limited to PG as well as Research students of Science faculty in Dr. Babasaheb Ambedkar Marathwada University, Aurangabad. The main focus of this study is to identify the needs & requirements of users in general & to know e-resources. While teachers of all faculties including science faculty, PG & Research students of other faculties have been excluded from the present study.

7. METHODOLOGY

Present study has used survey method. This method plays a significant role in research as can be seen from the statement. "The survey method is one of the most effective and sensitive instruments of research survey research can produce much needed knowledge" (Kasyap, 1969).

7.1. Data collection

To know the needs of students covered, a structured questionnaire was designed and factual questions, opinion questions were asked. The researcher has distributed 360 questionnaires to PG & research Scholars, 312 questionnaires duly filled returned by students i.e. the response rate was 86.66%.

8. DATA ANALYSIS & FINDINGS

The data collected was analyzed & findings were noted as follows:

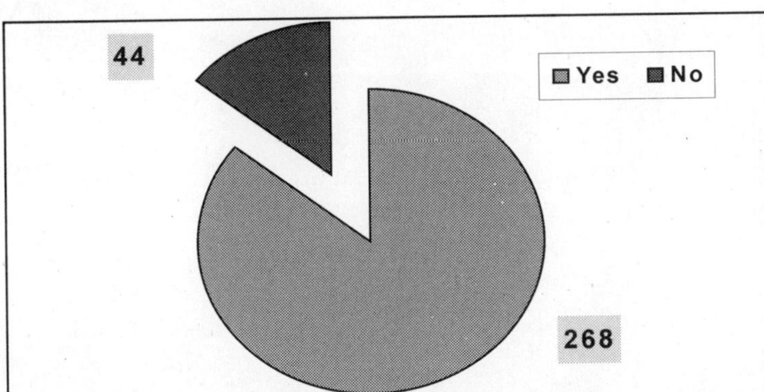

Fig. 8.1. Fluency of Using Computer

1. It was found that that majority i.e. 85.90% respondents are fluent in use of computer.

Table 8.1. Frequency of Using Computer

Frequency	*No. of Users*
Daily	195
Once in a week	68
Once in a month	41
Once in a while	8
Total	**312**

2. It can be noted from table 8.1 that majority 62.50% respondents using computer daily, while 37.50% respondents were using computer rarely i.e. either weekly, once in a month or once in a while.

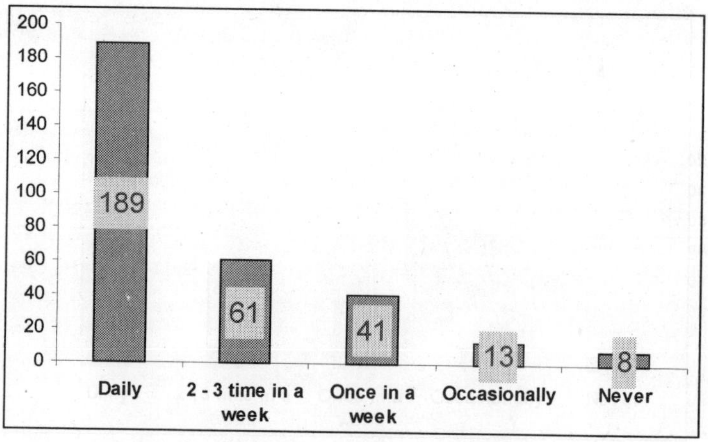

Fig. 8.2. Frequency of using Internet

3. It can be revealed from figure 8.1 that majority 60.58% respondents using internet daily, while 39.42% respondents were using internet rarely i.e. either 2 – 3 time or once in week or occasionally. This proves the hypothesis "**Awareness of Internet use is prominent**" (Hypothesis No.1).

Table 8.2. Time Spent on Internet

Time Spent	*No. of Users*
Less than 1 hour	12
2 - 4 hours	28
5 - 6 hours	28
7 - 9 hours	28
More than 10	28
Total	**312**

4. It can be noted from Table 8.2 that majority 50.32% respondents spend 7 - 9 hours a week on Internet, while 49.68% respondents were spent less than 1 hour, 2 - 4 hours, 5 - 6 hours & more than 10 hours in a week respectively. This proves the hypothesis "**Awareness of Internet use is prominent**" (Hypothesis No.1).

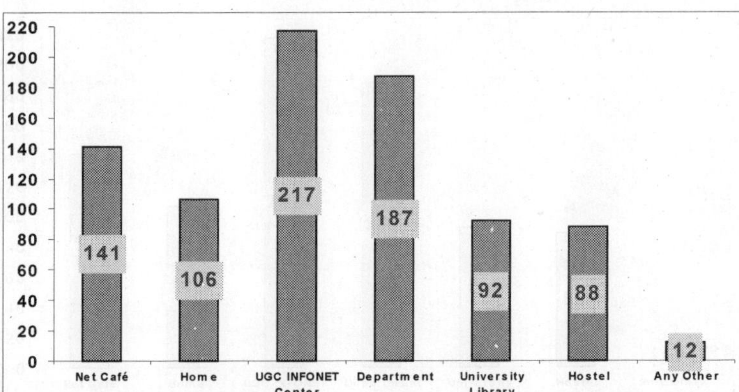

Fig. 8.3. Place of Accessing Internet

5. In this question users were allowed to select more than one option therefore the percentage is more than 100%. It can be revealed from figure 8.2 that majority i.e. 69.55% & 59.94% respondents accessing internet at UGC INFONET Center & Department respectively.

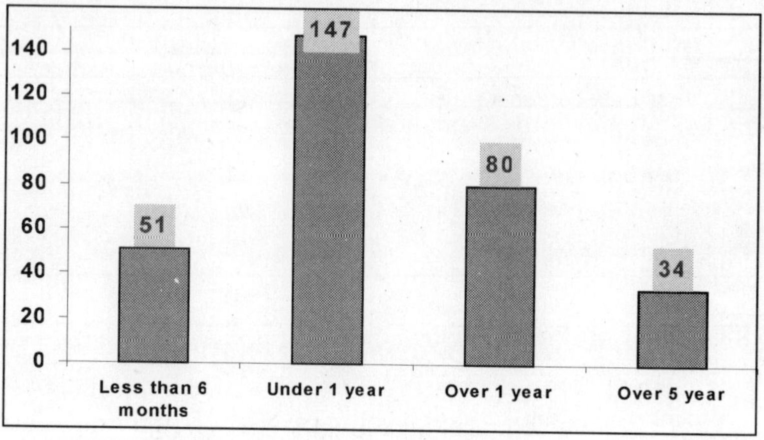

Fig. 8.4. Experience of Internet Use

6. It can be revealed from figure 8.3 that majority 47.12% students having under 1 year experience, while 23.72% students having over 1 year experience of using Internet.

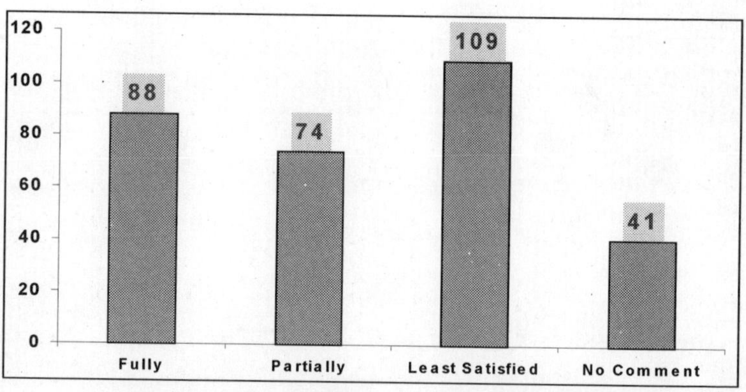

Fig. 8.5. Satisfaction level of using Internet

7. It can be noted from figure 8.4 that majority i.e. 34.94% students were least satisfied, while 28.21% students were fully satisfied. Remaining 23.71% students partially & 13.14% students says no comment.

Table 8.3. Internet Skills of Users

Internet Skills	*No. of Users*
Excellent	126
Very Good	74
Good	53
Fair	44
Poor	15

8. It can be noted from Table 8.3 that 40.38% & 23.72% students were having Excellent & Very Good Internet skills respectively. This proves the hypothesis "**Awareness of Internet use is prominent**" (Hypothesis No.1).

Table 8.4. Purpose of Browsing Internet

Purpose	*No. of Users*
E-mail	279
E-resources	191
OPAC	146

9. It is observed from Table 8.4 that 89.42% & 61.22% students browsing internet for the purpose of E-mail & E-resources respectively. This proves the hypothesis "**Awareness of Internet use is prominent**" (Hypothesis No.1).

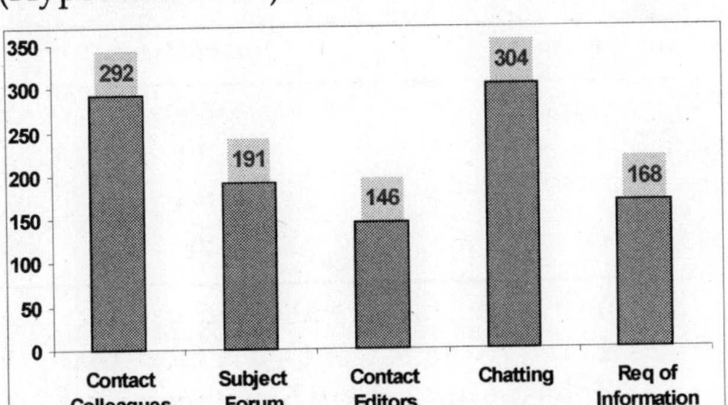

Fig. 8.6. Purpose of Using E-mail

10. In this question users were allowed to select more than one option therefore the percentage is more than 100%. It can be noted from figure 8.5 that 97.44% & 93.59% respondents using e-mail service for chatting & contact colleagues.

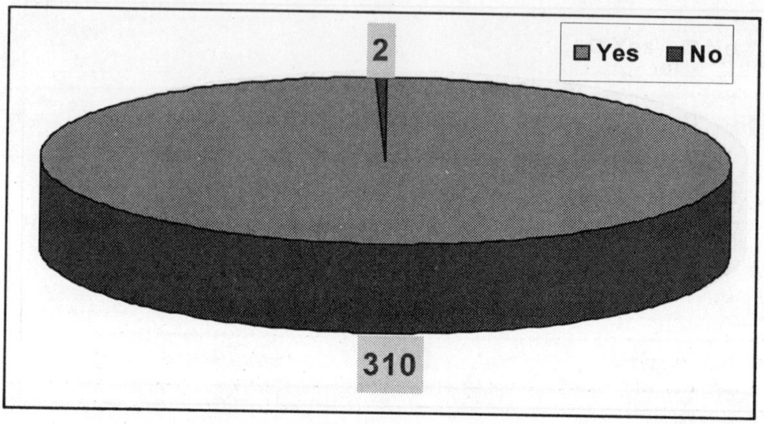

Fig. 8.7. Use of Search Engines

11. It can be revealed from figure 8.6 that 99.36% users are using search engines, expect 0.64% i.e. only 2 students are not using search engines. This proves the hypothesis "**Awareness of Internet use is prominent**" (Hypothesis No.1).

Table 8.5. Preferable Format for Downloading

Preferable Format	*No. of Users*
PDF	279
HTML	191
DOC	146
RTF	81

12. In this question users were allowed to select multiple options therefore the percentage is more than 100%. It can be resolved from Table 8.5 that majority 89.42% of the users' use PDF format for downloading document.

HTML format is used by 61.22% users & 46.79% of users used DOC type. While RTF format is used by only 25.96% of users.

9. CONCLUSIONS

It can be concluded that, in digital era users must have the knowledge of ICT as well as experience of using Internet & it's Technology.

REFERENCES

- ACRL (2004). Information literacy competency standards for higher education. *http://www.ala.org/ala/acrl/acrlstandards/standards guidelines. htm* (accessed on 19th August, 2011).
- ALA (1989). *American Library Association Presidential Committee on Information Literacy – Final Report.* Chicago: American Library Association.
- Bawden, D. (2001). Information and digital literacies: a review of concepts. *Journal of Documentation. 57(2).* 218-259. *http://gti1.edu.um.es:8080/jgomez/hei/intranet/bawden.pdf* (accessed on 19th August, 2010).
- Beatty, Susan and Mountifield, Hester (2005). Collaboration in an information commons: Key elements for successful support of e-literacy. *Journal of eLiteracy.* 2. 232-248.
- Faust, Judith (2001). Teaching information literacy in 50 minutes a week: The CSUH experience. *Journal of Southern Academic and Special Librarianship.*
- Fortier, John D. (1998). *Wisconsin's Model Academic Standards for Information and Technology Literacy.* West Indies.
- Grafstein, Ann (2007). Information literacy and Technology: An examination of some issues. *Portal: Libraries and the Academy. 7(1).* 51-64.
- Joint, Nicholas (2005). eLiteracy or Information Literacy: Which concept should we prefer? *Library Review. 54(9).* 505-507.
- Kane, Sally (2009). E-Document. http://legalcareers.about.com/od/glossary/g/E-documents.htm (accessed on 19th August, 2011).
- Kasyap, M M (1969). Planning of survey *Library Herald,* 2 (1&2), 195-199.
- Martin, A. and Rader, H. (2003) *Information and IT Literacy: enabling*

learning in the 21st century. London: Facet.

- Seetharama, S. (1999). Information management: Tools and techniques. *In*: National Workshop on Information Management including ISO 9000 QMS, held at Documentation Research and Training Centre, Bangalore.
- Singh, Jagtar (2008). Sense-making: Information literacy for lifelong learning and knowledge management. *DESIDOC Journal of Library and Information Technology*. *28(2)*. 13-17.